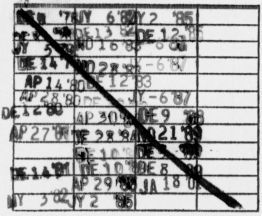

THE

FIRST AMENDMENT

AND THE FUTURE

OF AMERICAN

DEMOCRACY

The
First Amendment
and the Future
of American
Democracy

WALTER BERNS

Basic Books, Inc., Publishers   New York

The author gratefully acknowledges permission to reprint the following articles:

"Two Teachers Ousted Over Class on Sex," copyright © 1970 by The New York Times Company.

A revision of "Freedom of the Press and the Alien and Sedition Laws: A Reappraisal," from the *1970 Supreme Court Review,* Philip Kurland, editor. Copyright © 1970 by The University of Chicago.

Library of Congress Cataloging in Publication Data

Berns, Walter Fred, 1919-
    The First amendment and the future of American
democracy.

    Includes index.
    1. Civil rights—United States. 2. United
States. Constitution. 1st amendment. I. Title.
KF4770.B396   342'.73'085   76-22593
ISBN: 0-465-02410-6

To my wife, Irene

Contents

Preface

THE core of what constitutes liberty for Americans today, especially for those who call themselves liberals, is embodied in the First Amendment. The Constitution as a whole was called a charter of liberty by the men who wrote and adopted it, and its clauses providing for free elections and representation may be said to constitute the essence of self-government; but the rights guaranteed by the First Amendment somehow seem to come closer to defining what it means to be an American today. We have had, and continue to have, an experience of totalitarian governments in other places, and it is altogether reasonable to define the difference between them and us mainly in terms of the rights to believe, to think, and say what we will and without fear. To secure these rights, we depend only secondarily on the Congress or the Presidency and primarily on the Supreme Court. Its interpretation of the Amendment in what are now hundreds of cases constitutes the law of liberty on which we all depend.

But the Court not only interprets the Amendment as it decides the cases; it also provides the authoritative definitions of what is permissible in the name of liberty and what is impermissible, and in doing this it has a profound effect on our opinions, our habits, and our tastes, and ultimately, therefore, on the future of republican government in the United States. This is an awesome responsibility, and to fulfill it properly requires qualities that we cannot expect the justices to possess simply by virtue of their legal training, even when it is combined with practical experience in public affairs. The Founders, too, knew the law and had vast experience in public affairs, but the Constitution they wrote was informed by their reflections of a philosophic character, and its proper interpretation, therefore, requires us to look at the problems that arise under it within the same broad perspective— if we can. At any rate, it was inevitable that the Founders be consulted in this study, and not merely in those chapters, the first and third, which deal with the original understanding of the Amendment. For the same reason, Tocqueville appears frequently in these pages, in direct quotation and in the analysis of the problems presented in the cases; because of the range and depth of his understanding of political things, he was and remains democracy's best teacher. To read the cases with his assistance is to see that the Supreme Court justices are not merely the guardians of our liberty as we are inclined to define it today. They are also custodians of republican government, and it is a function of scholarship to make this known to them.

Legally we enjoy a greater liberty than ever before in our history; the Court has seen to that. The wall between church and state has never been higher or stronger, the political process is open to parties of any persuasion, the popular arts are free to a degree undreamed of in the past, and public discourse is carried on without regard to form or rule. That we can readily see. What is not so apparent is that the foundation on which liberty rests is endangered by the character of what is being communicated and what is not being communicated. It is the thesis of this book that the Court, in the name of civil liberty, is steadily eroding the conditions of civil liberty, to the point where it is appropriate to wonder about the future of liberal democracy in the United States. It is highly critical of the Court, but as Philip Kurland reminds us annually in *The Supreme Court Review,* the Court's work is too important to be accepted uncritically; and it is also too important for that criticism to be informed only by knowledge of the law. I, of course, accept Learned Hand's admonition that those who would dare to bring the judges severely to book must "take the trouble to understand them."

The first chapter and sections of the fifth on obscenity appeared in volumes edited by Harry Clor and published by Rand McNally; the third chapter appeared originally in *The Supreme Court Review, 1970,* edited by Philip Kurland and published by the University of Chicago Press. They have undergone considerable revision, but I am nevertheless grateful for the permission to use them here. I profited from the informed criticism of three fellow students of the Supreme Court and of the Constitution, Professors Robert Horwitz, Jacob Landynski, and Robert Scigliano; I wish to express my gratitude to them for their willingness to help me. I am especially aware of my indebtedness to the Earhart Foundation and its enlightened president, Richard A. Ware, for moral and financial support over the years. To my colleague Allan Bloom and to our teacher, the late Leo Strauss, I owe more than I am willing to express here.

THE

FIRST AMENDMENT

AND THE FUTURE

OF AMERICAN

DEMOCRACY

CHAPTER 1

Religion and the Founding Principle

I<small>T</small> is unfortunate, and a measure of our contemporary difficulties, that too many Americans today would hesitate to agree with the Englishman Gladstone that the American Constitution was "the most wonderful work ever struck off at a given time by the brain and purpose of man." It is not fashionable, even in America, to praise American things these days. It is also true, I think, that most of those who would agree with Gladstone about the Constitution would do so because of the Bill of Rights, an addition to the original Constitution, and especially the First Amendment. The First Amendment has become the most famous and praiseworthy part of the Constitution. There is good reason for this, for, to speak here only of its religious provisions, the principle of the separation of church and state provides the foundation on which free government rests. That principle has been celebrated in countless books and scholarly articles and is embodied in our public life as a nation—so much so, perhaps, that we tend to forget (or, at least, to fail fully to appreciate) the role played by the religious question in the beginning of free government. We acknowledge that the United States is a liberal democracy, but we may forget that the term *liberalism,* in its modern sense, was coined to denote the liberation from the power of church and churchmen. In the beginning of free and liberal government, no question was more important than the question of religion, and none played so prominent a role in the thought of the pertinent theorists—Hobbes, Locke, Spinoza, Bayle, and to a lesser but still significant extent, even Montesquieu. Even if it could be said that they solved the problem in principle, it was left to the American Founders to be the first to solve it, or to try to solve it, in practice.

The Separation of Religion and State

The Constitution, as it was sent by the Philadelphia convention to the people of the states for their ratification, contained a single provision dealing with religion: the proscription in Article VI of religious tests for office. This did not satisfy the six states (or five states plus the minority in Pennsylvania) that included a demand for a guarantee of the rights of conscience in their general call for a bill of rights. The typical demand made by these states was for an amendment protecting freedom of conscience, but no one, ratifier or nonratifier (or, as the nonratifier Elbridge Gerry inelegantly put it, "rats or antirats"[1]) expressed an opinion opposed to freedom of conscience! There was simply no debate on the subject, nor even a recorded difference of opinion, and this is not unrelated to the fact that freedom of conscience has not been an issue in the subsequent history of the country. More strikingly, especially to anyone with a memory of British and even American history during the seventeenth and eighteenth centuries, the fact that freedom of conscience was not an issue shows the great extent to which the religious question had already been settled in America at the time the Constitution was being written. There was a debate as to whether an amendment was necessary to protect it, but that posed no serious problem. There was considerable controversy over the question of whether the House should take time from the consideration of the pressing necessity to establish the offices of government in order to honor a pledge (which some of them did not regard as a pledge) to add a bill of rights to the Constitution; but that too proved tractable. The real difference was not discussed at all, although it can be glimpsed in the variety of formulations given the amendment; this was a difference that divided the participants among themselves and divided the more profound of them within themselves. In one sense, they were opposed to religion, to the organized religions of the day; in another sense, they recognized the role religion could play—and perhaps would have to play—in free government. Unlike freedom of conscience, this difference, the ambiguity on this aspect of the religious question, gave rise to an issue that has played a role in the subsequent history of the country and underlies the disagreement concerning the meaning of the First Amendment.

In 1947, for example, the Supreme Court said of the establishment clause that it means that neither a state nor the federal government may set up a church, pass laws aiding one religion or all religions, or prefer one religion over another.[2] This is a view widely held among constitutional scholars, but it is by no means the only view. It was not the view held by Edward S. Corwin or by Mark DeWolfe Howe,[3] or by others still living and writing. It was not the view of the Court when it upheld the statute granting tax exemptions to churches for properties used for worshiping purposes.[4] Presumably, it was not the view of Mr. Justice Douglas when, in the second "released time" case, he wrote that Americans "are a religious people whose institutions presuppose a Supreme Being," although it was his view, a few years later, when he wrote that the purpose of the religious clauses was "to keep government neutral, not only between sects, but between believers and nonbelievers."[5] Of course, the federal government may not "set up a church"; there has never been any argument about that. But may it aid religion, provided it does so on a nondiscriminatory basis? May the states? These are the

3

questions agitated today, and a good deal depends on the answers given. Because they are so important, we are not surprised to learn that they were raised—and answered—during the debates on the religious clauses in the First Congress.

In the Virginia ratifying convention, Patrick Henry had complained that under the proposed Constitution the states would lose their sovereignty which would thereby make insecure the rights of conscience protected under the state constitutions and, specifically, under the Virginia constitution. In response to Henry, and to others who in other states had expressed similar apprehensions, Madison opened the debates in the First Congress by proposing an amendment forbidding the establishment of "any national religion" or the infringement of "the full and equal rights of conscience." The issue here had to do with the relation of nation and states; but it was not much of an issue. The states had sought some reassurance, and the Founders had no objection to providing it. The House Select Committee formulated Madison's proposal as follows: "no religion shall be established by law, nor shall the equal rights of conscience be infringed." This led Benjamin Huntington of Connecticut to express the fear that this language could be read—not by him but by others—to forbid state laws requiring contributions in support of ministers of religion and places of worship. In addition, although he favored the free exercise of religion, he was anxious, he said, to avoid any language that might "patronize those who professed no religion at all."[6] He too was concerned with the nation-state relationship, but the source of his concern was his desire to allow the states to provide aid to religion.

Samuel Livermore of New Hampshire and Elbridge Gerry of Massachusetts were also intent on preserving their state laws in aid of religion and fostering the public worship of God. Gerry proposed to change the establishment clause to make it read "that no religious doctrine shall be established by law." Livermore, with Gerry's support, wanted to change it to read "that Congress shall make no laws touching religion,"[7] which, if adopted (and the House at one point did adopt it by a vote of 31-20),[8] would have prevented national laws "touching" or affecting or regulating or interfering with state laws on the subject of religion, including those laws that could be said to have established religion.[9] Madison's answer to Huntington's fear was the suggestion that the word "national" be "inserted before religion," thus leaving room for these state establishments; but Gerry, for the same reason that had earlier led him to vote against ratification of the Constitution in the Massachusetts ratifying convention, objected to the very use of the word "national."

Madison's amendments, as he had introduced them at the outset of the debates, would have forbidden the states, as well as the federal government, to "violate the equal rights of conscience." This suggests what we know from his other writings to be the case—that he was opposed to state as well as to federal establishment. In fact, he regarded this restriction on the states as "the most valuable amendment in the whole list,"[10] a judgment in line with his well-known opinion that the states were much more likely than the federal government to be ruled by factions, which would deprive religious minorities of their rights. This restriction on the states was adopted by the House and was lost only in the Senate.

Finally, on August 20, 1789, the House adopted the amendment in the style proposed by Fisher Ames of Massachusetts: "Congress shall make no law establishing religion, or to prevent the free exercise thereof, or to infringe the rights of conscience."[11] With insignificant stylistic changes, this is the form in which it was sent to the Senate. The following conclusions may be drawn from the House action: both the state and the federal governments were forbidden to infringe the rights of conscience, and, assuming there was a distinction (the Senate was to see none), the federal government was also forbidden to prevent the free exercise of religion; and the federal government (but not the states) was forbidden to establish religion. But did Ames, Huntington, Gerry, and Livermore, as well as some others, think that the federal government was also being forbidden to aid religion? Although we have no record of their debates, we know from the actions taken that this was made an issue by the Senate.

The House amendments were formally read in the Senate on August 25, and, after a debate that was interrupted more than once, the Senate completed its consideration of them on September 9. As mentioned, the single amendment placing restrictions on the states was dropped;[12] the amendment dealing with religion and that dealing with speech and press were combined into one; various changes were made to others; but, on the whole, they were adopted by the Senate in the form in which they came from the House. The establishment clause, however, was the subject of a number of amendments proposed and occasionally adopted. The first of these, offered on September 3, would have forbidden Congress to make any law "establishing one religious sect or society in preference to others"—which is certainly less ambiguous on the meaning of establishment than either the House version or the First Amendment as finally adopted—and it dropped the free exercise clause while retaining that part of the House version prohibiting infringement of the rights of conscience. It was defeated, then accepted; but the acceptance did not have the effect of ending the debate. After defeating a series of proposed changes, the Senate ended the day by returning to the House version, including the free exercise clause, but this time dropping the clause protecting the rights of conscience. From this it would appear that the senators regarded the latter as redundant, and it does not appear again. There continued to be some dissatisfaction with the establishment clause, however, with some senators anxious, and ultimately a majority of senators willing, to be more precise as to what would constitute an establishment. Hence, on September 9, the Senate adopted the following version, and this was the one it sent back to the House: "Congress shall make no law establishing articles of faith, or a mode of worship, or prohibiting the free exercise of religion...."[13] This seemingly would have left intact the various state establishments and would have permitted federal aid to religion on a nondiscriminatory basis. However, since we have no record of what was said in the Senate, we cannot know for certain that this was the intent.

The House refused to accept this version and asked for a conference. The Conference Committee, with Madison one of the ✓ House conferees, proposed the amendment in the form that was finally adopted by the required two-thirds vote in each house and ratified by the required three-fourths of the states: "Congress shall make no law respecting an establishment of religion, or prohibiting the free exercise thereof...." Here, then, is the origin of the troublesome phrase "respecting an establishment of religion."

Irving Brant, in his biography of Madison, says "there can be little doubt that this was written by Madison," and that, "of all the versions of the religious guaranty, this most directly covered the thing he was aiming at—absolute separation of church and state and total exclusion of government aid to religion."[14] But this is not altogether accurate. For example, Madison did not succeed in his attempt to place restrictions on the powers of the states with respect to the rights of conscience. Moreover, even if it is true that Madison was the author of this final formulation of the First Amendment, it is not necessarily the case that it was intended to promote the "absolute separation of church and state" or to forbid all forms of governmental aid to religion, even aid from the federal government. After all, this same First Congress, with Madison's approval, readopted the Northwest Ordinance of 1787, first passed by the Continental Congress, the third article of which reads as follows: "Religion, morality, and knowledge, being necessary to good government and the happiness of mankind, schools and the means of learning shall

7

forever be encouraged.''[15] It is not easy to see how Congress, or a territorial government acting under the authority of Congress, could promote religious and moral education under a Constitution that promoted "the absolute separation of church and state" and forbade all forms of assistance to religion. Whatever his own views—and we shall turn to those shortly—the situation that prevailed in the country and was reflected in the debates on the First Amendment would have required Madison to accommodate the views of others in whatever formulation he arrived at. The Senate wanted to prohibit federal laws "establishing articles of faith, or a mode of worship''; the House wanted to prohibit federal laws establishing religion; they agreed to the final version prohibiting laws "respecting" *an* establishment of religion. The question concerns the meaning of the words "respecting an establishment of religion.''

The House debate had begun on the Select Committee's version of the amendment, which read as follows: "No religion shall be established by law, nor shall the equal rights of conscience be infringed.'' The debate was opened by Peter Sylvester of New York, who objected to this formulation because "it might be thought to have a tendency to abolish religion altogether.''[16] So to construe the clause seems unnecessarily apprehensive—unless Sylvester had reason to believe that to forbid the establishment of religion by law would be to forbid all governmental assistance to religion, and that without this assistance religion would languish and eventually die. What is of interest is Madison's reply:

Mr. Madison said, he apprehended the meaning of the words to be, that Congress should not establish *a* religion, and enforce the legal observation of it by law, nor compel men to worship God in any manner contrary to their conscience. Whether the words are necessary or not, he did not mean to say, but they had been required by some of the State conventions, who seemed to entertain an opinion that under the clause of the constitution, which gave power to Congress to make all laws necessary and proper to carry into execution the constitution, and the laws made under it, enabled them to make laws of such a nature as might infringe the rights of conscience, and establish *a* national religion; to prevent these effects he presumed the amendment was intended, and he thought it as well expressed as the nature of the language would admit. [17]

Madison here twice adds the article—*a* religion—which, as a recent student of the debates has written, had it appeared in the original, would have made it virtually impossible for Sylvester to read the clause as forbidding "nondiscriminatory assistance to religion."[18] By the addition of the article, Madison seems to have expressed a willingness to accommodate those who wanted to permit such assistance. Can this also be said of the phrase "respecting an establishment of religion"? Perhaps; perhaps even probably. There were those who insisted on room for such assistance, and the language permits it. What is beyond question is that both the states and the federal government have traditionally acted as if the language permitted assistance of some sort. "Our system," as Justice Douglas had cause to complain, is "honeycombed" with laws that provide that assistance[19] at both the federal and the state levels. And when he and others insist that this is in violation of the Constitution, which was intended "to keep government neutral, not only between sects, but also between believers and nonbelievers,"[20] they are required to look elsewhere for supporting authority—to Madison's "Memorial and Remonstrance," for example. Written in opposition to the Virginia bill "for establishing a provision for teachers of the Christian religion," this famous statement of Madison's own views calls for the separation not only of church and state but of religion and state. But what is clear is that more than Madison's own views went into the First Amendment.

In the past, and especially in that recent English-speaking past well known to the Founders, religion had been the most divisive of political issues, the cause of civil strife and wars, of test oaths and recusancy, of revolutions and regicides, of political prob-

9

lems that threatened to defy solution, of, as Madison put it in the "Memorial and Remonstrance, "torrents of blood" spilled in the vain attempt to "extinguish Religious discord."[21] What is noteworthy in the debates leading to the adoption of the First Amendment is the absence of that kind of religious problem. It is not the differences among the participants in that debate but rather the extent of their agreement that is remarkable. What divided them were differences on what can only, in the light of that history, be called secondary issues: whether government depended in some way on religion and, therefore, whether government should be permitted, in some way, to foster religion, and whether this should be done at the federal as well as the state level. On these questions Madison especially differed from Samuel Livermore and his friends; but even Madison made no attempt in the First Amendment debates to have Congress adopt the policy he favored so eloquently and effectively in his "Memorial and Remonstrance." Compared to these differences, the agreement among them was massive. There was no dispute about freedom of conscience or the free exercise of religion; the adoption of the clause protecting free exercise was an altogether perfunctory matter, giving rise to no difference whatsoever. There was no dispute with respect to the principles on which the Constitution was built; stated in its most radical form, they all agreed that our institutions do *not* presuppose a providential Supreme Being. This is a fact of considerable significance, and, as I shall argue in Chapter 3, it allows us to understand why the Founders distinguished between religious and political opinion, and why they could accord absolute freedom to the one and not to the other.

One of the striking facts about the original, unamended Constitution is the absence of any passage invoking the name of God, providing for the public worship of God, according special privileges or places to churchmen, or stating it to be the duty of Congress to promote Christian education as part of a design to promote good citizenship. There is nothing in it similar to the provision in the Massachusetts constitution in 1780 declaring it to be not only the right but also the duty of the "towns, parishes, precincts and other bodies politic" to support, and to provide money for the support of, "the public worship of God."[22] Instead, the Constitution merely makes it possible for legislative majorities to enact—or not enact—laws of this sort. Yet what is regarded as primary or essential is not left to the discretion of legislative majorities or to chance. We have grown so accustomed to what we today call the secular state that we tend to ignore the significance of the absence of such provisions in the federal Constitution. If the Founders had intended to establish a Christian commonwealth (and, under the circumstances, it could not have been any other variety of religious commonwealth), it was remiss of them—indeed, sinful of them—not to have said so and to have acted accordingly. If they thought that all government was derived from God, they would have been remiss in not establishing constitutional institutions calculated to cause or help Americans to live according to His laws. Instead, the first of Madison's amendments, proposed in response to the demands of the states for a bill of rights, was a declaration insisting not that all power derives from God, but "that all power is originally vested in, and consequently derives from, the people."[23] Instead of speaking of men's duties to God and to each other, the Founders spoke—and again in this first of the proposed amendments—of men's indubitable, unalienable, and indefeasible rights, including the right freely to acquire and use property.

All this is not to say that Americans were not, in some sense—in most cases, some subordinate sense—a "religious people." Sylvester, Huntington, Livermore, and Gerry were indeed speaking on behalf of religion, but even their cause was a far cry from the causes defended by religious enthusiasts of the past. Massachusetts did require in its 1780 constitution that men had a duty publicly to worship God—but this was significantly qualified by the concession that each man do this according to "the dictates of his own conscience." What is more, this duty was imposed for a political reason. The towns "and other bodies politic" were to provide support for "the public worship of God" *because* "the happiness of a people, and the good order and preservation of civil government, essentially depend upon piety, religion, and morality."[24] This position was better stated in the Massachusetts ratifying convention when John Turner said that "without the prevalence of Christian piety and morals, the best republican constitution can never save us from slavery and ruin."[25] On the basis of such statements, it might even be said that whereas our institutions do not presuppose a Supreme Being, their preservation does. This is a venerable opinion. Tocqueville goes so far as to say that it was the opinion of all Americans:

Indeed, it is in this same point of view that the inhabitants of the United States themselves look upon religious belief. I do not know whether all Americans have a sincere faith in their religion—for who can search the human heart?—but I am certain that they hold it to be indispensable to the maintenance of republican institutions. This opinion is not peculiar to a class of citizens or to a party, but it belongs to the whole nation and to every rank of society.[26]

To some extent, Americans were taught this political lesson by the Founders.

In his First Inaugural, Washington paid homage "to the Great Author of every public and private good" and suggested that Americans, above all peoples, must "acknowledge and adore the Invisible Hand which conducts the affairs of men." Statements similar to these can be collected in the hundreds—and have been[27]—to the end of supporting the proposition that the United States is, or was intended to be, a Christian or, less specifically, a religious commonwealth—at any rate, the sort of commonwealth whose institutions "presuppose a Supreme Being." At the beginning, there must have been Americans who truly believed this, and believed it in an altogether unsophisticated way; but this cannot be said of the men whom we call the

Founders. It cannot be said of Washington, who, rather than God, to say nothing of Jesus of Nazareth, invoked the name of "that Almighty Being," and "the Great Author," and "the Invisible Hand," and "the benign Parent of the Human Race." There were others who made specific references to the God of the Scriptures, but Washington here sounds more like the Freemason he was than a pious Christian in an orthodox sense. His reasons for acknowledging divine assistance in the constituting of the United States, and for doing it in this manner, are suggested by the following statement in his Farewell Address:

Of all the dispositions and habits which lead to political prosperity, religion and morality are indispensable supports. In vain would that man claim the tribute of patriotism who should labor to subvert these great pillars of human happiness, these firmest props of the duties of men and citizens. The mere politician, equally with the pious man, ought to respect and to cherish them. A volume could not trace all their connections with private and public felicity. Let it simply be asked where is the security for property, for reputation, for life, if the sense of religious obligation *desert* the oaths, which are the instruments of investigation in courts of justice? And let us with caution indulge the supposition that morality can be maintained without religion. Whatever may be conceded to the influence of refined education on minds of peculiar structure, reason and experience both forbid us to expect that national morality can prevail in exclusion of religious principle. ✓

In the light of this statement, we are permitted to say that Washington, too, looked at religion from a political viewpoint, and from this perspective saw reason to doubt that a civil society founded on the rights of man could sustain itself in the absence of the extraneous support provided by religious belief. Clearly, he was one of Tocqueville's Americans who held religion to be "indispensable to the maintenance of republican institutions." Even more significantly, considering his reputation, Jefferson, too, was persuaded of the necessity of some sort of religious conviction—not for himself or Washington and others with "minds of peculiar structure" and "refined education," but for the great body of Americans. "And can the liberties of a nation

13

be thought secure when we have removed their only firm basis, a conviction in the minds of the people that these liberties are of the gift of God?'' Jefferson asks this question in his discussion not of religion—he had apparently disposed of that subject in the previous query (or chapter)—but of slavery, and in that context its appearance is especially striking. Slavery exists in Virginia, but it is contrary to the rights of man and natural justice. Not only is it contrary to natural justice, but its effects are also deleterious to master and slave alike. It must be abolished. Yet Jefferson has no illusions about the strength of the passions that stand in the way of that just conclusion. Greed and, especially in a warm climate, sloth stand in the way: ''For in a warm climate, no man will labour for himself who can make another labour for him.''[28]

Thus, natural rights are opposed by these passions, liberty by economic interest; and liberty can win in this contest only if it gains the support of religious conviction—specifically, the conviction in the minds of the people that liberty is the gift of God. Wisdom might dictate that it be the policy of the government to promote this conviction, which it can do by supporting religion in the form of a ''multiplicity of sects'' while favoring no particular one of them. Pennsylvania and New York, Jefferson had pointed out in the previous query, had shown the way for Virginia (and the United States as a whole). They had ''long subsisted without any establishments,'' but religion was well supported there—''of various kinds indeed, but all good enough'' from his political point of view, ''all sufficient to preserve peace and order [and] morals.''[29] Harvey C. Mansfield, Jr. has stated the conclusion to be drawn from this: ''For the sake of liberty, government must support religion in general, but no particular religion.''[30] That this was Washington's opinion we know from the Farewell Address, and it explains the style of his First Inaugural. Government cannot afford to be neutral ''between believers and nonbelievers''; good government depends on the existence of a certain kind of believer because there is, or was thought to be, a connection between religious belief and the moral character required to restrain the passions inimical to liberty. If religion "does not impart a taste for freedom," Tocqueville was to observe a few years later, "it facilitates the use of it."[31] As we might expect from a man whose thought was strongly influenced by a tradition derived from Rousseau, Tocqueville's opinion was that liberty cannot govern "without faith [and] is more needed in democratic republics than in any others."[32]

But the Constitution was ordained and established to secure liberty and its blessings, not to promote faith in God. Officially, religion was subordinate to liberty and was to be fostered—by public assistance, for example, and by exemplary admonitions on state occasions—only with a view to securing liberty. Moreover, before religion could be publicly fostered, it had to be reformed and rendered harmless. On the basis of all the evidence available to us, however, it would appear that this "reformation" had largely taken place in America prior to the writing of the Constitution.

The Religious Problem

> When indeed Religion is kindled into enthusiasm, its force like that of other passions is increased by the sympathy of a multitude. But enthusiasm is only a temporary state of Religion, and whilst it lasts will hardly be seen with pleasure at the helm [of state]. Even in its coolest state, it has been much oftener a motive to oppression than a restraint from it. [33]

Instead of establishing religion, the Founders established religious *freedom,* and the principle of religious freedom derives from a nonreligious source. Rather than presupposing a Supreme Being, the institutions they established presuppose the rights of man, which were discovered by Hobbes and Locke to exist prior to all government—in the state of nature, to be precise. To secure these rights, it is necessary for men to leave the state of nature, which they do by giving their consent to civil government. Nevertheless, the rights presuppose the state of nature, and the idea of the state of nature is incompatible with Christian doctrine. According to Christian doctrine, "the first and great commandment" is to love God, and the second, which is like unto it, is to love one's neighbor as oneself. In the state of nature, however, man is not obliged to love anyone, but merely to preserve himself and, what is more to the point, "to preserve the rest of mankind [only] when his own preservation comes not in competition."[34]

Just as they spoke frequently of natural rights, of founding government in order to secure these rights, and of compacts being "the vital principle of free government as contradistinguished from governments not free,"[35] the Founders spoke of and took seriously the state of nature. For them this was neither a "verbal construct" nor a purely hypothetical supposition; rather, it was the situation in which man found himself originally and into which he would lapse under certain conditions. One of the earliest debates in the First Congress turned on the question of whether Americans, upon declaring their independence of Great Britain, had "reverted" to a state of nature. The question was posed when a petition was introduced calling upon the House of Representatives to declare William Smith of South Carolina ineligible to take his seat in the House because he did not meet the constitutional requirement of seven years' citizenship. As a young boy of twelve in 1770, Smith had gone to England to be educated; he had lost both his parents during his absence from America, had endeavored to return during the Revolutionary War, but had suffered a series of misadventures and difficulties, including a shipwreck. He finally managed to reach Charleston, South Carolina, in November 1783. After serving in the state legislature, he was duly elected to the House of Representatives and appeared to take his seat in the First Congress, only to be met, in May 1789, with the challenge that he had not been a citizen at his birth in 1758—indeed, he, like most if not all the others in Congress, was born a British subject—and had not, unlike the others, acquired it by fighting in the Revolution, by taking an oath to one of the states, by tacit consent, or, finally, by adoption.

Madison, who supported him, replied that Smith was a citizen "on the Declaration of Independence" (by which he apparently meant on account of, or by virtue of, the Declaration) and that he continued to possess citizenship unless he had somehow forfeited it. The Declaration of Independence had absolved his "secondary allegiance" to George III but not his allegiance to the society of which, even as a child, he had been a member. "This reasoning will hold good," Madison said, "unless it is supposed that the separation which took place between these States and Great Britain, not only dissolved the union between these countries, but dissolved the union among the citizens themselves: that the original compact, which made them altogether one society, being dissolved, they could not fall into pieces, each part making an independent society; but must individually revert into a state of nature." Madison did not "conceive that this was, of necessity, to be the case." Such a revolution did not, he believed, "absolutely take place." The colonies remained "as a political society, detached from their former connexion with another society, without dissolving into a state of nature; but capable of substituting a new form of Government in the place of the old one, which they had, for special considerations, abolished."[36] The difficulty of the question is one that must be acknowledged by any reader of the last chapter of Locke's *Second Treatise* ("Of the Dissolution of Government"), and Madison spoke without his customary assurance.

Not so James Jackson of Georgia. His reading of the situation was that there had been only one allegiance to Great Britain and, that being dissolved, they had all, Smith included, experienced "a total reversion to a state of nature amongst individuals." After this, "every man made his election for an original compact, or tie, which, by his own act, or that of his father for him, he became bound to submit to.''[37] This Smith had not done, or had done only on his return in 1783, a mere six years earlier, and therefore he was not eligible to take his seat in the House. Fortunately for Smith, the House voted overwhelmingly in his favor—that is, overwhelmingly in favor of Madison's reading of Locke and of the events of 1776. What is of primary interest here is the source of the guidance the legislators sought on such questions, or the source of the principles on which they acted politically: so far as the Constitution of the United States is concerned, in the beginning was not the word (''and the word was with God, and the word was God''); in the beginning was the state of nature, and the word was with the philosophers of natural rights. It was from them that the Founders learned the new ''science of politics,''[38] and with it the principles of free government.

These principles require the establishment of religious freedom, the right of men to hold whatever opinions they choose respecting God or gods. That men must have this choice is not itself a matter of choice or indifference. Jefferson insisted on this, and Jefferson is acknowledged to be the authoritative American spokesman on this subject. In his *Notes on the State of Virginia* (the only book he ever wrote), which contains probably his deepest reflections on political questions, he said that because their institutions are not built on a religious truth, Americans are not entitled to regard it as an injury—or an injury for which the law will provide a remedy—for their neighbors to say there are twenty gods or no God. Such religious opinions neither pick their pockets nor break their legs, as he put it in his famous formulation;[39] and because such religious opinions do not injure them or the commonwealth, their neighbors are entitled to an absolute right to hold them. Any denial of this would, of necessity, be based on a particular religious doctrine. For example, a law forbidding the opinion that there are twenty gods would arise out of the opinion that there is one God, or no God,

18

or some other number of gods; and to legislate on such a basis would be to transform what in the eyes of the Constitution is merely an opinion—and, officially at least, must remain so—into an official truth, and this would be incompatible with the Constitution and the political philosophy underlying it. Futhermore, religious freedom must be established because "difference of opinion is advantageous in religion," not advantageous to religion (although that may be true incidentally), but *politically* advantageous. That is, it is politically advantageous to have religious differences in the country, to have a variety of religious sects, because the "several sects perform the office of a Censor morum over each other."[40] The rights of man are protected by a "multiplicity of sects," as Jefferson's friend and colleague Madison said in the 51st *Federalist,* and what matters is the rights of man (and not a particular religious doctrine concerning eternal salvation or anything else). Thus, the establishment of religious freedom rests on the proposition that there can be no officially recognized creed or doctrine—that, officially, all religious doctrines are equal—and Jefferson and Madison did their best to establish this principle not only in federal public law but in the public law of Virginia as well. The state religious establishments might have to be accommodated in practice, but they were, nevertheless, incompatible with the principle on which the country was founded.

While the United States recognizes no religious truth, it is founded on the "self-evident" philosophical truth respecting the natural freedom and equality of all men. Being naturally free, men contract one with another to form civil society—"all power is originally vested in, and consequently derives from, the people." This contract represents their agreement to be governed—their consent to be governed—and this agreement or consent, which is the beginning of all legitimate government, is required by the fact of their natural freedom and equality. Being equal with respect to natural right, and however unequal they may be according to any religious doctrine or in any other

19

respect, no man may justly rule another without his consent (although, prior to the formation of the United States, this right was not recognized or acknowledged in practice). Kings, in the course of time and from place to place, may have been required to make laws only with the consent of the lords spiritual and temporal and the commons in parliaments assembled, but they claimed to hold their crowns by the grace of God, independent of the consent of those they governed. In this fundamental political respect, men were held to be unequal.

Discovery of the rights of man changed that. "All eyes are opened, or opening, to the rights of man," Jefferson said. "The general spread of the light of science has already laid open to every view the palpable truth, that the mass of mankind has not been born with saddles on their backs, nor a favored few booted and spurred, ready to ride them legitimately, by the grace of God."[41] This "palpable truth" is a scientific truth, not a religious truth or opinion but a truth discovered by the new political science; and the United States was the first country to organize itself on it. It was the first country to recognize the self-evident truth of the natural freedom and equality of all men and, therefore, that legitimate government can arise only out of consent. It was, as the motto on its Great Seal proclaims, a *novus ordo seclorum,* a new order of the ages. In this decisive respect, it was the first "new nation," and its newness consisted in large part in the nonreligious character of its founding principle. The uniqueness of this fact is emphasized in the thought of John Locke, the Englishman frequently called "America's philosopher," whom Jefferson, referring to him as one of the three greatest men who ever lived, accepted as one of his teachers. In the first of his *Two Treatises of Government,* Locke goes to what today are regarded as extraordinary lengths to show what we would regard as self-evident—namely, that kings do not rule by virtue of any donation from God to Adam and his heirs. This having been shown, he says at the outset of the *Second Treatise,* it is necessary "to find out another rise of government, another original of political power,"[42] and by saying this, he suggests that the only alternative to government based on the religious doctrine of divine donation is, as it turns out, government based on the nonreligious doctrine of the rights of man and the contract men make with each other. To secure these rights, governments are instituted among men.

Such a government was not established with the settling of the American colonies, and although its principles were well known to Jefferson and his colleagues, it had not been fully established in Virginia even by the end of 1781, when Jefferson wrote his *Notes on the State of Virginia.* As he saw it, the people of Virginia had not yet been sufficiently instructed in these principles, even after they had declared their independence. "The convention of May 1776, in their declaration of rights, declared it to be a truth, and a natural right, that the exercise of religion should be free; but when they proceeded to form on that declaration the ordinance of government, instead of taking up every principle declared in the bill of rights, and guarding it by legislative sanction, they passed over that which asserted our religious rights, leaving them as they found them."[43] Heresy was, in principle, still punishable under the laws of Virginia; a Christian could deny the doctrine of the Trinity only at the price of his right to hold "any office or employment ecclesiastical, civil, or military" and, if he should persist in his denial, at the price of his liberty, his right to sue or inherit property, and even his "right to the custody of his own children." This, Jefferson complained, "is a summary view of that religious slavery under which a people have been willing to remain, who have lavished their lives and fortunes for the establishment of their civil freedom." Men are endowed with natural rights, and rulers have no authority over these rights except as men, in the compact forming civil society, have submitted to them. But it was Jefferson's view—and he was sustained in this by the existence of the Virginia law, as well as by the strength of the opposition he and Madison had to overcome in order to establish religious freedom in the state—that too many Virginians persisted in the error of regarding it as proper for the rights of conscience to be submitted to government.

This Virginia law and the religious establishments that continued to exist in some other states were vestiges of the orthodox Christianity that had come under attack in the seventeenth century from the new political science. It had to be attacked or somehow displaced, because, as Professor Mansfield has said, any revealed religion is incompatible with modern natural right. A revealed religion is revealed only to the godly, and the godly are only too likely "to take advantage of the favor of revelation to demand political power for themselves or their allies."[44] In a limited way—limited when compared with the claims staked out by the priests and princes against whom Hobbes, Spinoza, and Locke had to contend—this is what the nominally pious Virginians were doing. To destroy the political power of revealed religion, it was first necessary to destroy or displace the authority of revealed religion, which, in the Europe of the seventeenth century, meant the authority of Scripture and, especially, of the New Testament, wherein the proof of Jesus' authority is supplied by "the multitude of miracles he did before all sorts of people." This is necessary because "where the miracle is admitted, the doctrine cannot be rejected." Thus Hobbes wrote a critique of "miracles, and their use";[45] Locke wrote a *Discourse of Miracles,* from which the passage quoted above is taken;* and Spinoza attempted to demonstrate that

---

*Locke, *Works* (1812 ed.), vol. 9, p. 259. The nature of Locke's critique of miracles is suggested in the following passage (as well as in the fact that he specified that the *Discourse* be published only after his death): "For miracles being the basis on which divine mission is always established, and consequently that foundation on which the believers of any divine revelation must ultimately bottom their faith, this use of them would be lost, if not to all mankind, yet at least to the simple and illiterate, (which is the far greatest part,) if miracles be defined to be none but such divine operations as are in themselves beyond the power of all created beings, or at least operations contrary to the fixed and established laws of nature. For as to the latter of those, what are the fixed and established laws of nature, philosophers alone, if at least they, can pretend to determine." (Ibid., p. 264.)

"God cannot be known from miracles."[46] Christianity had to be made reasonable, which is why Locke, in addition to writing *Some Considerations of the Consequences of the Lowering of Interest and Raising the Value of Money* and helping to found the Bank of England, found it necessary to write *The Reasonableness of Christianity.*

Jefferson, of course, was a statesman, not a philosopher, but his statesmanship was informed by what he had learned from the natural rights philosophers who preceded him. From them he had learned that Christianity had to be made reasonable, and he was willing, albeit in words that he was careful to keep from the public, to commit his thoughts to paper. He denied the divinity of Christ. He nevertheless described himself as a Christian—not the sort of Christian that any of the Christian churches could have recognized, but a Christian "in the only sense [Jesus] wished anyone to be." He was perfectly willing to attribute to Jesus "every *human* excellence," which, he insisted against the churches, was all Jesus ever claimed for himself.[47] The so-called Christians think otherwise, said Jefferson, because they had been corrupted, taught to believe in the Bible and that the Bible is a record of God's self-revelation to man. This doctrine, wholly false in his judgment, Jefferson traced to the fact that Jesus, like Socrates, "wrote nothing himself," thereby making it possible for "the most unlettered & ignorant men [writing] from memory & not till long after the transactions had passed [to commit] to writing his life and doctrines...."[48] Hence, the doctrines "he really delivered...have come to us mutilated, misstated, & often unintelligible," and they were further "disfigured by the corruptions of schismatising followers, who have found an interest in sophisticating & perverting the simple doctrines he taught by engrafting on them the mysticisms of a Grecian sophist, frittering them into subtleties, & obscuring them with jargon, until they have caused good men to reject the whole in disgust, & to view Jesus himself as an imposter."[49] His moral doctrines, Jefferson went on, are in fact "pure & perfect" and

23

inculcate a "universal philanthropy, not only to kindred and friends, to neighbors and countrymen, gathering all into one family, under the bonds of love, charity, peace, common wants and common aids."[50]

To say that Jefferson advocated religious freedom and the separation of church and state, and to leave it at that, is to miss what was then the radical character of his views on religion. Americans, no more than the immediate addressees of Locke's writings, would not accept a policy of freedom and separation, or of toleration (and Jefferson made copious notes and significant use of Locke's *Letter Concerning Toleration*[51]), until or unless they were persuaded of the ground of this toleration, and the ground of this toleration is the opinion that traditional Christian doctrine is false. When it is shown to be false and, more practically, when the truth of this falseness is "by the light of science" spread among and accepted by the mass of mankind, it will be possible for men to attach themselves more firmly to the God of the Declaration of Independence—"Nature's God"—and the religious problem will be solved and free government secured.

No book is needed to read the will of "Nature's God." The American who set out·most vigorously and openly to expound the new religious principles was not Jefferson, however, but Tom Paine. Unlike Jefferson, and much more openly than the equally radical but far more subtle critiques written by his more learned seventeenth-century predecessors, Paine does mount an attack on miracles, prophecy, and mystery. Also unlike Jefferson, who concealed his most radical religious views from the eyes of the public, Paine, dedicating his book to his "fellow citizens of the United States of America," informs them that Christianity is the most "absurd," "repugnant," "derogatory," "unedifying," and "inconsistent" religion ever "invented."[52] The Bible, he says, is a book of fables, not the revealed word of God. God has revealed himself in his works, as first cause of these works. God can be discovered only by studying his created world, and the Bible and the churches are positively detrimental to this project; they have traditionally stood as obstacles in the path of science and will continue to do so as long as they hold power over the minds of men.

Paine does his best to destroy that power in page after page of argument, ridicule, anger, and unconcealed contempt for the enemies of what he regards as scientific truth. This truth does not need the "crutch" of fable[53]—or, as Jefferson put it, "truth can stand by itself."[54] God, "the Almighty Lecturer," speaks to man not indirectly through the Bible, but directly in His display of "the principles of science in the structure of the universe [and] has invited man to study and to imitation."[55]

Jefferson never deigned publicly to speak so boldly, but there is nothing in the *Age of Reason* that does not find a place in the thoughts Jefferson committed to letters and other such papers. If we are no longer shocked by them, as Paine's contemporaries were for a while shocked by his writings, that merely shows the extent of the change that has occurred in our opinions. Despite the extravagance of his presentation, Paine was a representative spokesman of his age, the Age of Reason. It is not by chance that he wrote another book, entitled *Rights of Man,* or that he thought it appropriate to dedicate it to George Washington.

Under the reign of the doctrine of the rights of man, the day might come, and Paine and Jefferson in their different ways worked to hasten its coming, when the typical Anglican priest of Virginia would have long since ceased his agitation for the presumed benefits of establishment and would be less concerned with what separates the various religions than with what they have in common. He might come in time to speak of the "Judeo-Christian tradition," for example. Whatever might be said of this from the point of view of orthodox Anglo-Catholicism and orthodox Judaism (which, Jefferson said, was also in need of "reformation" and to "an eminent degree"[56]), it would bespeak (and, of course, does bespeak) a situation in which both Anglo-Catholic and Jew, as well as others, were allowed to enjoy the rights to which they are entitled as men: to live in liberty and to worship as they please, because neither would be inclined to prevent the other from exercising these rights, or to think it important or even legitimate to do so. Washington stated this perfectly in his answer to an "Address" from the Hebrew Congregation of Newport, Rhode Island:

It is now no more that tolerance is spoken of, as if it was by the indulgence of one class of people, that another enjoyed the exercise of their inherent natural rights. For happily the government of the United States, which gives to bigotry no sanction, to persecution no assistance, requires only that they who live under its protection should demean themselves as good citizens, in giving it on all occasions their effectual support.... May the children of the Stock of Abraham, who dwell in this land, continue to merit and enjoy the good will of the other inhabitants, while everyone shall sit in safety under his own vine and fig-tree, and there shall be none to make him afraid. [57]

The origin of free government in the modern sense coincides with and can *only* coincide with, the solution of the religious problem, and the solution of the religious problem consists in the subordination of religion. In prior times, it was thought to matter whether a nation believed in twenty gods or one God or no God, or whether the one God was this God or that God. That is why the question of religion used to figure so prominently in the works of the political philosophers. Then it was a political question; now it is not. One can say that the natural rights philosophers spent so much time on the religious question in order to make it possible for the politicians who followed them to ignore it.

That this lesson was learned by Americans (and not by the besieged residents of Northern Ireland, for example) was obvious even in Tocqueville's time;[58] but it is not at all obvious that it was learned directly from Paine's intemperate presentation. It is more likely that Americans—whose strong attachment to material comforts led Jefferson in 1781 to predict that, on the successful conclusion of the Revolutionary War, they would be concerned solely with making money—were led by this attachment to accept an "understanding of Christianity which [was] not in conflict with it."[59] Paine could have profited from Montesquieu's advice: the way "to attack a religion is by favor, by the commodities of life, by the hope of wealth; not by what drives away, but by what makes one forget; not by what brings indignation, but by what makes men lukewarm, when other passions act on our souls, and those which religion inspires are silent. *Règle générale:* with regard to change in religion, invitations are stronger than penalties."[60] Professor Pangle's comment on this makes the point even clearer, and more clearly relevant to America: "Christianity will be overcome by making men 'forget' everything which is at a tension with securing 'the commodities of life.' All that is required on the part of 'political writers' like Montesquieu is to show the way to an understanding of Christianity which is not in conflict with devotion to commerce and comfort; the inherent attractions of these things will do the rest."[61] And the Constitution of the United States certainly did nothing to discourage a life devoted to the acquisition of material comforts.

The Founders did not establish religion, but they did establish commerce and the commercial republic; by so doing, they facilitated the acquisition of the material comforts it would provide. In a statement whose significance cannot be overemphasized, Madison, in the most famous of the *Federalist Papers,* says that the "protection of different and unequal faculties of acquiring property...is the first object of government."[62] Previous generations, no less than our own, have regarded such a statement as outrageous. Many people have simply refused to concede that Madison meant what he said. It is too blunt for us, too shocking to our sensibilities, too seemingly lacking in a concern for the less well endowed or less fortunate, those who do not fare well in the competition. But this was not an ill-considered statement tossed off in the press of meeting a journalistic deadline; he had said essentially the same thing on the floor of the constitutional convention.[63] Commerce and the material comforts it promises will entice men away from their austere religions and, in addition, will provide the needed substitute for the moral habits religion inculcated. This was Locke's and, later and in more precise detail, Adam Smith's teaching,[64] but it was left to Madison to apply it to an actual political situation. This he did in the tenth *Federalist*.

The argument goes as follows: The United States, a nation founded on the principle of self-interest ("to secure these [individual] rights, governments are instituted among men"), faces the severe problem of somehow moderating self-interest. The problem will manifest itself—and in 1788 had already manifested itself in the various states—as the problem of faction, defined as "a number of citizens... united and actuated by some common impulse of passion, or of interest, adverse to the rights of other citizens, or to the permanent and aggregate interests of the community." The "mischief" can be cured by removing its causes—but only at the price of liberty—or, the old religious way, by giving everyone the "same opinions, the same passions, and the same interests." For example, the state might require everyone to be an Anglo-Catholic, as Britain and, more recently, even Virginia had tried to do. Madison, speaking for the United States, rejects that "cure." Besides, the states were demonstrating that it was, in fact, a cure no longer available in America. "From the conclusion of this war," said Jefferson at the end of his discussion of religion, "we shall be going down hill [and] the people will forget themselves, but in the sole faculty of making money."[65] The states, despite their affirmations, were not succeeding in restraining this passion. Massachusetts may have required public support of public worship—because the preservation of civil government was thought, or said, to depend "upon piety, religion and morality"—but Massachusetts was the scene of Shays's Rebellion, and in the Founders' minds no event better illustrated the extent to which a democratic people could trample on the rights of man. There was, Madison argued on the floor of the constitutional convention, no security in the states for private rights and the steady dispensation of justice. "Interferences with these were evils which had more perhaps than anything else, produced this convention." In a republic the majority rules; when the majority is united by a common interest or passion, the rights of the minority are in danger. What, he asked, will restrain it? Not a "prudent regard to the maxim that honesty is the best policy"; not a "respect for character"; not "conscience"; not religion. Indeed, "religion itself may become a motive to persecution and oppression."[66] The states called for morality, but they had not succeeded in providing it. The states praised sumptuary laws, John Adams noted, but such laws were more often praised than enacted.[67] That was why an entirely different approach, an approach embodying a substitute for or a supplement to morality, had to be found.*

Fortunately, a substitute or supplement was available. The "mischief" could be cured by controlling the effects of faction: instead of attempting to make men moral by preaching to them to love their neighbors as themselves, which cannot be relied on to work in the United States ("we well know that neither moral nor religious motives can be relied on as an adequate control"), instead of trying to control the passions, especially acquisitiveness or greed, the state could direct the passions of men to the pursuit of material goods. It is in this context that Madison says that the "protection of different and unequal faculties of acquiring property...is the first object of government." There would be no unrestrained majority operating within each state and riding roughshod over the rights of others, since a large commercial republic like that delineated in the tenth *Federalist* would make the formation of such a majority extremely difficult. And instead of civil strife and wars caused by disputes between Catholics and Protestants, Christians and Jews, or high

*This issue of the republic founded on public spirit and virtuous citizens or the republic founded on self-interest and the commercial spirit was the issue debated in the ratification struggle, with the Antifederalists contending for the former and the Federalists for the latter. The Antifederalists, of course, lost the debate, which proved to be decisive for the subsequent history of the country.

church or low church, men could live in peace and liberty if permitted to pursue successfully their passion for material well-being (and they would succeed, and have succeeded) in the large commercial republic dedicated to promoting "different degrees and kinds of property."[68] In short, instead of pursuing eternal salvation and fighting over how to achieve it, if men seek material gratification and win it, republican government will be possible. We know the result under the name of capitalism. Capitalism, understood as the right of unlimited acquisition, will promote the "Wealth of Nations" and, by so doing, secure the rights of man. This is what it means to say that acquisition is the substitute for morality—or, to speak more soberly, was intended to be a substitute for morality.

Conclusion

Liberalism knows nothing about happiness; indeed, according to the "laws of nature and Nature's God," the only knowledge of this available to man is knowledge of the conditions appropriate to the pursuit of what each man may call happiness. It follows from this that there can be no official answer to the most important question: How shall I live? The role of the properly constituted government is therefore confined to guaranteeing the conditions that allow each man to pursue his privately defined happiness. Liberalism preserves the private sphere and fosters the self-defined private life. Stated within the terms of the First Amendment, the United States may not establish any church or recognize any creed or any articles of faith, but it must protect the rights of conscience, or the right of every man to believe what he will. These "operations of the mind," as Jefferson put it, unlike "the acts of the body," are not "subject to coercion of the laws." Thus was religion subordinated through relegation to the private realm, where everyone is free to believe there is one god or twenty gods or no god at all.

But the acts performed by the body are not independent of the operations of the mind, so that even the truest of liberal governments may not be able to remain indifferent to this private realm where opinions are formed. As early as 1781, Jefferson was wondering whether American liberty did not depend on the "conviction in the minds of the people" that it was the gift of God; and after only eight years of government under the Constitution, Washington warned the nation that religion provided the "indispensable" support of those "dispositions and habits which lead to political prosperity." Then, on the eve of his death, Jefferson again said that he rejoiced "that in this blessed country of free inquiry and belief, which has surrendered its creed and conscience to neither kings nor priests, the genuine doctrine of one god only is reviving, and [he hoped] that there [was] not a *young man* [then] living in the United States who [would] not die an Unitarian."[69] It was still a private matter whether a man said there is one god or twenty gods or no god, but Jefferson was himself of the opinion that it would be politically beneficial if Americans privately were to decide that there is "only one God, and he all perfect," that "there is a future state of rewards and punishments," and that everyone should "love God with all [his] heart and [his] neighbor as [himself]."[70]

Liberal government protected the private realm, but there seems to have been an awareness that the health of liberal government required certain virtuous habits to be preserved in that realm. Stated otherwise, liberalism required both the subordination of religion and the maintenance of certain habits that religion alone could inculcate. This is why the First Congress, in drawing up the First Amendment, protected the right to be religious and, in forbidding laws respecting an establishment of religion, was careful to avoid language that would also forbid aid, including financial aid, to religion on a nondiscriminatory basis. Thus, Justice Douglas was right when he complained— even if from the point of view of the authors of the First Amendment he was wrong *to* complain—that our "system at the federal and state levels is honeycombed with such financing."[71] In God (reasonably defined) we do indeed collectively trust, and there is even room for those who trust in Him first and foremost, provided their piety stays within the bounds required for "peace and good order." Until those bounds are violated, Jefferson said, it is unnecessary for "the State to be troubled with [them]."[72]

Americans had, as Tocqueville observed, succeeded in combining the spirit of religion and the spirit of liberty, but they did so by subordinating the former to the latter. Not only were they wise to do so, he suggested, but the two could not be combined in any other fashion.[73] Still, if he was right, "the whole nation" held religion "to be indispensable to the maintenance of republican institutions,"[74] and it was his opinion that only so long as this combination was maintained would the crisis of liberalism be avoided. The First Amendment question of our own day is whether the Supreme Court will permit the means of maintaining both religion and liberty.

CHAPTER 2

Religion and the Supreme Court

WHEN Madison spoke deprecatingly of religion being "kindled into enthusiasm," he gave voice to one of the fears that lay behind the First Amendment; when Peter Sylvester spoke anxiously that nothing be done that would "abolish religion altogether," he gave voice to another. In the first case, religious enthusiasm would have to be tempered if free government were to be constituted and survive; in the second case, the spirit of religion, being an indispensable support of free government, would have to be preserved. The desiderata arising from these two fears are not incompatible, but they do not coexist easily, especially in the particular setting in which they are placed in America. The principal characteristic of democratic times is the love of material well-being, Tocqueville said; and in America, a very democratic country ("the most democratic country in the world"),[1] the love of God has had to accommodate itself to the love of material well-being, and the churches have had to make their peace with the passion they could not suppress. According to Tocqueville, their survival depends on it:

It may be believed that a religion which should undertake to destroy so deep-seated a passion [as "the love of well-being"] would in the end be destroyed by it; and if it attempted to wean men entirely from the con-

33

templation of the good things of this world in order to devote their faculties exclusively to the thought of another, it may be foreseen that the minds of men would at length escape its grasp, to plunge into the exclusive enjoyment of present and material pleasures. [2]

It is not by chance, then, that America has not been much bothered by religious enthusiasm in the old sense. The exceptions come readily to mind, but they do so because they are exceptions.

It may yet prove otherwise with respect to the second desideratum. That religion has survived at all in this subordinate position may be attributed, in part, to the modesty of the role it has played. On the whole, it did not resist the establishment of government on the new principles, which meant that there was absent at the beginning the sort of revolutionary struggle involving the churches that characterized the liberal revolutions in Europe, most markedly in France and, in the twentieth century, in Spain. Americans, as Tocqueville rightly remarked, were "born equal without having to become so" and were therefore able to avoid a "democratic revolution." Moreover, religion in America accommodated itself to the governing passions of democratic times. Its principal concern has indeed been merely "to purify, to regulate, and to restrain the excessive and exclusive taste for well-being that men feel in periods of equality."[3]

The politically significant aspect of this is that in consigning religion to the care of private institutions, America also consigned to them, and to the private realm generally, the inculcation of those habits or popular virtues needed even by liberal government. It was in this context that Tocqueville said that when "any religion has struck its roots deep into a democracy [as it had in the American colonies], beware that you do not disturb it; but watch it carefully, as the most precious bequest of aristocratic ages."[4] Liberal democracy must preserve what it cannot itself generate, and it must do this without jeopardizing the private character of religion. As we have seen, the First Amendment did not forbid the advancement of this policy, but what is constitutionally permissible is not always politically possible, and what is politically possible has not always proved constitutionally permissible.

Religious Enthusiasm and the Constitution

There is no way of knowing how many truly pious persons there are or have been in America. Nor is there any way of knowing the number of religious bigots there have been among us, although, in this case, because bigotry sometimes manifests itself politically when given the opportunity and the occasion, we do know their works. There has been an Anti-Mason party, for example—it even elected a couple of governors and collected a few electoral votes during the Jacksonian era. The Ku Klux Klan was in part anti-Semitic and anti-Roman Catholic, and the Know-Nothing Party was an anti-immigrant, and particularly anti-Roman Catholic, movement; the Jehovah's Witnesses of our own day have both manifested bigotry and been its victims. On the whole, however, the history of the United States, especially on the national level, is marked by the absence of religious politics; unlike Western Europe even today, a Christian Democratic party (to say nothing of a Christian Anti-Democratic party) is conspicuous by its absence. This is not to deny the political activities of the churches—the statute books are studded with laws that originated in such activity, and the schools issue has long provided and continues to provide a battleground for sectarian and nonsectarian armies. Nevertheless, religious passions in the United States have been translated into political passions comparatively rarely. The groups that do not accept the liberal principle of the depoliticization of religion have been few in number and few in members. We know them as Amish, Mennonites, and Hutterites; they exist in enclaves, seeking to withdraw from the secular world. But that withdrawal cannot be complete, because the secular world has laws that apply even to them. The problem of religious enthusiasm in America has arisen typically on those occasions when someone demands, on religious grounds, exemption from the laws which are supposed to be obeyed by everyone. These are not laws requiring a confession of faith or a tithe, both of which are clearly forbidden by the First Amendment. Rather, they are laws demanding military service, salutes to the flag, or school attendance, or laws forbidding the use of the mails for fraudulent purposes. It is something of a paradox that as the country has become increasingly secular, the Supreme Court has become increasingly solicitous of demands for exemption from such laws.

It was Jefferson who supplied the principle by which these disputes should be resolved. He said that it is an error to assert that "the operations of the mind ... are subject to the coercion of the laws," but that it was otherwise with "the acts of the body," including those acts that arise out of religious opinion.[5] This has consequences that we have come to overlook, and to overlook increasingly often. The subordination of religion does not mean that the law can be indifferent to religion. It cannot be indifferent to—indeed, it must deny—the claim that religious belief constitutes a title to rule. It must also deny that religious belief, or "conscience," can give rise to a legitimate claim to be exempt from rule. When principles, including religious principles, "break out into overt acts against peace and good order," civil government is certainly entitled "to interfere," as Jefferson put it,[6] and there is no evidence that anyone at that time disagreed with him. But it is sometimes denied today, not only by those who have a self-interested reason to deny it—for example, sectarians who refuse to salute the flag or go to school, or escape military service or burn Selective Service records—but also by Supreme Court justices. The following examples will illustrate the point.

Louis A. Negre sought discharge from the Army after receiving orders for Vietnam duty. He was not conscientiously opposed to wars as such (and therefore could not qualify for exemption under the Selective Service Act of 1967, which extends to anyone who, "by reason of religious training and belief, is conscientiously opposed to participation in war in any form"), but he claimed that it was his duty, as a faithful Roman Catholic, to discriminate between just and unjust wars and to refuse to serve in the Vietnam war because it was, in his view, an unjust war. To serve in that war would contravene his conscience, he said. His application for discharge was denied, and the Supreme Court upheld this denial on appeal.[7] Justice Douglas alone refused to go along with this decision. "No one can tell a Catholic that this or that war is either just or unjust," Douglas said. Because that was a personal decision which only the individual Catholic can make "on the basis of his own conscience after studying the facts," it followed for Douglas that only the individual Catholic can decide whether he will serve in this or that war.[8] As Douglas said in a companion case, "the welfare of the single human soul [is] the ultimate test of the vitality of the First Amendment."[9] In the course of his brief dissent, he cited Francisco Victoria, Dominican master of the University of Salamanca during the sixteenth century, Pope Paul VI, and Cardinal Ottaviani, among others; he did not cite anyone having anything to do with the Constitution of the United States.

The next year, a Supreme Court majority allowed Jonas Yoder, a member of the Old Order Amish religion, to disobey a valid law of the state of Wisconsin requiring parents to cause their children to attend school until the age of 16. The Court, having stressed the significance of compulsory school attendance laws in its decision in the public school segregation cases of 1954,[10] minimized the school laws here, then claimed that all "that has been said and written on the subject [of church and state confirms] that only those interests of the highest order...can overbalance legitimate claims to the free exercise of religion."[11]

In this day of profound dissatisfaction with what is commonly referred to as the quality of American life, it is not difficult to understand how the Court could be sympathetic with the Amish and their pious, gentle, yet industrious ways. No doubt the Amish had good reason to believe that it would have been profoundly contrary to their way of life for their children to attend local high schools, and one wishes the Wisconsin Superintendent of Public Instruction could have been prevailed upon to allow the sort of accommodation reached in Pennsylvania, where Amish children are permitted to satisfy the high school attendance requirement by attending an Amish vocational school and, during the balance of the week, performing farm and household duties under parental supervision, keeping a journal of their daily activities. Our sympathy for their cause should not, however, blind us to the fact that the *Yoder* decision is a palpable and unprecedented misconstruction of the Constitution, palpable because in this one respect it can be said that Old Order Amish is now an established religion of the United States (insofar as they alone are exempt from the operation of this law), and unprecedented because this was the first time the Court had held that one's religious convictions entitle one to an exemption from a valid criminal statute. The Jehovah's Witnesses who refused to obey the World War II Selective Service Law managed to avoid the criminal penalty because a majority of the Court concluded that they had not been given procedural rights to which they were entitled; the Court did not say that the First Amendment entitled them to an exemption.[12] The *Yoder* case must also be differentiated from perhaps the best known of such cases, in which West Virginia required schoolchildren to salute the flag and recite the pledge of allegiance. Children who refused to comply were expelled and treated as delinquents; their parents were made liable to prosecution and, upon conviction, to a fine and jail sentence. Jehovah's Witnesses refused to render the salute on the ground that to do so would constitute worship of a graven image, and they were upheld in their refusal by the Supreme Court. But the Court was very careful to avoid making them the special beneficiaries of its decision. The flag-salute requirement was held to be a violation of the free speech provision of the First Amendment, not of the free exercise clause. Stated otherwise, the Court held that no one, be he an enthusiastic sectarian or a militant atheist, could be required to salute the flag.[13]

No fair-minded person can deny the difficulty presented by these cases, for, especially during an era when sincerity is believed to have acquired the characteristics of a virtue, respect for the rights of conscience might incline one to respect what is done or left undone on the basis of conscience. Indeed, the difficulty is scarcely mitigated in cases where there is reason to doubt whether the defendants are proceeding in good faith, either legally or theologically. Consider the situation the Court faced in the case of the heirs of Guy W. Ballard, "alias Saint Germain, Jesus, George Washington, and Godfrey Ray King," the founding father of the "I Am" movement. Ballard claimed to possess miraculous powers and carried on a rather extensive mail-order ministry, passing the collection plate through the mails, so to speak. After his death, his wife and son, who had carried on his work and his collections, were indicted and convicted of mail fraud. The trial judge charged the jury to find whether the Ballard claims were made in good faith (and it was decided that they were not) and to ignore the question of the truth of these claims; but the Court of Appeals reversed the convictions on the ground that the prosecution had to prove, in addition, the falsity of at least some of the claims. But how does a jury determine whether Jesus had in truth stood behind Ballard and dictated the tracts he (not He) distributed through the mails, or whether Saint Germain had in truth shaken hands with Ballard in San Francisco? A bare majority of the Court, obviously embarrassed by the case, reversed the Court of Appeals and held that to inquire into the truth of these representations would constitute a denial of the free exercise of religion.[14] This had the effect of reinstating the convictions, but because the Ballards had maintained that the Court of Appeals had not considered other grounds on which reversal of the convictions was justified, the Supreme Court remanded the case to that court. The Court of Appeals affirmed the convictions, and the Ballards brought the case back to the Supreme Court. This time a bare majority of the Court managed to find a fault in the indictment—it had, said the Court, been handed down by a grand jury from which women had been excluded; therefore, it had to be dismissed.[15] That, as it turned out, ended the government's war with the Ballards.

Most of us would probably be inclined to say that the persons who contributed money to the Ballards were the victims of a palpable fraud. The jury thought so; but is the government entitled to say that the contributors did not get what they paid for? In his dissent in the first case, Chief Justice Stone said he could not say "that freedom of thought and worship includes freedom to procure money by making knowingly false statements about one's religious experiences."[16] But as Justice Jackson said in his dissent, how can the government "prove these persons knew something to be false which it cannot prove to be false?"[17] Jefferson's principle would allow the government to intervene when religious beliefs "break out into overt acts against peace and good order." This is easy to apply to a case where, for example, some zealot commits a religiously inspired assassination, but not so easy to apply here. Is fraud an act against "good order"? Surely it is. But does that depend on there being a complaining victim of the fraud? Or is the government entitled to act in order to protect potential victims? But who is to say that they *are* victims—that such contributors do not get what they pay for? At this point Justice Jackson cited William James's *The Will to Believe.*

Such questions lead one to be thankful that the government did not seek another indictment of the Ballards. Nevertheless when the issue is drawn and must be resolved, there is good reason to resolve it on the basis of Jefferson's principle, with whatever reluctance when the defendant is Yoder (and with less reluctance when the defendant is Ballard). After all, Yoder was not convicted for his beliefs but for failing to send his daughter to school. The Ballards were not indicted and convicted for their beliefs, which they may have held and certainly propagated, but for fraud. Jackson to the contrary, it would not have been impossible for a jury to find that Ballard "knew" Jesus had not shaken his hand or dictated that tract to him, and to do so without making a judgment respecting the possibility of such a miraculous event. The jurymen and women might themselves be awaiting precisely that promised reappearance and yet have reason to doubt that Ballard was telling the truth when he said it had already occurred. By introducing testimony that prior to the alleged miracles to which the Ballards were parties, they had been involved in a variety of the more familiar confidence games, the government might have been able to convince the jury of their bad faith.

Again, on principle, we would prefer to avoid such cases, but they are certain to arise on occasion. The same year as *Ballard,* the Court did not hesitate to uphold a decision of a Massachusetts court that forbade a young Jehovah's Witness to distribute religious literature on the streets at night, and it did so against what certainly appeared to be the girl's honestly held conviction that failure to distribute the literature would bring her condemnation "to everlasting destruction at Armageddon."[18] One suspects the Court did not believe this; the alternative is that the Court did not care. In either case, the Court applied Jefferson's principle and upheld the law, which is good, both because of the importance of maintaining respect for the law and because to rule in favor of the Princes and Yoders, thereby avoiding one religious thicket, is merely to march headlong into another. If one is entitled not only to disobey a law because of one's religious beliefs but also to *define* one's own religious beliefs, eventually the courts will have to become involved in the illegitimate business of distinguishing the honest profession of faith from the spurious. (It is easy to envisage a sect that takes its bearings from Christ's injunction to render unto God that which is God's and concludes that its federal income taxes should not be rendered unto the Internal Revenue Service.)

In Yoder's case the Court took the first step in this heretofore prohibited direction when it emphasized that the exemption being carved out for the Amish could not be claimed by other kinds of groups, "however virtuous and admirable" may be their "way of life." Even Thoreau, who, like the Amish, "rejected the social values of his time and isolated himself at Walden Pond," would not have been entitled to the exemption, because, unlike Yoder's, his "choice was philosophical and personal rather than religious."[19] Justice Douglas took exception to this. He agreed that the Amish could not be compelled to go to high school, but he insisted that this privilege could not properly be restricted to those whose objection to a law rests on religious belief in a formal sense; Thoreau too should qualify. Thus, the point might be reached where the Court would have to grant exemption from a *valid* law to everyone who regards the law as "immoral and totally repugnant" (this is Douglas's position)[20] or would have to draw distinctions between honest and dishonest, sincere and insincere, profound and shallow, or, if you will, true and false beliefs. At this point, we can better appreciate the validity of Jefferson's rule, which the Court used to apply, and without apology.

Yoder's fate (his $5 fine was, presumably, remitted) can be compared instructively with the fate of George Reynolds, who, a hundred years earlier, was fined $500 and sentenced to two years in jail at hard labor for violating a federal statute prohibiting any person "having a husband or wife living" to marry any other person. Reynolds acknowledged the constitutionality of this law but insisted that it could not be applied to him without depriving him of the free exercise of religion. He was a Mormon—in fact, he was Brigham Young's personal secretary—and the Mormons regarded polygamy as part of God's design and command, the argument being that the best way to fulfill the biblical command to "replenish the earth" was for one man to have and to use as many wives as possible. But polygamy was also against federal law, and the Supreme Court unanimously upheld the law. Chief Justice Waite, who wrote the opinion of the Court, took his bearings from Jefferson, and specifically from the two sentences from Jefferson's preamble to the "Bill for Establishing Religious Freedom." In these two sentences, concerning belief and "overt acts," was to be found "the true distinction between what properly belongs to the Church and what to the State."[21] He then quoted from the famous letter to the Danbury Baptists: "'Adhering to this expression of the Supreme will of the Nation in behalf of the rights of conscience [the religious clauses of the First Amendment], I shall see, with sincere satisfaction, the progress of those sentiments which tend to restore man to all his natural rights, convinced he has no natural right in opposition to his social duties.'"[22] Next he rang some rhetorical changes on examples from Locke's toleration letter by way of Jefferson, and concluded by asking whether a man can excuse practices contrary to law because of his religious beliefs. The answer was clearly no. "To permit this would be to make the professed doctrines of religious belief superior to the law of the land, and in effect to permit every citizen to become a law unto himself. Government could exist only in name under such circumstances."[23]

So it went in this first and leading case. Whatever our sympathies for Reynolds, and however much we would like to have these questions resolved administratively below the level of principle, we must agree that the principle embodied in the free exercise clause was properly applied to his case. It is doubtful that the decision would be the same today. Today it is not generally recognized that the subordination of religion leads, and was intended by the philosophers of natural rights (Hobbes, Locke, Montesquieu, and Rousseau) to lead, to the concentration of political power in the hands of the sovereign, or in the law; and that this concentration of power in the hands of the civil authority—this denial of "private judgment"—has the effect of denying the legitimacy of any appeal from the sovereign or the law to a body of religious doctrine or to "conscience." According to the philosophy of natural rights—and to put the case even more baldly, according to liberalism—one renders unto Caesar whatever Caesar demands and to God whatever Caesar permits. This is an aspect of the separation of church and state that has been forgotten. We have grown accustomed to looking at the problem of church and state solely from the perspective of its advantages to the citizen, and we tend to ignore, or to be oblivious to, what the citizen has to forgo in exchange for the advantages. He may worship as he pleases or not worship at all; he may not be disqualified from holding "any office or public trust under the United States" because of his religious opinions or lack of them; he may not be required, or in the public schools even encouraged, to recite a prayer, however innocuous; he may not be required to support a church or contribute money to its support; he may not be penalized in any of the ways familiar to subjects of an illiberal government. All these advantages—and they are not inconsiderable—are familiar to us, and especially to us students of constitutional law. But it necessarily follows that he may not refuse, because of his religious beliefs, to obey the law. That follows because no religious beliefs have any status in the law—except, as in the case of conscientious objection to military service, when the law, as a matter of grace, grants that status. Whether a law is just or unjust is a judgment that belongs to no "private man," however pious or learned or, as we say today, sincere he may be. "For the private judgment of any person concerning a law enacted in political matters, for the public good, does not take away the obligation of that law, nor deserve a dispensation."[24] So said Locke, following Hobbes; and Jefferson, who made careful notes on Locke's *Letter Concerning Toleration,* was equally emphatic on the subject (see Chapter 1). But the contemporary Supreme Court has refused to be guided by this fundamental principle of liberalism.

The Court's solicitude for vestigial religious enthusiasm is nowhere more unmistakably displayed than in the modern conscientious objector cases. Continuing a practice that began in 1775 in a resolution adopted by the Continental Congress, resumed during the Civil War, and affirmed in the Militia Acts of 1903 and 1916 and again in the Selective Draft Act of 1917 and the Selective Service Act of 1940, Congress, in the Universal Military Training and Service Act of 1948, exempted from "combat training and service" anyone who, "by reason of religious training and belief, is conscientiously opposed to participation in war in any form."[25] Throughout this long legislative history two principles are unambiguously preserved: military service is a duty that may be required of all citizens, and exemptions from this duty are made as a matter of legislative grace, not of constitutional necessity. The exemptions were originally drafted to favor the members of the historic peace churches—Quakers, Mennonites, and Schwenkfelders, "people who, from Religious Principles, cannot bear arms in any case," as the Continental Congress put it in 1775, or "a member of any well-recognized religious sect or organization . . . whose existing creed or principles forbid its members to participate in war in any form," as Congress put it in the World War I act. In the 1940 act this was broadened to embrace anyone who "by reason of religious training and belief, is conscientiously opposed to participation in war in any form." This formulation was retained in the 1948 act, and Congress added a sentence to clarify the meaning of the phrase "religious training and belief." The clarification was needed because in 1943 the Court of Appeals for the Second Circuit, in what has been described as "gratuitous dicta," had made religious belief and conscientious belief synonymous terms.[26] To make it plain—as plain as language can be, one would have thought—that it did not regard them as synonymous, Congress in the 1948 act added the following sentence: "Religious training and belief in this connection means an individual's belief in a relation to a Supreme Being involving duties superior to those arising from any human relation, but does not include essentially political, sociological, or philosophical views or a merely personal moral code."[27]

In 1965, Daniel Seeger, who explicitly denied belief in a Supreme Being and based his claim to be a conscientious objector on his "belief in and devotion to goodness and virtue for their own sakes, and a religious faith in a purely ethical creed," was nevertheless held by the Supreme Court to be entitled to the exemption under this section.[28] What Congress meant by religious belief, the Court held, was a "sincere and meaningful belief which occupies in the life of its possessor a place parallel to that filled by the God of those admittedly qualifying for the exemption...." Since Seeger's objection to war occupied "the same place in his life as the belief in a traditional deity holds in the lives of his friends, the Quakers," he, like them, was entitled to the grace of Congress.

Elliott Ashton Welsh II went further than Seeger; he said he did not believe in a Supreme Being and, at the outset, expressly disclaimed any religious aspect to his pacifist views, acknowledging that they had been formed by his reading "in the fields of history and sociology."[29] The Court, five years after Seeger, disagreed with him; Welsh was apparently one of the many Selective Service registrants who were unaware of the "broad scope of the word 'religious' as used in [the statute]." Therefore, contrary to Welsh's own original disavowal, the Court held that his views *were* religious within the meaning of the statute and that he was entitled to exemption on this ground. The statutory "religious beliefs" included moral and ethical beliefs "about what is right and wrong" if these beliefs were "held with the strength of traditional religious convictions."[30] It was a sharply divided Court that arrived at this destination.

These cases, and the host of lower court decisions dealing with the same question, make an interesting chapter in the story of statutory interpretation, or in what the New Deal generation of constitutional lawyers called "the struggle for judicial supremacy," to refer to Mr. Justice (but at the time, plain Robert H.) Jackson's book under that title. The plain fact is, the Court was playing ducks and drakes with the conscientious objector section of the Selective Service Act. As Justice Harlan demonstrated in his concurring opinion in *Welsh*, Congress left no doubt whatever in its actions of 1940, 1948, and, between *Seeger* and *Welsh,* in 1967, that it did not intend to grant grace to persons holding the beliefs of Seeger and Welsh. In fact, as Michael Malbin has shown beyond any argument, a review of the history of such exemptions shows that Congress was consistent in its refusal to grant them exemption "every time the issue came up for discussion between 1789 and 1967.[31]

We are, of course, accustomed to the practice in American courts of interpreting statutes seemingly against their plain meaning. Unlike the situation prevailing under a system of legislative (or parliamentary) supremacy, American courts have the power to declare statutes unconstitutional; as a corollary of this power, courts are expected to "read" a statute in a constitutional manner, or, stated otherwise, to make it constitutional, if at all possible. Such an intention played a role in *Seeger* and, more evidently, in *Welsh*. In the latter case, the vote that tipped the balance in Welsh's favor was cast by Justice Harlan, who concurred separately and made it clear that he did so solely on constitutional grounds. "In my opinion," he wrote, "the liberties taken with the statute both in *Seeger* and [in] today's decision cannot be justified in the name of the familiar doctrine of construing federal statutes in a manner that will avoid possible constitutional infirmities in them."[32] He voted for Welsh because a statute granting the exemption to those holding religious beliefs and withholding it from those holding "secular beliefs" would constitute an establishment of religion, therefore violating the First Amendment. It was his view—a view best elaborated by Professor Philip Kurland in his *Religion and the Law*[33]—that religion is an unconstitutional classification that may not be utilized either to confer a benefit or impose a burden.

Congress may refuse to grant exemptions to everyone, but if Congress chooses to grant exemptions from military service, it must grant them to everyone with a conscientious and intense moral belief against war. "The common denominator must be the intensity of moral conviction with which a belief is held."[34] According to Harlan, to narrow the ground of conscientious objection to religious objection is to establish religion, placing nonreligious objectors at a disadvantage; in so doing, it violates the constitutional requirement that legislation be "neutral." Two possible conclusions followed from this: (1) invalidate the statute because it did not extend to a sufficiently broad class of objectors, in which case, there being no valid statutory exemption, neither Welsh nor anyone else would be entitled to an exemption from military service; or (2) accept the statute as amended by the Court to cure "the defect of underinclusion." For reasons we need not consider here, Harlan chose to do the latter, and thereby to supply the vote Welsh needed. He thus made it possible for the majority of the Court to impair the principle of the rule of law.

Harlan was right to concede that Congress need not grant exemptions to anyone, even someone who, in the language of the statute, believes "in a relation to a Supreme Being involving duties superior to those arising from any human relation"; but he failed to see the consequences of this. Congress does not have to grant an exemption to someone who follows the command of God rather than the command of the law because the Congress established by the Constitution of the United States denies—to state the matter harshly, as the Court has forced us to do—*that God issues any such commands.* A private person may think He has (and the Constitution protects his right to think He has), but he may not act on the basis of this opinion, not when the law commands otherwise. His belief, however profound, has in the eyes of the Constitution the status of a mere opinion. His belief that God forbids him to kill another human being occupies the same status as another person's belief that he must worship a golden calf, or still another's belief that she must immolate herself on her dead husband's funeral pyre. Constitutionally, these are mere opinions, and the law may require the one to bear arms and forbid the second to hoard gold and the third to commit suttee.

The second consequence of Harlan's concession (a concession liberalism requires him to make) is that whether there are or should be any exemptions from a law is a matter solely within the jurisdiction of the lawmaking body. The First Amendment requires Congress to tolerate religious opinions—all of them—but it is a matter for Congress to decide whether various acts ("acts of the body") shall be permitted. Congress decides whether to exempt women, forty-year-old men, fifteen-year-old boys, or conscientious objectors from bearing arms, and it does not impair or derogate from the rule of law for Congress to make any of these exemptions. It is still the law speaking. Congress decides to grant the exemptions because in its judgment women should not fight, forty-year-old men are too old to fight, fifteen-year-old boys are too young to fight, and a truly conscientious objector will not fight even if given a weapon. In the last case, Congress may have an additional reason for granting the exemption: considering the small number of religious pacifists in the country and that they are exemplary, law-abiding citizens in every other respect, nothing will be lost and something might be gained if we avoid placing them in a situation where, because of their private opinions, they will have to make an anguished choice between the duty imposed by the law and what they believe to be a duty imposed by God. By granting an exemption from the law, Congress keeps them within the law and thereby enhances the rule of law.

What the Supreme Court did in *Seeger* and *Welsh* was to move some distance toward the position where not the law but the citizen himself decides whether he must obey. *Seeger* enlarged the legislatively defined category to include a "sincere and meaningful belief which occupies in the life of its possessor a place parallel to that filled by the God of those admittedly quali-fying for the exemption...." So vaguely stated a category is certain to be self-administered in practice. There is no substance to it; it permits (or if there were still a Selective Service Act, would permit) any objector to claim that his beliefs are "parallel" to those of a Quaker's—for example, that they are as honestly and "deeply" held—and there is almost no basis for a Selective Service Board to disagree. Nor did *Welsh* change this significantly. Liberalism began in the effort to subordinate reli-gious opinion to the law—"the private judgment of any person concerning a law...does not take away the obligation of that law," Locke said—and the Court has now exalted the vaguest of moral sentiments over the law. This seems certain to enhance civil disobedience, and civil disobedience is detrimental to good government.

Should this appear to be harsh doctrine—and no doubt it will in certain quarters, since it denies a constitutional right of conscientious objection—the answer is that, however harsh, it is compatible with the principle of the equality of all men, and conscientious objection is not. If the person objecting to the law claims, on the basis of his religious convictions or his conscience, an exemption from the law, he is asking to be treated differently and therefore unequally. He is saying that the law may demand military service or taxes or marital restraint of others, but that the law may not demand them of him. If, on the other hand, the person objecting to the law claims that no one need obey it because the law is unjust, the position taken by the defenders of civil disobedience, he is claiming a moral superiority, in flat defiance of the proposition that all men are created equal. He is claiming that his private judgment is superior to the public judgment, or to the private judgments of the majority that, in a democracy, are transformed into the public judgment when they are made law.

To argue that in principle there can be no private judgment against the law is not to argue that a healthy polity cannot accommodate—perhaps by simply ignoring—a good deal of recusancy. Nor is it to argue that the law is always right; it is merely to argue that the alternative is unacceptable in principle. Locke admits that the law can err, and he makes this admission in the very context of arguing that there can be no right of private judgment:

Thus the safeguard of men's lives, and of the things that belong unto this life, is the business of the commonwealth; and the preserving of those things unto their owners is the duty of the magistrate; and therefore the magistrate cannot take away these worldly things from this man, or party, and give them to that; nor change property amongst fellow-subjects, no, not even by a law, for a cause that has no relation to the end of civil government; I mean for their religion; which, whether it be true or false, does no prejudice to the worldly concerns of their fellow-subjects, which are the things that only belong unto the care of the commonwealth. [35]

But what if, nevertheless, the magistrate believes "he has a right to make such laws, and that they are for the public good, and his subjects believe the contrary? Who shall be judge between them?" God alone, he answers; on this earth there is no judge. Which is to say: the magistrate is not authorized to misrule, but there is no sure way to prevent it. Locke could provide a general outline of the institutional safeguard carried further by Montesquieu and perfected by the American Founders—namely, the separation of powers. But as Tocqueville was to say much later, institutions exercise "only a secondary influence over the destinies of man." Tocqueville added that if he could believe them to be all powerful, he "would have more hopes for our future, for we might someday chance to stumble upon the precious recipe which would cure all our ills...."[36] Still, the United States, with the variety of "auxiliary precautions" extolled by Madison in the 51st *Federalist,* plus judicial review, which was extolled by his colleague Hamilton in the 78th *Federalist,* has come as close to solving this problem as any other nation, and probably closer. To say nothing here of Madison's "auxiliary precautions," the institution of judicial review comes as close as any device can come to accommodating the demands of the law and the demands of conscience.

No nation can adopt the rule that citizens need not obey the law when, in their opinion, it is immoral; such a rule, in Waite's words, would in effect "permit every citizen to become a law unto himself." Nor can a constitution that recognizes rights against government allow the private citizen to define those rights; that is the duty of courts. What a constitution can do, and what the institution of judicial review does, is to permit the private citizen to ask a court—an official body, yes, but one separate from the body that enacts the law, and as separate as human ingenuity can make it without making it irresponsible—to determine not whether the law is immoral, but whether it is unconstitutional. It permits the citizen to raise the moral question by requiring him to transform it into a constitutional question and to submit that question to a court, not to his own conscience. What can a *citizen,* especially a citizen in a self-governing democracy, ask beyond that? In judicial review, Americans have an institution that comes as close as possible to allowing them to render unto Caesar that which is Caesar's without making it impossible to render unto God that which is God's.

And what, finally, if the Supreme Court errs? Those who so easily assume they know the answer to this question should ponder Lincoln's response to the greatest constitutional and political error ever committed by the Court: *Dred Scott* v. *Sandford.*[37] To Lincoln and his associates in the newly organized Republican Party, the law announced in the *Dred Scott* decision had a more devastating impact than any law encountered in the recent past by the opponents of the Vietnam war. *Dred Scott* destroyed the principle of the Republicans' existence as a political party. They were pledged to prevent the further spread of slavery into the territories, and *Dred Scott* forbade the government to enact laws forbidding the spread of slavery into the territories. To accept it meant to cease to exist as an antislavery political movement and to acquiesce in what they regarded, rightly, as a moral abomination profoundly at odds with the founding principle respecting the equality of all men. Yet, precisely because of their attachment to the Declaration of Independence, the Republicans had to stand with the Constitution, and the Supreme Court expounded the meaning of the Constitution. Even in this extremity, and with the best of reasons knowing the Court's decision to be wrong, constitutionally wrong, Lincoln did not claim a right to disobey it:

We oppose the Dred Scott decision in a certain way, upon which I ought perhaps to address you a few words. We do not propose that when Dred Scott has been decided to be a slave by the court, we, as a mob, will decide him to be free. We do not propose that, when any other one, or one thousand, shall be decided by that court to be slaves, we will in any violent way disturb the rights of property thus settled; but we nevertheless do oppose that decision as a political rule which shall be binding on the voter, to vote for nobody who thinks it wrong, which shall be binding on the members of Congress or the President to favor no measure that does not actually concur with the principles of that decision. We do not propose to be bound by it as a political rule in that way, because we think it lays the foundation not merely of enlarging and spreading out what we consider an evil, but it lays the foundation for spreading that evil into the States themselves. We propose so resisting it as to have it reversed if we can, and a new judicial rule established upon this subject. [38]

Lincoln proposed to resist *Dred Scott* by refusing to accept it as final and irreversible; he proposed to work politically and within the law and the Constitution to have it reversed. The alternative was revolution, not civil disobedience. As he said in his First Inaugural, "This country, with its institutions, belongs to the people who inhabit it. Whenever they shall grow weary of the existing government, they can exercise their *constitutional* right of amending it, or their *revolutionary* right to dismember or overthrow it." He said nothing about a right to break the law, and nothing in this statement supports those who have cited it as part of their case for civil disobedience; for Lincoln spoke of a *revolutionary* right, and he italicized the word for emphasis.* In

*Even so careful and nondoctrinaire a constitutional scholar as the late Alexander M. Bickel was reluctant to accept the position espoused here and embodied in Lincoln's response to the egregious provocation of *Dred Scott;* and taking this position, Lincoln was merely following Jefferson, for the Declaration of Independence does not justify disobedience to law; it justifies revolution, and the men who wrote and adopted it knew what would happen to them if they lost, which is why they pledged to each other their lives, their fortunes, and their sacred honor.

It remains only to consider Harlan's constitutional argument that religion is an unconstitutional classification insofar as, by bestowing a benefit in the form of an exemption on religious believers, the statute constitutes a law respecting an establishment of religion. This is another version of Douglas's argument that the First Amendment requires Congress to be neutral between religion and irreligion. As we saw in the preceding chapter, this is demonstrably not the intent of the Amendment. Furthermore, we *know* that the First Congress did not share the view that the First Amendment forbade religious exemptions from military service; we know this from the debates in the First Congress on the Bill of Rights. What is now the Second Amendment read as follows when Madison first proposed it on June 8, 1789: "The right of a people to keep and bear arms shall not be infringed; a well regulated militia being the best security of a free country; but no person religiously scrupulous of bearing arms shall be compelled to render military service in person."[39] After an extensive debate on a variety of matters, the House adopted this, and the exemption clause was lost only in the Senate.

Of course, we have no record of the Senate debates of that period, so there is no way of knowing the Senate's reasons; but if we conjecture that the senators were persuaded by some of the

as a result of this reluctance, he misread Lincoln's response. He said the line drawn by Lincoln lies "between the general law, the law of the land...enunciated in a judicial decision...and the judicial judgment addressed to the parties in an actual case. There is no moral duty always and invariably to obey the former. There is a moral duty to obey the latter" ("Watergate and the Legal Order," *Commentary 57* [January 1974]: 22). This is surely wrong. It is wrong because it does not conform to what Lincoln says, and it is wrong because if there is no moral duty to obey the law of the land, there cannot be a moral duty to obey a judgment based on that law.

arguments made in the House debates, which we do have, then we can say what these reasons were. They were a desire to leave the question of exemptions to legislative discretion, the fear that the provision might provide Congress with a weapon to weaken the state militias, the difficulty of defining "religious scruples," with the possibility that the term might be exploited by "those who are of no religion," and a dispute over the issue of whether exempted pacifists should be required to make some sort of monetary payment in lieu of military service. No one suggested that to exempt pacifists on religious grounds would constitute a law respecting an establishment of religion. The following remarks of Egbert Benson of New York, made on August 17, 1789, during the debate on Madison's proposal, are typical of the mood of the House:

Mr. Benson moved to have the words "but no person religiously scrupulous shall be compelled to bear arms," struck out. He would always leave it to the benevolence of the Legislature, for, modify it as you please, it will be impossible to express it in such a manner as to clear it from ambiguity. No man can claim this indulgence of right. It may be a religious persuasion, but it is no natural right, and therefore ought to be left to the discretion of the Government. If this stands as part of the Constitution, it will be a question before the Judiciary on every regulation with respect to the organization of the militia, whether it comports with this declaration or not. It is extremely injudicious to intermix matters of doubt with fundamentals.

I have no reason to believe but that the Legislature will always possess humanity enough to indulge this class of citizens in a matter they are so desirous of; but they ought to be left to their discretion. [40]

The constitutional argument against religious exemptions can only be advanced in defiance of the historical record.

Religion and the Public Morality

This public recognition of religious worship...is not based entirely, perhaps even mainly, upon a sense of

55

what is due to the Supreme Being himself,...but the same reasons of state policy which enduce the government to aid institutions of charity and seminaries of instruction will also incline it to foster religious worship and religious institutions, as conservators of the public morals, and valuable, if not indispensable assistants to the preservation of the public order. [41]

Prior to the adoption of the Fourteenth Amendment (or, more precisely, prior to the time when it was held to embrace the religious provisions of the First Amendment), the Supreme Court lacked all supervisory authority over the states in religious matters. Whether the states imposed religious tests for voting or holding office, or required or permitted their schools to teach the tenets of any faith or to conduct prayer services or to read from the Bible at designated devotional ceremonies, or with their financial support discriminated against other than Christian churches or even among the various denominations of Christians—all these were questions "to be acted upon according to [each state's] own sense of justice...."[42] The First Amendment by itself left "the whole power over the subject of religion...exclusively to the State governments." They began to lose their power only in 1940, when the Supreme Court said that the liberty protected against state action by the Fourteenth Amendment included religious liberty, meaning, moreover, not only liberty to worship but liberty (it can only be awkwardly formulated) from laws respecting an establishment of religion. Speaking for a unanimous Court, Justice Roberts said that the Fourteenth Amendment renders "the legislatures of the states as incompetent as Congress" to make laws respecting "an establishment of religion or prohibiting the free exercise thereof."[43] It remained only to be decided what exactly it was that they were equally forbidden to do, for with only one insignificant exception, the Court had never had the occasion to define the policy limitations imposed by the establishment clause on the national government. The exception is the 1899 case of *Bradfield* v. *Roberts,* in which the Court allowed the government to enter into a contract with and to grant funds to a hospital in the District of Columbia controlled by a Roman Catholic order of nuns.[44] The import of what the Court did in 1940 may have been concealed from it by the narrow view taken of the establishment clause; this, Roberts said in a dictum, merely forbade "compulsion by law of the acceptance of any creed or the practice of any form of worship," which would seem to be already forbidden by the free exercise clause. Within a few years the Court had the chance to define establishment, and it proved to forbid a good deal more than compulsory worship.

The New Jersey statute involved in the 1947 case, *Everson* v. *Board of Education,* authorized school districts to reimburse parents for the bus fares paid by their children traveling to and from schools, including church-related schools. Everson, a taxpayer, was granted standing to challenge the right of the school board to reimburse parents of parochial schoolchildren, contending, in part, that such reimbursement constituted a law respecting an establishment of religion. The Court, in an opinion written by Justice Black, said there was "every reason" to give the same broad interpretation to the establishment clause as it had previously given to the free exercise clause; so interpreted, the establishment clause meant that neither Congress nor a state legislature may "pass laws which aid one religion, aid all religions, or prefer one religion over another." Nor may any tax "in any amount, large or small...be levied to support any religious activities or institutions, whatever they may be called, or whatever form they may adopt to teach or practice religion."[45] In support of this reading of the establishment clause, Black cited Jefferson's metaphor of "a wall of separation between church and state," his "Bill for Establishing Religious Freedom in Virginia," and Madison's "Memorial and Remonstrance," in addition to the secondary literature; he did not cite the debates in the First Congress.

What is striking in Black's opinion for the Court and in Rutledge's powerful dissenting opinion is the reliance on Jefferson's wall metaphor, Madison's "Memorial and Remonstrance," and the evidence drawn from the Virginia disestablishment struggle. Black did not even refer to the First Amendment debates. While Rutledge referred to them and twice quoted parts of them in footnotes, he managed to overlook all the evidence contrary to his interpretation of the Amendment. Thus, Black found that it was the "feelings" of the Virginians which "found expression in the First Amendment," and that the First Amendment "had the same objective and was intended to provide the same protection against governmental intrusion on religious liberty as the Virginia Statute;"[46] and Rutledge, who dissented because he thought the busing scheme unconstitutional, said the purpose of the Amendment "was to create a complete and permanent separation of the spheres of religious activity and civil authority by comprehensively forbidding every form of public aid or support for religion." The Virginia experience and Madison's "Memorial and Remonstrance" provided "irrefutable confirmation of the Amendment's sweeping content."[47] In this fashion, then, in this first and decisive case, the Virginians became not merely the principal but the sole authors of the religious provisions of the First Amendment. As Mark DeWolfe Howe put it, in *Everson* the justices made "the historically quite misleading assumption that the same considerations which moved Jefferson and Madison to favor separation of church and state in Virginia led the nation to demand the religious clauses of the First Amendment."[48] This, he said, was a "gravely distorted picture." So far as any of the three opinions in *Everson* is concerned, the policy advanced in the House by Gerry, Sylvester, Huntington, and the others, and by what appears to have been a majority of the Senate, found no place in the version of the First Amendment which was adopted with their support. This proved to be decisive, because *Everson* has been the case on which the law of the establishment clause has been made.

There can be no doubt of the relevance of Madison's "Memorial and Remonstrance"; it was and has remained an authentic American statement of liberal principles respecting religion and politics. Nor can there be any doubt that the various laws establishing and thereby preferring the Anglican Church of Virginia were violative of those principles.[49] Nevertheless, to accept Madison and Jefferson as the sole authorities among the Founders on the meaning of the religious clauses of the First Amendment is, as Professor Howe said, to distort the picture. It is worth mentioning here that the particular bill against which Madison directed his "Memorial and Remonstrance," a tax for the benefit of "teachers of the Christian religion," was proposed by Patrick Henry and had the support of Washington and Marshall, and that all this occurred in 1785, before there was a First Amendment. The fact is, Madison even more than Jefferson stands out from the other men of his time because of the radical character of his views on church and state. It is sufficient to recall that as President he vetoed a bill to grant a charter of incorporation to the Episcopal Church in Washington, D.C., and opposed the appointment of chaplains in the Army and Navy and the granting of tax exemptions to "Houses of Worship"; he even objected to presidential proclamations of days of thanksgiving. The extent to which others did not share all his views is reflected in the fact that he found it necessary to yield to the pressure and issue such a proclamation.

To suggest that, with its reliance on the history of the Virginia struggle, the Court in *Everson* emphasized one aspect of the First Amendment at the expense of another, albeit subordinate aspect, does not mean that the Fourteenth Amendment was intended to have no effect on a state's powers respecting religion. If anyone today were to insist that the states may still discriminate against non-Christian sects in public "encouragement" programs, it would not be improper to suspect him of being influenced by something other than a scrupulous devotion to the constitutional text. Or assuming Story is right (and there is reason to believe that he is right), and that originally Congress itself was merely forbidden to prefer one Christian church over another in whatever policy it adopted by way of encouraging religion,[50] it does not follow that Congress today might limit its aid under the Elementary and Secondary Education Act of 1965, for example, to schools affiliated with Christian churches only. A more latitudinarian policy is required not only by the prevailing religious pluralism but also because it is, in fact, more in keeping with the founding principle: the United States recognizes no religious truth. The earlier interpretation can be explained only as an illiberal concession to the conditions prevailing in the country during the early years of the Constitution. But in *Everson* the Court did more than bring the First Amendment up to date, so to speak; by relying so heavily on Madison and on Jefferson's wall metaphor, it launched an interpretation under which the First Amendment forbids precisely what many a man in the First Congress went to such pains to protect—namely, public support of religion, albeit on a nondiscriminatory basis. In the cases decided in the wake of *Everson,* the Court has insisted that it is precisely the religious activities of religious organizations that may *not* be supported, neither by Congress nor by the states.

This rule is well illustrated in the 1963 Bible-reading case, *Abington School District* v. *Schempp,* where the Court, in the course of invalidating the program, said that the constitutionality of any government aid program depends on its "purpose and primary effect": if either its purpose or primary effect is the advancement of religion, "then the enactment exceeds the scope of the legislative powers."[51] This leaves room for "encouragement" of a religious organization if the legislative purpose is secular and its primary effect is not to advance religion. The trouble with this formulation is that it forbids the fostering of religious belief in order to advance a secular end; yet, whatever might be said of some programs that existed in the past, this is what the states have sought to accomplish by promoting Bible reading and prayer ceremonies in the public schools. And, although it may be fruitless to dwell on the point, this is what

Sylvester, Gerry, Livermore, Ames, Huntington, and others in the House, and those anonymous members of the Senate, thought they were permitting when, in the First Congress, they supported the adoption of the First Amendment.

Justice Brennan, in a long concurring opinion in the *Schempp* case, conceded that the Bible-reading and prayer exercises may sometimes be intended to serve "broader goals than compelling formal worship of God," but the "crucial fact," he insisted, is that such exercises are "nevertheless religious."[52] This is their constitutional vice. Unlike the Sunday closing laws, whose constitutionality the Court had upheld,[53] "these exercises appear neither to have been divorced from their religious origins nor deprived of their centrally religious character by the passage of time."[54] Thus, when no religious purpose would be served by doing so, the Bible may be read and the prayers recited in the public schools. But if any religious significance is attached to the Bible, or if the students pray in anything resembling a reverent manner, the Constitution is violated just so much. At this point Brennan opened the door a bit, only to slam it shut immediately: a religious means may be adopted to secure a legitimate secular end only if it has been shown that that secular end cannot be achieved through nonreligious means. But it "has not been shown that readings from the speeches and messages of great Americans, for example, or from the documents of our heritage or history," cannot accomplish the same purpose for which the Bible was being read; nor has it been shown that the "daily recitation of the Pledge of Allegiance, or even the observance of a moment of reverent [but, of course, not too reverent] silence at the opening of class, may not adequately serve the solely secular purposes of the devotional activities [and do so] without jeopardizing...the proper degree of separation between the spheres of religion and government."[55] But one of the "messages of great Americans"—in fact, one of the greatest messages of one of the greatest Americans—is Washington's Farewell Address, and in it Washington warned the nation not to "indulge the supposition, that morality can be maintained without religion." Both "reason and experience," he said, "forbid us to expect that National morality can prevail in exclusion of religious principle." In fact, Brennan quoted this passage in a footnote on the preceding page. Perhaps he quoted it only to prevent its being quoted against him. In any case, having quoted it, he proceeded to ignore it, and we are left to speculate as to the evidence he could have adduced to show that Washington was wrong, or what experience he could have pointed to in order to convince us that Washington's apprehensions were misguided. Perhaps a steadily declining crime rate?

There is no way of knowing how far these school religious exercises go in serving Washington's purpose, and candor requires us to recognize that they exact a price from children who would prefer to be excused from them but are, for obvious reasons, reluctant to ask to be excused.[56] There is, then, a "free exercise" argument against these public religious ceremonies, one that cannot be fully met by making them voluntary. But once we recognize that the schools have always been charged with providing more than a technical or vocational training in the narrow sense (see pp. 65-67), that somehow they are expected to play a role—and, willy-nilly, do play some sort of a role—in the forming of tastes and shaping of opinion, then it becomes important to pay attention not only to the curriculum but also to the setting within which that curriculum is taught, and by whom. The exemplary method of education—or, better, the exemplary role of the educator—cannot be denied, especially with younger children; and at the risk of being ridiculed for peddling niaiseries, I would argue that it is better that teachers be seen leading prayers than agitating for some of the popular causes of our day. Some knowledge of the history of the disputes surrounding public education, as well as a reading of the daily newspaper, lead me to believe that the American people share this naive opinion. But be that as it may, it is when the principle of the prayer cases is applied to cases involving public assistance to private religious institutions, especially educational institutions, that the damage is done. For if the vice is said to be the religious character of the ceremony rather than the public character of the school, then no religious institution may be the recipient of public assistance.

Although its ramifications seemed clear, *Schempp* actually left unresolved the issue of the constitutionality of public aid to church-related schools. It was possible to argue that the Court's "purpose and primary effect" test leaves room for some aid programs, and in *Board of Education* v. *Allen* in 1968 a sharply divided Court refused to strike down a New York program whereby secular textbooks were "lent" without charge to all schoolchildren enrolled in grades seven to twelve in private (including church-related) as well as public schools. What apparently saved this program was the Court's judgment that its "purpose and primary effect" was not the advancement of religion, a judgment that was made possible, at least, because the nominal beneficiaries were the children rather than the institutions they attended.[57] There were, of course, ominous rumblings from the dissenters that boded ill for any program, however formulated, which promised to provide the substantial financial assistance apparently needed by church-related schools if they are to survive.

From the point of view of the proponents of this aid, these forebodings were not dispelled by the Court's 1970 decision that tax exemptions granted to church properties do not constitute a violation of the establishment clause, even though all but one of the justices (the exception was Douglas) agreed to this.[58] In terms of the actual benefits received, there may not be much difference between an exemption from a tax and an affirmative grant of state funds, but there is a great difference—and a politically significant difference—between the number of churches operating schools and the number of churches receiving tax benefits. This difference probably accounts for the constitutional difference the Court was able to discern between the tax exemption and the "secular purpose" programs enacted after the textbooks loan case.

The rule that the "purpose and primary effect" of a program may not be the advancement of religion led, as it might be expected to lead, to a variety of legislative attempts to disguise religious aid in secular trappings. Pennsylvania "purchased" instruction in secular subjects from private, including church-related, schools.[59] Rhode Island subsidized private school teachers for their "secular" teaching by making available payments of up to 15 percent of their regular salaries.[60] New York paid private schools to compensate them for various state-mandated "secular" services they performed, such as enforcing compulsory attendance laws, keeping health records, and administering state "Regents" examinations.[61] New York also provided direct grants to nonpublic schools for the "maintenance and repair" of facilities and equipment when these schools served high concentrations of pupils from low-income families. In addition, the same New York statute offered tuition grants to low-income parents of nonpublic school children, and state income tax deductions to financially better endowed parents.[62] Pennsylvania, again, came up with a "Parent Reimbursement Act for Non-Public Education,"[63] and the same state, in two statutes, authorized loans of textbooks, instructional materials, and equipment and provided such "auxiliary services" as guidance counseling and speech and hearing therapy to nonpublic schools, including church-related schools.[64]

With the exception of the textbook loan provision in the last-named act, none of these programs passed constitutional muster; nor, given the secular purpose rule (and the "excessive entanglement" rule applied in *Lemon* v. *Kurtzman*), did any of them deserve to pass muster. Of course church-related schools perform some functions that are performed in the public schools, and these might truly deserve the designation "secular"; but the schools are maintained for a religious purpose. It is impossible to support the one without making it easier for the churches and the children's parents to support the other. The justices were not slow to see this. With the exception of the textbook loan programs, the only public aid programs to survive recent constitutional challenge were those involving higher education, and they were able to do so only because, in the Court's opinion, the colleges and universities were not essentially religious institutions. The principal case involved the Higher Education Facilities Act, enacted by Congress in 1963; under this measure, "brick and mortar" grants were made, in the test case, to four Roman Catholic colleges in Connecticut to enable them to construct buildings to be used for secular activities. Chief Justice Burger, speaking for a mere plurality of the Court, emphasized that college students were less impressionable than their younger brothers and sisters; besides, the institutions were less likely to spend their time propagating the faith among them.[65] More or less on the same grounds, a South Carolina revenue bond program was upheld. The Baptist college whose receipt of the bonds was being challenged was not, the Court felt, primarily engaged in an effort to advance religion.[66] Thus, under the Constitution of the United States, public aid (both state and federal) may be extended to religious schools to the extent that they fail to fulfill what they would at one time have regarded as their primary mission. More simply: aid may be extended to religious schools to the extent to which they are not religious. There would be no disposition to quarrel with this rule except for the strong possibility that the advancement of the religious objective may make it easier to advance a political objective shared by all good citizens—namely, the preservation of free government in the United States—and that it may be one of the few means of doing so available to public policy makers.

The history of American education is, in one of its significant aspects, a history of gradual secularization of the schools and their curricula; but to say this is to acknowledge that there have been religious elements in that education from the beginning, elements that have not yet entirely disappeared. During the colonial period and continuing into the nineteenth century, education, to the extent to which it existed at all outside the family (or the tutors employed by the wealthy families), was the direct responsibility of the churches themselves. Where public schools were established, as they were in Boston as early as 1635, their curricula "consisted largely in the Bible and moralizings based on the Bible."[67] The schools of Massachusetts continued to be characterized by a Calvinist pietism until an 1827 statute forbade the purchase of books calculated to favor a particular sect or tenet; but the purpose of the law was merely to put an end to the monopoly enjoyed by the Congregationalists, not to make the schools secular. Even Horace Mann, whose contribution to the cause of public education is commemorated in many a school bearing his name, was opposed not to religion in the schools but to sectarian schools. He was, he said, "in favor of religious instruction in our schools to the extremest verge to which it can be carried without invading those rights of conscience which are established by the laws of God and guaranteed by the Constitution of the State [of Massachusetts]."[68] Secularization arose, then, not so much out of disputes between religion and irreligion as between different varieties of religion, and in this respect the school disputes resembled the earlier struggles to disestablish state churches.

Church education gave way to public sectarian education, which in turn gave way to religious education less narrowly—but not yet altogether broadly—defined. For example, it was not defined broadly enough to make it acceptable to Roman Catholics, and with their arrival in significant numbers a new chapter in the schools dispute began. Unlike most Protestant sectarians, they objected to the practice of reading from the Bible because they objected to the Bible that was being read; similarly, they objected not to religious teaching but to the religion being taught. For the instruction of Catholic children they sought either the right to bring their Bible and their dogma into the public schools or a share of public funds to enable them to establish their own schools. Failing in this, they argued that all religious materials should be eliminated from the tax-supported public schools. In doing so, they apparently played a role in the secularization of these schools. In Leo Pfeffer's words, the "triumph of the secularization of the public school was in no small measure due to the persistence of the Church and the courage of Catholic parents in refusing to sacrifice their claims of conscience by yielding to a settlement that was entirely satisfactory to the Protestant majority."[69] While today Catholics are inclined to complain that the public school is "Godless," before and after the Civil War they complained of the Protestant character of the schools. Mann's nonsectarianism was Christianity, a Protestant Christianity.[70] The policy that the Catholics were driven to adopt involved the establishment of a separate system of privately funded parochial schools that, by the early 1960s, enrolled almost 6 million students, or approximately 12 percent of all elementary and secondary students in the country. So it came about, and for a long time remained, that the "Catholics [had] their parochial schools and the Protestants [had] the public schools."[71] The alternative to the sectarian school, contrary to what is sometimes suggested, proved not to be the secular school, as this is defined by the "separationists" of our day, but the school implicitly recognizing a nondenominational Protestantism. The extent of the religious element in the public schools is indicated in the fact that the Readers and Spellers of that famous Ohio Protestant minister, William McGuffey, sold 122 million copies between 1836 and 1920. The principal historian of American public education, Elwood P. Cubberley, estimates that half the schoolchildren in America "drew their inspiration and formulated their codes of morals and conduct from this remarkable series of Readers."[72] Americans were, as Justice Sutherland reiterated for the Court as late as 1931, "a Christian people,"[73] and in practice this meant a Protestant Christian people.

In a brief survey of this history in his separate opinion in the

67

first "released-time" case, Justice Frankfurter spoke of the "development of the public school as a symbol of our secular unity."[74] It *is* that, and should be praised for being that; but the development of the quasi-secular public school may be more accurately attributed to our religious disunity. The fact that it occurred is, of course, a reflection of the willingness of most (even if not of all) Americans to accept—and in most cases eagerly to accept—the Founding principle respecting the subordination of religion; but the history of school disputes reveals a determination on the part of those who were parties to them to preserve religion in the subordinate place to which it had been consigned. So long as the argument was confined to the political arena, irreligion—to this day not a popular position for a politician to espouse—played an insignificant role. What the Protestants wanted was the nonsectarian public school, and what the Catholics wanted was, at one stage, the multisectarian school; very few wanted the secular school, as that term is currently understood. Thus, it is somewhat misleading for Leo Pfeffer to refer to a proposed constitutional amendment, adopted by the House of Representatives in 1876, as an illustration of America's "devotion...to the secular public school." That amendment (which failed of adoption in the Senate) would have forbidden the teaching of "the particular creed or tenets" of any religious organization, but would have expressly permitted "the reading of the Bible."[75]

One striking consequence of the intervention of the Supreme Court in these school disputes is the enhancement of the role in them played by extreme "separationists"; their standing in the courts is much greater than they ever attained in the political arena. In one respect, of course, this is as it should be. The Constitution forbids laws—at least, it forbids congressional laws—respecting an establishment of religion; the Constitution is itself law, law enforceable in the courts; and the courts must be open to the victims of laws contrary to the law of the Constitution. "The very essence of civil liberty," Marshall wrote in

Marbury v. *Madison,* "certainly consists in the right of every individual to claim the protection of the laws, whenever he receives
an injury."[76] In another respect, however, because the Court
proved eager to adopt so large a part of the views of the extreme
separationists on the establishment clause, granting standing to
them in these school disputes has prevented accommodations
achieved politically, and this may be one of those areas where
political accommodations are superior to settlements resting on
principle. As Alexander Bickel reminded us,[77] not all political
disputes are best resolved on the level of principle, and it is precisely and sometimes solely principle to which the extreme
separationists appeal. Surely the Los Angeles chapter of the
American Civil Liberties Union was not seeking a remedy for an
injury in any tangible sense when it filed suit to enjoin the use of
the words "under God" in the Pledge of Allegiance, nor was the
New Jersey ACLU when it sought to prevent the employment of
chaplains in the armed forces. Such suits would appear to have
been intended mischievously and, had they been allowed to proceed through the courts, would certainly have provoked a good
deal of avoidable discord. And how grave an injury was suffered
by the Wisconsin Council of Churches when it objected to a plan
whereby children attending private and parochial schools would
be allowed to use the *regular* school buses to travel not to the
schools they attended but to the public schools they were entitled
to attend, a plan that forbade them to leave such buses before
they arrived at the public schools even though they might pass
directly in front of the private schools on the way? This
compromise was achieved only after years of sometimes bitter
controversy, but a divided Wisconsin Supreme Court struck it
down as a violation of the state's constitution.[78] There are times
when an ostensible appeal to principle, appears to be mainly a
means of concealing other motives.

This, of course, cannot be said of the typical advocates of the
secularization of the public schools. Many men and women have

labored long and selflessly to achieve an end they see required not only by the First Amendment but by a sound polity. Leo Pfeffer speaks for them when he argues that a "secular state requires a secular state school," and also when he assures us that "the secularization of the state does not mean the secularization of society."[79] This is a venerable opinion, but it was not shared by Rousseau, for example, or by Washington, and even Jefferson had his doubts; and Pfeffer, too, in the context of his argument that religion does not need the state, implies nevertheless that the liberal state needs a religious people. This we are, he says, and this, he assures us, we can remain.[80] Perhaps, but there is profound opinion to the contrary. Our experience can be no guide here because we have no experience of living under wholly secular auspices. It is only in our own day that we have approximated the secular state, the state that is not only forbidden to aid religion (on either the local or national level) but, in the United States and elsewhere, is also under constant pressure to sever the connection between the laws and a morality that finds its origins in religious doctrine. (I have in mind the abortion laws, for example, and laws forbidding the public display and distribution of obscene materials, laws against vulgar speech, and laws forbidding incest and restricting the right of marriage to members of opposite sexes. Such laws exist in large numbers.) And if Pfeffer should prove wrong when he says that "society" can remain religious though the "state" be indifferent to religion, we shall then be in a position to learn whether Tocqueville was right when he said that, unlike despotism, liberty cannot "govern without faith."[81]

In fact, however, there is no necessity to concede the principle to the strict separationists, however many Supreme Court opinions they can cite in their support. Those opinions, as we have seen, depend too much on Madison and on Jefferson's metaphor, and too little on the First Amendment. That Amendment was not intended to require government to be neutral between religion and irreligion. "An attempt to level all religions, and to make it a matter of state policy to hold all in utter indifference, would have created universal disapprobation, if not universal indignation.''[82] Story exaggerates if he means to attribute this opinion to everyone, but the substance of what he says is accurate. ''The historical record shows beyond peradventure that the core idea of 'an establishment of religion' comprises the idea of *preference;* and that any act of public authority favorable to religion in general cannot, without manifest falsification of history, be brought under the ban of that phrase.''[83] So said Edward S. Corwin, one of the most respected of our constitutional scholars. Properly applied, the First Amendment forbids a national church and any preference in the aid or recognition extended to religion; applied to the states by way of the word ''liberty'' in the Fourteenth Amendment, it forbids state churches and state preferences and, therefore, sectarian state schools. Whatever else it may forbid, there is nothing in the principle *or in the reasons for its adoption* to forbid indirect aid that has the effect of supporting religion without raising it above the subordinate position to which the principle consigns it. And there may be sound reason to supply this aid.

Whether it should be given is a matter of policy, not principle. Of course, there is a strong argument for making it a matter of principle; the Court frequently, and most recently in *Meek* v. *Pittinger,*[84] has pointed to the divisiveness bred by proposals to supply aid to church-related schools, for example, and there is no doubt whatever that the Founders saw the dangers of and hoped to avoid political divisions along religious lines. One way these divisions might be avoided is to hold that the Constitution simply forbids the adoption of the policy the proposing of which gives rise to such divisions, and the Court has been moving in this direction; in short, this is to hold that the Constitution forecloses discussion—or at least adoption—of such a policy. But would this ''principled'' decision not be likely to have the effect of shifting the conflict elsewhere, by provoking a major effort to amend the Constitution? Such a conflict would likely breed more divisiveness than any policy issue we have yet experienced, precisely because, disputed on the level of principle rather than policy, it would preclude the kind of accommodation so imperatively required not only by our contemporary situation but by the liberal principle itself.

In this context, it is fair to raise the question as to how much of the divisiveness surrounding our recent policy debates has not in fact been provoked by the Court and its insistence on a "principled" resolution of the controversies. Is there not reason to wonder whether the recent policy debates, which have been debates not between religions but rather between religion and irreligion, have not been embittered by the fact that irreligion has been emboldened by the Court's decisions? These decisions all stem from the *Everson* case, and it is interesting to learn that the First Amendment argument was not even raised in that case until it reached the Supreme Court.[85] Only at that stage, and especially in the *amicus* brief filed by the American Civil Liberties Union, was the argument made that the First Amendment forbade busing because the First Amendment was "designed to bring about the complete separation of church and state"; and only at that stage, in the same brief, was reference made to the Virginia experience and to Madison's "Memorial and Remonstrance."[86] But the framers of the First Amendment did not speak of the complete separation of church and state—indeed, they did not use the term at all—and precisely because they were not restricted by this formulation of the principle, they would have been able to appreciate and to give appropriate weight to the factors that characterize our present situation and then legislate accordingly. And what is our present situation? Is there any possibility that a policy of aid to religion, a policy that is able to win legislative approval, will have the effect today of exalting religion above the place to which the First Amendment consigns it? Is it not more likely, today, that any such policy would be designed to rescue religion from the oblivion to which it seems to be heading?

72

It has been said that the parochial schools cannot "meet the basic requirements of religion," and even that the Court erred when, back in 1925,[87] it did not permit Oregon to close them. No doubt there would be a problem if these schools, after the fashion of the Communist Party, taught the necessity of over-throwing constitutional government in the United States, or, after the fashion of the Ku Klux Klan, bred hatred of Jews and Negroes; and no doubt there would be a problem if they were administered by churches that did not accept the constitutional principle of religious tolerance and all that this implies. But assuming, as the evidence suggests we must, that nothing comparable to any of these lessons is taught in them today, the question should be asked whether it is good or bad for the United States for children to attend schools where, among other lessons, they are taught that it is right to honor their fathers and mothers and wrong to kill, commit adultery, steal, bear false witness, or covet their neighbors' possessions—where, to state the teaching simply, they are taught to love God and to love their neighbors as themselves. That is a policy question. It is not a politically irrelevant question; and the Constitution, properly interpreted, does not forbid it to be raised. It is the modern Court that is largely responsible for transforming it into a matter of principle or, at a minimum, for allowing the antireligionists to transform it into a matter of principle. Surely, in an age characterized so strongly by the spirit of ecumenism (and what is this but another word for toleration?), most Americans ought to be less concerned with what separates the various religions than with what they have in common and need in common, thereby avoiding divisions when proposals are made to aid religion in common.

It is no secret that the Catholic schools especially, both elementary and secondary, are in deep trouble. Between 1965 and 1972 over 2,700 of them closed their doors, a rate of more than one a day, and their student enrollments declined from 5,574,000 to 3,790,000. One obvious cause of this decline, and probably the principal cause, is the cost of operating them; that this cost has risen and is rising faster than the general price level is reflected in the necessity to hire a greater proportion of lay teachers. Whereas in 1965 lay teachers comprised some 30 percent of the total teaching staffs, they now comprise about 50 percent, and their proportion, and with it the cost of operating the schools, is steadily rising.[88] (But so, probably, is the quality of the instruction in secular subjects.) Whether they and other church-related schools should be assisted by public funds is a fair question, one that is not foreclosed by a proper reading of the First Amendment; and it ought to be possible for someone in no way involved with these schools, or with the church by which most of them are supported, to ask that the question be given a fair hearing. It may in fact be found that, in the light of the present racial integration problems, no plan of state aid to church-related schools could be implemented without jeopardizing the very existence of the public schools in some areas of the country, and that ought to be conclusive. This may well be true of voucher plans or income tax credit plans, which have not been declared unconstitutional.[89] On the other hand, some scheme might be devised that could provide assistance to church-related schools without injury to the public schools. Despite his reputation as a "strict separationist," Jefferson, for example, saw merit (and no violation of principle) in a program featuring a sharing of facilities. The establishment by the various churches of religious schools within the confines of the University of Virginia, he wrote, "would complete the circle of the useful sciences embraced by this institution, and would fill the chasm now existing, on principles which would leave inviolate the constitutional freedom of religion." Such an arrangement, he added, "by bringing the sects together, and mixing them with the mass of other students, [would] soften their asperities, liberalize and neutralize their prejudices, and make the general religion a religion of peace, reason and morality."[90] To paraphrase Madison from the 49th *Federalist,* the American

74

people "will not find it a superfluous advantage" to achieve a school system characterized by peace, reason, and morality.

In this quest it cannot expect much help from the Supreme Court. In one of its most recent school decisions, the Court held that the public schools may not even temporarily suspend students for misconduct without giving them "oral and written notice of the charges" against them—due process requires "at least" this much,[91] and how much more we will learn in the course of time. "One can," said Justice Powell in dissent, "only speculate as to the extent to which public education will be disrupted by giving every school child the power to contest *in court* any decision made by his teacher which arguably infringes the state conferred right to education."[92] But such decisions tell only part of the story. The Court has also forbidden public universities to expel, even after a *full* due process trial, student newspaper editors who fill their columns with the most vulgar expressions to be found in the language.[93] With the extension of this rule to the public elementary and secondary schools (and there would appear to be no basis on which to prevent its extension), we shall have a public school system marked by free speech and due process—and a good deal more—but very little of the kind of education parents expect in exchange for their school taxes. Forty years ago, Cubberley could say it was the "settled conviction of our American people" that nothing "contributes so much to the moral uplift [and] to a higher civic virtue" than does the public school system.[94] In 1975, Senator Birch Bayh, on the basis of the studies conducted by his Judiciary subcommittee, reported to the Senate that in the public schools approximately 70,000 "serious physical assaults on teachers" occur each year, and hundreds of thousands of assaults on students, including more than 100 murders in 1973 alone, and this merely in the 757 school districts surveyed.[95] A further indication of the situation is revealed in the statistics respecting maliciously broken windows in Chicago public schools: in the school year 1973/1974, these numbered 89,517.

Conclusion

Anyone accustomed to reading the older political philosophy would have remarked not merely the conspicuous absence in the constitutional debates of any concern for the education of the citizens who were to constitute the material of this new nation in America, but the conspicuous reliance on what was understood to provide a substitute for this education—namely, the carefully contrived institutional arrangements, or Madison's "auxiliary precautions." True, it was also Madison who, acknowledging the "depravity" as well as the "other qualities of human nature which justify a certain portion of esteem and confidence," admitted that "republican government presupposes the existence of these [latter and unspecified] qualities in a higher degree than any other form [of government]."[96] Nevertheless, except to the extent to which they expected these qualities to be generated by the institutional arrangements,[97] the Founders made no provision for them. In this context especially it is interesting to take note of the reason for their confidence that for the first time in history, free government was a possibility. The advocates of despotism, Hamilton said in the ninth *Federalist,* have portrayed vividly the weaknesses of republican government built on civil liberty; and these apprehensions would have required abandonment of the cause of free government were it not for the great improvements recently made in the "science of politics." These improvements, it turns out, were all institutional in character: separation of powers, checks and balances, independent judges and representation. These, plus the virtues of the large commercial republic, "are wholly new discoveries, or have made their principal progress towards perfection in modern times." It is doubtful that a better statement could be found to illustrate the fact that the United States was, and was understood to be, the first "new nation." The Founders were concerned with the structure, they did not attempt to fashion the materials; good character may have been a public necessity, but its formation was a private business.

It was after the ratification of the Constitution that the connection between moral education and good government begins to find public—by which I mean, official—recognition. The men of the First Congress argued that the First Amendment must not be so worded as to preclude public recognition and public (which is to say, political) use of religion, especially on the part of the states; nor must it "patronize those who professed no religion at all."[98] Washington expressed this concern in his last address to the nation: "religion and morality...these greatest pillars of human happiness [are the] firmest props of the duties of men and citizens." Not merely the "pious man" but also the "mere politician...ought to respect and to cherish them." The politicians of the nineteenth century may not have respected and cherished them to the full extent wished by Washington, but they did preserve an element of religious education in the schools they built, Horace Mann being a conspicuous case in point. His work also illustrates the constraints under which they worked: the religious element had to be preserved without violating the principle of the free exercise of religion. The schools disputes serve to demonstrate that this is not readily accomplished. Moreover, the contemporary Supreme Court has added to the difficulty by incorporating Jefferson's metaphorical wall into the Constitution and raising it to a height it was not intended to reach. For all that appears in some of the opinions the justices have written, whether religion and religious training languish and pass altogether into desuetude is not a matter with which politicians may concern themselves. Religion is a private matter.

Strangely, the same Court that yields only grudgingly on the issue of aid to religion has proved to be unusually solicitous of religious beliefs, and even the vaguest of moral sentiments, when the issue is obedience to law. Justice Douglas, who would not allow a cent to be given to the Catholic Church, even in the form of an uncollected tax, would allow the individual members of that church to pick and choose the wars they will fight in. He was alone in this position, but the majority's opinion did not reject it altogether; on the contrary, it implicitly criticized the government's belief, which seemed to contend that Congress need not "accord any breathing space whatever to noncompliant conduct inspired by imperatives of religion and conscience."[99] But there is nothing new or unjustified in the government's contention; whether "breathing space" is given to conduct based on conscience has always been seen as a matter of legislative grace, not constitutional right. Instead of apologizing for the government's contention, the Court should have buttressed its holding by citing Jefferson on the difference between "operations of the mind" and "acts of the body," the latter being subject to the *coercion* of the laws. One year later the Court proved that this lapse into constitutional heresy was not inadvertent when it held that the First Amendment guarantees "breathing space" for the Amish. They (and so far only they) do not have to obey a *valid* school law. They do not have to obey it because "only those interests of the highest order" can prevail against a claim of free exercise.[100] As applied in this case, this is surely one of the strangest formulations to be found in the body of constitutional law. Valid statutes must be obeyed, but only valid statutes embodying "interests of the highest order" have to be obeyed by some of us. Familiarity with the cases and the problems they present leads to an appreciation of the difficulties the Court faces in expounding the meaning of the religious clauses; still, it is a peculiar First Amendment that subordinates religious belief to the point where it may not be encouraged by law and, at the same time, exalts religious belief—and even "religious" belief—to a point where the believer need not obey law. Nothing in the original intention, and nothing in the requirements of sound public policy, justifies this.

Yet candor requires me to acknowledge that this development may be implicit in liberalism. The liberal state is indifferent to religious belief and will, therefore, tolerate all and any—so long as they do not "break out into overt acts against peace and good order." Belief will be left to the private conscience, and one effect of this will be to exalt the belief that is idiosyncratic, resting solely on the individual will, which in turn rests on the passions, not, as orthodox Christianity or Judaism would have it, on the will of a providential God. The stronger the passions, the stronger the will and the belief. It is almost inevitable—at least it is not strange—that what is held to be important becomes the sincerity of belief (whatever the substance of belief) rather than its orthodoxy. In time, sincerity becomes the mark of the virtuous person, who, as Seeger and Welsh learned, are entitled to have their sincerity recognized by the law. Indeed, the Constitution requires the law to recognize their sincerity.

Unfortunately, the sincere citizen is not necessarily the good citizen in a liberal democracy.

CHAPTER 3

Free Speech and
the Founding Principle

W E know from the First Amendment debates and also from the theoretical writings—Jefferson's and those of his philosophical predecessors—what the Founders understood to be the purpose of the provisions respecting religion; but the debates tell us nothing about, and there are no equivalent writings of this period concerning, the purpose of the speech and press provision. The debates do suggest that the association of the religious and speech provisions in the same amendment was adventitious, the result of a decision taken in the Senate that was made for no apparent reason other than linguistic convenience. They had passed the House as separate articles and were not associated in any debate of which we have record. In fact, the speech and press provision was scarcely debated. Its association with the religious provisions originated in the article adopted by the House and defeated in the Senate imposing restrictions on the states: "no state shall infringe the right of trial by jury in criminal cases; nor the rights of conscience; nor the freedom of speech, or of the press." But here it was also associated with trial by jury, which, of course, is altogether remote. Since this was the only amendment touching state legislative power, there is no reason to believe that the combination served any purpose other than, in this case, stylistic convenience; all the other evidence suggests that they were understood to be discrete items. The debates, then, shed little light on the speech and press clause.

This has not been understood to constitute a problem because of the widespread belief, resting on other evidence, that religious and other varieties of opinion are entitled to the same degree of protection under the Amendment. This belief, which was adopted formally as part of the law of the Constitution in 1940 in the case of *Cantwell* v. *Connecticut*,[1] derives from the well-known statement in Jefferson's preamble to the "Bill for Establishing Religious Freedom in Virginia":

> ...that to suffer the civil magistrate to intrude his powers into the field of opinion and to restrain the profession or propagation of principles on supposition of their ill tendency is a dangerous falacy [sic], which at once destroys all religious liberty, because he being of course judge of that tendency will make his opinions the rule of judgment, and approve or condemn the sentiments of others only as they shall square with or differ from his own....[2]

Although this statement occurs in the context of the (successful) effort to establish religious liberty in Virginia and makes explicit reference only to "religious liberty," it is not difficult to see its apparent applicability to political and other types of opinion. Zechariah Chafee, Jr., for example, in his celebrated study, *Free Speech in the United States,* says that Jefferson's "words about religious liberty hold good of political and speculative freedom, and the portrayal of human life in every form of art."[3] And Dumas Malone, Jefferson's principal biographer, says that since "freedom of thought was an absolute" for Jefferson, "it may be assumed that he applied not merely to religious opinion but to all opinion this maxim: 'Reason and free enquiry are the only effectual agents against error.'"[4]

On the other hand, and casting doubt on this view of Jefferson's position, there is his statement in his Second Inaugural: "No inference is here intended that the laws provided by the States against false and defamatory publications should not be enforced; he who has time renders a service to public morals and public tranquillity in reforming these abuses by the salutary coercions of the law...." To the same point in his letter to Abigail Adams after she had criticized him for pardoning those convicted under the 1798 Sedition Law:

Nor does the opinion of the unconstitutionality, and consequent nullity of that law, remove all restraint from the overwhelming torrent of slander, which is confounding all vice and virtue, all truth and falsehood, in the United States. The power to do that is fully possessed by the several State Legislatures. It was reserved to them, and was denied to the General Government, by the Constitution, according to our construction of it. While we deny that Congress have a right to control the freedom of the press, we have ever asserted the right of the States, and their exclusive right, to do so.[5]

It is the apparent incongruity of these statements that led to the charge of inconsistency and worse on Jefferson's part. "Between his words and deeds on religious liberty there was almost a perfect congruence, but it was not a congruence that was characteristic."[6] There is the "darker side" of his record, the side characterized especially by his alleged failure to adhere to principle when he himself was the victim of abusive speech. Oscar Handlin, in his foreword to the book just quoted, accuses him of violating the principles of the Declaration of Independence:

Jefferson, after all, was the author of the brilliant phrases of the Declaration of Independence; and he has for generations been venerated as the apostle of American liberty. Yet a confrontation with the facts leads to the conclusion that he did not directly apply to practical political problems a libertarian creed to which he adhered consistently.[7]

Thus, it was not because he thought freedom of conscience and freedom of speech and press were governed by different principles but because of political expediency or worse that Jefferson failed in practice to accord political opinion the same protection he consistently accorded religious opinion.

Yet doubts remain. What does Madison mean when he says,

in a later-day letter to Jefferson, that, although it is as difficult to frame a "political creed" as it is to frame a religious creed, "the public right [is] very different in the two cases"?[8] Does this mean that the public has a right to frame and enforce a political creed? The lack of a public right to frame a religious creed follows, as we have seen, from the fact that the United States is not founded on a religious truth; this being so, all religious beliefs are mere opinions and, in the eyes of the law, are to be treated equally. Freedom of religious opinion is absolute, and neither Jefferson nor Madison ever denied that principle in their practice. The difference that may explain Jefferson's alleged inconsistencies respecting speech and press derives from the fact that the United States *is* founded on a "political creed," the self-evident truths acknowledged in the Declaration of Independence. The truths that "we hold" to be "self-evident" constitute a creed on which the country was founded. ("To secure these rights, governments are instituted among men....") This may explain why Jefferson could say that difference of opinion is advantageous in religion and harmless in physics and geometry, and *not* say it regarding the fundamental principles of government.[9] This could mean that the freedom of political speech and press was not intended to be absolute.

Traditionally, the issue was understood to turn first on the status under the Constitution of the common law of seditious libel. Under the influence of Justice Holmes on the Supreme Court and Zechariah Chafee, Jr. in the academic world, most Americans who were concerned with these matters assumed that the First Amendment had not left the common law of libel in force; considering the amount of illiberal mischief done with that law, it was not unreasonable to assume that the Founders would have denied it a place in America. This comfortable assumption was rudely shaken in 1960 by the publication of Leonard Levy's *Legacy of Suppression.*[10] Levy demonstrated that the authors of the First Amendment simply accepted the traditional English law of freedom of speech and press, which

83

was certainly not libertarian in the modern sense of that term. Blackstone was their authority here as in so many areas of the law.

One example will suffice. James Wilson, responding in the Pennsylvania ratifying convention to the charge that the Constitution left freedom of the press unprotected, said that *"what is meant by the liberty of the press is that there should be no antecedent restraint upon it;* but that every author is responsible when he attacks the security or welfare of the *government,* or the safety, character and property of the individual."[11] When the words used were directed against the government, or the "public," as he put it, "the mode of proceeding is by a prosecution" by the government. This is wholly in accord with Blackstone's statement of the common law.[12] To put the matter simply here, Levy found that originally freedom of the press meant freedom from previous restraints upon publication, but that words alone (except as statements of religious belief) could constitute criminal matter. Thus, although Jefferson may have been illiberal in his practice respecting political speech, he was not the only Founder against whom this charge can be laid. The Founders, according to Levy's title, left us a "legacy of suppression."

At the time of its original publication, *Legacy of Suppression* was the best book ever written in the United States on freedom of speech and press. Other studies had reviewed the early cases, but none with so scrupulous an attention to the rules of law applied or the principles asserted or assumed, and to the place of these rules and principles in the historical development of the law. Levy did not confine himself to the court cases; he looked carefully at the activity in an arena that, for a time, was more important to freedom of speech and press than were the courts. I refer to the legislatures that invoked parliamentary privilege against writers and printers who had the temerity to print words criticizing the legislatures—words tending, or allegedly tending, to impeach their behavior, question their authority, derogate from their honor, or defame their members. This was a major chapter in the history of the subject of freedom of speech and press in America, and Levy deserves praise for having assayed it. Finally, he reviewed the writings of the theorists, Milton, "Cato," Hume, and others whose works had not been noticed sufficiently, and the words and deeds of the American Founders, and he did this without preconception. The result is what he himself called revisionist history, but one is bound to say that it is not in the spirit of so much of this familiar genre—it lacks the obvious delight in shocking, in novelty, in the challenging of received opinion.

Levy set out to write history, not revisionist history, and this allowed him to find what he did not want to find. It was a difficult book to write, he said, not merely because the facts dictated conclusions that violate his own predilections, but also because they do clash with the accepted version of history.[13] The Founders may have looked upon themselves as authors of a charter of liberty, a Constitution ordained and established, in part, to "secure the Blessings of Liberty to [themselves] and [their] posterity," but, at least so far as speech and press are concerned, their legacy to us was one they had inherited from Locke, Milton, Blackstone and others: "an unbridled passion for a bridled liberty of speech."[14] They, like Locke and Milton, were men of their time, Levy said, and apparently no one at that time was bold enough to challenge the right of the state to proscribe seditious speech. The times began to change, and with the times, the men, in 1798, when Congress enacted the Alien and Sedition Laws. Faced with the necessity of defending themselves against sedition charges, the Jeffersonians (but not Jefferson himself) generated a theory of speech and press that may truly be called libertarian. For the first time, the idea that government might justly punish its critics was squarely rejected. That, at least, is Levy's argument.

Thus, the debate that is missing in the First Congress concerning the meaning of freedom of speech and press may be found in the controversy engendered by the Sedition Law. This controversy began in 1798 and continued to 1804, with aspects of the controversy extending even into the decade of the 1830s.

Aliens and Sedition

The political situation that gave rise to the Alien and Sedition Laws is known with textbook familiarity. The treaty of peace with Britain, the Jay Treaty, antagonized the French and those Americans who were shortly to become acknowledged Republicans; the attempt to settle the differences with the French involved the ill-fated mission of Gerry, Pinckney, and Marshall; Talleyrand's request for money as a condition of a settlement issued in the XYZ Affair, the disclosure of which discredited the American "Francophiles" and very nearly provoked an American-French war ("Millions for defense, but not a cent for tribute"). With an inflated notion of both their virtue and their strength in the country, the Federalists enacted, over the intense opposition of the Republicans, the Alien and Sedition Laws as a defense measure designed to protect the country against alien opinion and the aliens themselves (whether French, "Wild Irish," or criminal English—but in any event, Republican). Federalist prosecutors and Federalist judges proceeded to use the Sedition Law in an effort to silence some of their opponents. Their opponents accused them of intending to silence opposition itself and to effect a revolutionary change in the regime—namely, to establish a monarchy or a "monocracy" in the place of the republic. With the exception of the Civil War and the periods immediately preceding and succeeding it, and until the period beginning in the late 1960s, America probably had not known a time when its politics was conducted with such vehemence and hatred.[15]

It is entirely possible that not even the press of the late 1960s could match that of the late 1790s, with its Benjamin Franklin

Bache and William Duane of the Philadelphia *Aurora* and James Callender on the one side, and its William Cobbett of *Porcupine's Gazette* and John Ward Fenno of the *Gazette of the United States* on the other. Callender referred to Washington and Adams as "poltroons" and "venal" and called Adams a "libeller" whose "hands are reeking with the blood of the poor, friendless Connecticut sailor," a liar whose office was a "scene of profligacy and...usury," and a "hoary headed incendiary" whose purpose was to "embroil this country [in a war] with France."[16] Cobbett, in his *Porcupine's Gazette,* the most scurrilous of the Federalist journals, referred to his political opponents as, among other things, the "refuse of nations" and "frog-eating, man-eating, blood drinking cannibals." An action was begun against him in 1797 for libeling the Spanish minister to the United States, Don Carlos Martinez d'Yrujo. Despite the efforts of Thomas McKean, a leading Pennsylvania Republican and chief justice of that state's supreme court (and also Martinez's father-in-law), the grand jury refused to return a true bill.[17] When McKean ran for governor of Pennsylvania, John Ward Fenno wrote an editorial against him that concluded with these words:

Twenty thousand FRENCHMEN, and *twenty thousand* UNITED IRISHMEN: What a precious horde of Sans Culotte cutthroats are these to teach what true liberty is! And Americans remember, there are men among you, your countrymen too, who declare they wish these ruffians would come into the United States to teach Americans what *true liberty is*!!!—Pennsylvanians, would you like to be governed by a man whose wish it is to have these villains for your political teachers [Cobbett more than once accused McKean of making such a statement]:—If you do not wish it, look well to your election for GOVERNOR. [18]

It would be asking for a greater measure of equanimity—or better, magnanimity—than we have a right to expect from public men to ask them to be undisturbed by such slander and, the law willing, to take no action against it. Washington was unwilling to ignore it, and he was surely the most magnanimous man of the

87

age. So it is not strange that the victims of it, of both parties, resorted to the law, as well as to duels and less organized violence. The "Francophiles" turned to the common law administered by state courts; the "monocrats," or Federalists, because they were uncertain as to whether the federal courts enjoyed a common law jurisdiction, invoked federal legislation and federal courts.

The Federalists' concern with aliens and sedition gave rise to four distinct but related pieces of legislation, all enacted in less than a month's time during the summer of 1798. The first of these was a naturalization law that increased the period of residence required for citizenship from five to fourteen years.[19] The principal provision of the second, the so-called Alien Friends Act, authorized the President to deport all aliens whom he regarded as "dangerous to the peace and safety of the United States." It was a temporary measure, to be in force for two years after its passage.[20] The third, entitled "An Act Respecting Alien Enemies," was genuinely a wartime measure operative only during a "declared war" or a real or threatened invasion, which event was to be officially proclaimed by the President. It authorized the President, after issuing the proclamation, to apprehend, restrain, secure, or remove any national of a country at war with the United States.[21] The fourth was the notorious Sedition Act, consisting of four sections. The first section provided for the punishment of anyone who unlawfully combined to oppose the laws of the United States. The fourth section provided that the act was to be in force until March 3, 1801—that is, until one day before the inauguration of the next President. It is the second and third sections that have come to be known as the Sedition Act:

SEC. 2. *And be it further enacted*, That if any person shall write, print, utter or publish, or shall cause or procure to be written, printed, uttered or published, or shall knowingly and willingly assist or aid in writing, printing, uttering or publishing any false, scandalous and malicious writing or writings against the government of the United States, or either house of the Congress of the United States, or the President of the United States, with intent to defame the said government, or either house of the said Congress, or the said President, or to bring them, or either of them, into contempt or disrepute; or to excite against them, or either of them, the hatred of the good people of the United States, or to stir up sedition within the United States, or to excite any unlawful combinations therein, for opposing or resisting any law of the United States, or any act of the President of the United States, done in pursuance of any such law, or of the powers in him vested by the constitution of the United States, or to resist, oppose, or defeat any such law or act, or to aid, encourage or abet any hostile designs of any foreign nation against the United States, their people or government, then such person, being thereof convicted before any court of the United States having jurisdiction thereof, shall be punished by a fine not exceeding two thousand dollars, and by imprisonment not exceeding two years.

SEC. 3. *And be it further enacted and declared*, That if any person shall be prosecuted under this act, for the writing or publishing any libel aforesaid, it shall be lawful for the defendant, upon the trial of the cause, to give in evidence in his defence, the truth of the matter contained in the publication charged as a libel. And the jury who shall try the cause, shall have a right to determine the law and the fact, under the direction of the court, as in other cases. [22]

Under these provisions, indictments were brought against fourteen persons (one of them, William Duane, was indicted twice), ten of whom were convicted and sentenced to pay fines ranging from $5 to $1,000 and to be imprisoned for periods ranging from six hours to eighteen months.[23] No one, apparently, neither "Wild Irishman" nor "Jacobin," was deported under either of the Alien Acts.

The Opposition to the Alien and Sedition Acts in Congress

Are not we, the people of the United States of America, a sovereign and independent nation? Have we not, as a nation, all the rights pertaining to that state, equally with any other nation?

The first congressman to speak out in opposition to the alien friends bill, the estimable Albert Gallatin, who was subsequently to have so distinguished a career in the service of his adopted country, sounded the theme that was to dominate the Republican attack on both the Alien and the Sedition Acts:

> ...it must be agreed by all that every nation had a right to permit or exclude alien friends from entering within the bounds of their society. This is a right inherent in every independent nation; but that power is vested, according to the Constitutions of different countries, in one or other branch of the Government. In this country...the power to admit, or to exclude alien friends, does solely belong to each individual State, and...the General Government has no power over them, and, therefore...all the provisions in this bill are perfectly unconstitutional.[25]

In short, while every sovereign nation has an inherent right to exclude aliens, in the United States this element of sovereignty was bestowed on the states, not the nation. Whatever else might be said about this, it is not a civil liberties argument.

Indeed, with respect to the merits of such legislation, there is no difference between Gallatin's principle and that subsequently adopted and applied by the Supreme Court of the United States. In 1892 the Court said that it "is an accepted maxim of international law, that every sovereign nation has the power, as inherent in sovereignty, and essential to self-preservation, to forbid the entrance of foreigners within its dominions, or to admit them only in cases and upon such conditions as it may see fit to prescribe."[26] A year later the Court quoted this passage and added that the "right to exclude or to expel all aliens, or any class of aliens, absolutely or upon certain conditions, in war or in peace, [is] an inherent and inalienable right of every sovereign and independent nation...."[27] Unlike Gallatin, however, and his Republican associates in Congress, the Court by then understood the United States to be the "sovereign and independent nation" that was authorized to exercise this power in the United States.

Whether a persuasive argument could have been made against the Alien Friends Act, an argument objecting to it on principle or expediency, is not here the question; what is relevant is that the Republican leader in the House chose to lead off the debate by denying what would appear to be an essential part of sovereignty to the nation he was later to serve with such great distinction, and that his argument was the one principally made by the Republicans. It was the argument that led Robert Goodloe Harper, one of the Federalist leaders in the House, to doubt whether his opponents were serious, and to claim that they had adopted it only because the bill could not be "opposed on the ground of expediency."[28] It was not until June 21, five days later, on the bill's third reading, that anyone voiced an objection to it on its merits. This was done by Edward Livingston of New York, who had just arrived. He protested that the bill would give the President despotic power over aliens insofar as it would allow him to decide what conduct merited expulsion from the country.

Despite Harper's doubts, however, the opponents of the alien friends bill were "serious" in their stand on states' rights. They were serious because they saw, or imagined, a connection between the principle of power being asserted here, the authority that permitted Congress to expel aliens, and the authority to affect an interest dearer to them than any other, an interest as far removed from civil liberties as any interest could be: slavery. Whether pro- or antislavery, most southerners, including Jefferson and Madison and all who were shortly to acknowledge formally a membership in the Republican Party, were united behind a policy of denying to the national government any competence, legal and practical, to deal with the question of slavery. Except for the questions of fugitive slaves and the foreign slave trade, slavery was a "domestic" matter—that is, a local matter. Only the states could be trusted to deal with it; therefore, only the states possessed the constitutional authority to deal with it. From the time of the debates (beginning in February 1790) on the first of the petitions from the Pennsylvania Quakers calling for a "sincere and impartial inquiry" into the slave trade, to Taney's opinion for the Court in

91

the *Dred Scott* case in 1857,[29] and on a host of occasions in between, whether the issue was avowedly one of slavery or, as in the case of the alien friends bill, only tangentially one of slavery, southerners insisted on the competence of the states and the incompetence of the national government in this matter. Certainly Gallatin was no friend to slavery (although he said he would oppose a proposal to keep slavery out of Mississippi if it threatened the property of slave owners already in the territory).[30] But his southern colleagues were, and it was the southerners who supplied most of the votes against the alien friends bill. It was passed by a vote of 46-40, and 30 of those 40 voting against the measure came from southern slave states.[31] Of the 46 voting in favor of the measure, only ten came from slave states, and five of these were from Maryland. The vote in the Senate is equally instructive. The measure carried by a vote of 16-7, with all seven votes in opposition cast by slave-state senators.[32]

This is the kind of sectional split that is traditionally and rightly associated with the slavery issue, and it is somewhat strange that the principal historians of the event have not remarked it. The Jay Treaty dispute is seen by some commentators as largely a dispute over slavery, if only because of Jay's failure or refusal to insist on compensation from Britain for the slaves taken during the Revolutionary War. Yet in the House only three men (George Dent and Samuel Smith of Maryland and Andrew Gregg of Pennsylvania) voted for the Jay Treaty[33] but against the alien friends bill, and in the Senate only two men switched sides, Humphrey Marshall of Kentucky joining his southern associates on the alien bill, having voted for the treaty, and Alexander Martin of North Carolina voting for the alien bill, having voted against the treaty. To say, as many historians have done, that both issues provoked straight, or almost straight, party votes is to beg the question, for it in a sense assumes the prior existence of well-defined parties and ignores the question of what it was that led to the formation of these parties. More precisely, it ignores the question of the extent to which slavery and the desire to have slavery policy made at the state level led Jefferson and his friends to form a political party in order to wrest control of the national government from the men we call Federalists.[34] Even James Morton Smith, despite the detail of his study,[35] makes no reference to the expressions of concern for the institution of slavery uttered by southerners during the course of the debate on the alien bill.

The second Republican, and the first southerner, to speak against the bill in the House of Representatives was Robert Williams of North Carolina. A preceding speaker, Samuel Sewell of Massachusetts, had claimed constitutional authority for it in the commerce clause of the Constitution, and Williams replied that it was a "curious idea, that all emigrants coming to this country should be considered as articles of commerce." If this were accepted, he went on, nothing would prevent Congress from claiming the power to send slaves out of the country. "And as ready as the Southern States are to grant slaves are a dangerous property and an evil in their country, they will not consent to Congress assuming the power of depriving their owners of them, contrary to their will."[36] And when the proponents claimed constitutional authority under the first part of Article I, Section 8, Abraham Baldwin of Georgia said that this provision respecting the power to provide for the general welfare "had never been considered as a source of Legislative power. [In fact, the] first instance in which it had ever been attempted to be acted upon...was the application of the Abolition Societies to Congress for an abolition of slavery, the power of Congress to act upon which was said to be derived from these words...."[37] Baldwin had no doubt that "if this bill passed into a law, Congress would again be appealed to by the advocates for an abolition of slavery, with requests that the President may be authorized to send these persons out of the country, and strong arguments will be used in favor of the measure." Against this danger Baldwin had an obvious safe-

93

guard, the states, and a constitutional principle that later almost destroyed the Union, states' rights: "...this business of admitting or banishing aliens belonged to State Governments, and not to the General Government."[38]

Gallatin and others went so far as to argue that the power to expel aliens, like the power to expel slaves, was expressly forbidden until 1808 by Article I, Section 9 of the Constitution, because the prohibition on exclusion carried with it a prohibition on expulsion, and the phrase "such persons," they insisted, referred to aliens as well as to slaves.* As Mr. Mercer said in the course of the debate on the Virginia Resolutions in the Virginia House of Delegates, the Alien Law "virtually destroyed the right of the states under [Article I, Section 9]; for though the states might admit...such persons as they might think proper prior to a certain period, it was to little purpose, if the President...could send them away."[39] Like his colleagues in the House of Representatives, Mercer was concerned that in conceding a power over aliens, they were also conceding a power over slaves. Thus, the national government must be denied the power to expel aliens. And thanks to the rhetoric of the Republican editors, the bill came to be denounced as a "draconic measure."[40]

This was not the principal response of the opponents of the bill in the House. Those from Virginia especially were in no position to inveigh against the measure in such terms unless they

---

*Gallatin's words are these: "But if, by implication [the general power of preventing the migration of aliens] may be derived from any of the specific powers given to Congress...its exercise is prohibited to Congress, by this clause, till the year 1808..." (ibid., p. 1979). It is interesting that a South Carolinian, Robert Goodloe Harper, said the clause referred only to slaves (ibid., p. 1991). The provision reads as follows: "The migration or importation of such persons as any of the States now existing shall think proper to admit, shall not be prohibited by the Congress prior to the year [1808]." However dangerous this reading of the clause could be in the future (since, ignoring the Fifth Amendment's protection to property, it concedes a congressional power to expel slaves beginning in 1808), it was very convenient to southern interests because it denied a congressional power over the domestic slave trade—that is, over the *migration* of such persons (slaves) within the country, as well as the *importation* of such persons (slaves) into the country. See Walter Berns, "The Constitution and the Migration of Slaves," *Yale Law Journal* 78, (December 1968): 198-228.

were willing to apply the same language to a law of their own state. As George K. Taylor of Prince Georges County, Virginia, said during the debate on the Virginia Resolutions in the Virginia House of Delegates, the state had enacted an alien law in 1792, a law that "authorized the Governor to apprehend, and secure, and compel to depart out of the commonwealth, all suspicious persons etc. *from whom the President of the United States should apprehend hostile designs against the said states.*"[41] This state law made no provision for trials, even though the Virginia constitution, Taylor said, declared trial by jury to be a sacred right. Taylor noted that "...the legislature of the state could have no more power by the constitution to pass such a law than Congress had by the constitution of the United States. Yet no complaint against such a law had ever been heard until the law of Congress was passed. All the clamour had been reserved for that alone."[42] The federal law, he said, merely does what the Virginia law does: permits aliens to be sent out of the country "at the instance of the President." Taylor was answered by one Ruffin with the familiar states' rights argument to the effect that the power over aliens was a right reserved to the states,[43] which is an answer—by then a familiar answer—but not, again, a stirring declaration of the rights of man. It was states' rights, not civil liberties, that concerned the Republicans.

The debate on the sedition bill, which began immediately after the passage of the Alien Friends bill, was interrupted the following day (July 6) in order to discuss the question of whether the country was not in fact already at war with France and whether Congress should not formally make a declaration of this fact. Instead, the House contented itself with agreeing (after amendments) to the Senate bill abrogating various treaties with France. It was against this background of grave international problems that these bills were debated and adopted.

Edward Livingston began the debate on the sedition bill by moving to reject it in its entirety. John Allen of Connecticut responded in such a way that the issue of free expression under the

Constitution was immediately joined, or at least broached. Allen quoted a typical tirade against President Adams from the New York *Time-Piece* and asked whether anyone seriously contended that the liberty of the press extended to such publications: "Because the Constitution guarantees...the freedom of the press, am I at liberty to falsely call you a thief, a murderer, an atheist?...The freedom of the press and opinions was never understood to give the right of publishing falsehoods and slanders, nor of exciting sedition, insurrection, and slaughter, with impunity. A man was always answerable for the malicious publication of falsehood; and what more does this bill require?"[44] Allen was followed by Harper who, acknowledging that he had often heard in Congress and out "harangues on the liberty of the press," defined this liberty after the manner of Blackstone, which indeed was the accepted understanding of the subject at the time: "the true meaning of [liberty of the press] is no more than that a man shall be at liberty to print what he pleases, provided he does not offend against the laws, and not that no law shall be passed to regulate this liberty of the press."[45] Such an understanding did not preclude prosecutions of seditious libels, either at the common law or under the proposed legislation; according to Leonard Levy, it was only under "the pressure of the Sedition Act [that] writers of the Jeffersonian party were driven to originate so broad a theory of freedom of expression that the concept of seditious libel was, at last, repudiated."[46]

Such a theory did not, however, emerge from the debates in the House. Livingston insisted that the bill violated the First Amendment, and he was supported in this view by the next speaker, Nathaniel Macon of North Carolina; but the debates reveal that neither Livingston nor Macon—nor any of their Republican colleagues—adopted a broad "libertarian" understanding of the principle of freedom of expression. The bill "directly violated the letter of the Constitution," Macon said; he regretted that, "at a time like this, when some gentlemen say we are at war, and when all believe we must have war, the Congress are about to pass a law which will produce more uneasiness, more irritation, than any act which ever passed the Legislature of the Union." He challenged the Federalists to show "what part of the Constitution [authorizes] the passage of a law like this." But he then acknowledged that "persons might be prosecuted for a libel under the State Governments," and questioned the necessity of a federal law.[47] In short, he, like his colleagues during the debate on the alien friends bill, objected to the sedition bill on constitutional grounds and, more precisely, on states' rights grounds, but he did not argue that such legislation was objectionable in principle. He made this clear later in the debate, on July 10, when he asserted that liberty of the press was sacred and ought to be left where the Constitution had left it. And where did the Constitution leave it?

The States have complete power on the subject, and when Congress legislates, it ought to have confidence in the States. . . . He believed there was nowhere any complaint of a want of proper laws under the State Governments; and though there may not be remedies found for every grievance in the General Government, what it wants of power will be found in the State Governments, and there can be no doubt but that power will be duly exercised when necessity calls for it. [48]

And of course there were such state laws. Harrison Otis of Massachusetts had taxed the Republicans with inconsistency by quoting state constitutional provisions respecting the rights of free speech and press, then quoting statutes of the same states making libel a criminal offense and punishing licentiousness and sedition.[49] In accusing them of inconsistency, however, he was to some extent missing the thrust of their argument. They were not contending for free speech and press; they were contending for states' rights, for the right of the states to punish libels.

Livingston continued the argument as soon as Macon had resumed his seat. He insisted, in words that were to be echoed in our day by Justice Black, that Congress may pass *"no* law" abridging the liberty of speech and press (and no law establishing

97

"a national religion"), and the proposed bill was to him clearly such a law. But Livingston, as a typical member of the inchoate Republican party, was not objecting to the principle of such legislation, any more than his colleagues had objected in principle to the alien bill. On the contrary, such legislation was essential to a well-ordered republic:

> But, it is said, will you suffer a printer to abuse his fellow-citizens with impunity, ascribing his conduct to the very worst of motives? Is no punishment to be inflicted on such a person? Yes. There is a remedy of offences of this kind in the laws of every State in the Union. Every man's character is protected by law, and every man who shall publish a libel on any part of the Government, is liable to punishment. Not...by laws which we ourselves have made, but by the laws passed by the several States. [50]

The sedition bill violated the Constitution, Livingston argued, because the power to punish libels—the power to enact *criminal* libel laws and to enforce them—was reserved by the Constitution to the states. Furthermore, he went on, the fair administration of justice required this arrangement:

> Suppose a libel were written against the President, where is it most probable that such an offence would receive an impartial trial? In a court, the judges of which are appointed by the President, by a jury selected by an officer holding his office at the will of the President? or in a court independent of any influence whatever? [51]

Whether the state courts could fairly be described as "independent of any influence whatever"—that is, whether they could have provided impartial forums for the prosecution of criminal libels against the President of the Union—is a fair question. Surely they could scarcely have proved less impartial than the federal courts were soon to prove themselves to be. One historian, Charles Warren, has written that the "proper remedy for all the flood of scurrility and calumny, which swelled each succeeding year of the Adams administration, was a more rigid enforcement of the laws of criminal libel by state officials and courts,"[52] thus agreeing altogether with Livingston. But state prosecutions

98

depended on state officials, and no Virginia official, for example, would likely have proved assiduous in the defense of John Adams's good name. To cite another example: whereas the officials of Republican Pennsylvania did not hesitate to prosecute libels made against Republican Pennsylvanians, there is no record of their being equally zealous when it came to prosecuting libels made against the Federalist officials of the national government, the capital of which was temporarily located in the state's principal city. "A criminal libel proceeding," Warren continues, "was a weapon which could be employed by both parties." He is probably correct when he adds, as an account of the Federalists' motives, that they "wished absolution for their own words, and punishment only for their opponents"; but he might have said the same thing of the Republicans.* The difference was (and this attests to one of the virtues of the federal system) that with a national law, the Federalists (attributing the worst of motives to them) would have silenced their opponents throughout the length and breadth of the land, whereas the Republicans would have silenced Federalists only in those states which they, the Republicans, controlled. As Jefferson was shortly to learn through his mistaken reliance on resolutions issuing from state legislatures, to be effective on a national scale requires activity on a national scale and, ultimately, control of the national government. In the summer of 1798, however, he and his party were preaching states' rights; as would soon become apparent, some of them were also preaching nullification and disunion. They were not defending civil liberties—except, one must immediately add, to the extent that civil liberty, to them, depended on their states' right view of the Constitution and Union.

---

*In answer to Gallatin during the last stages of the debate, Harper stated that the purpose of the bill was to transfer "the trial of libels and sedition [from the] State courts...to the Courts of the United States." To leave such trials in the states, he said, "would be running into Scylla, in an attempt to avoid Charybdis. There was, certainly, as much danger of partiality on one side as the other" (*Annals of Congress,* 5th Cong., 2nd sess., vol. 2, p. 2166).

Thus, while the Jefferson party in the Congress argued the bill's unconstitutionality, insisting that no power to enact it could be found among the powers enumerated in the Constitution and that the First Amendment expressly prohibited it, they did so in the context of defending the right of the states to enact and enforce such laws. Only in one limited respect did they "originate" a broad libertarian theory in Levy's modern sense: one of the Virginia Republicans, John Nicholas, questioned the distinction (which Levy calls the "alleged" distinction)[53] between liberty and license,[54] thereby challenging the prevailing Blackstonian view of the right of freedom of the press. For to Blackstone and the Federalists, freedom of the press meant, to state the matter simply, no prior restraints but subsequent punishment for abuses, a view that presupposes a distinction between liberty and license and the ability of a court to discern and define it. Later the same day, Gallatin pursued this point, contending that the First Amendment could not (and must not) be understood as prohibiting merely previous restraints. Since laws could be enacted requiring a license to print—and this would be a previous restraint on the press—what, he asked, could possibly constitute a previous restraint on the liberty of speech? Since it was impossible to conceive of such a law, he contended, and because the First Amendment forbids the abridgment of the freedom of speech as well as of the press, it must be understood to forbid more than previous restraints.[55] Such an argument would certainly constitute evidence of the beginnings of a broader libertarian theory, simply by virtue of the fact that it rejects the essential principle of the Blackstonian view, except for the equally obvious fact that, having made the point, Gallatin unmade it by the characteristic Republican insistence that, anyway, the trial of criminal libels "belonged to the State courts"—exclusively.[56] Harper answered Gallatin in the last speech of the debate. In the course of a long rebuttal, he asked whether there could be "so great an absurdity, can such a political monster exist, as a Government which has no power to protect itself against sedition and libels?"[57] Whatever the true answer may be to this question, the answer of the Jefferson party was, once again, that the United States was not fully a government. Or more precisely, it was a collection of sovereign states, each of which had a government, but it was not an entity authorized to govern in matters respecting aliens and sedition.

The bill was then passed by a vote of 44-41.[58] Two men, Stephen Bullock of Massachusetts and William Matthews of Maryland, who had voted for the alien friends bill voted against the sedition bill, but otherwise, if a few absentees on each occasion are ignored, the division was the same as it had been on the earlier measure. In the Senate no one changed his vote.

A few years ago, the late Professor Harry Kalven hailed the Court's 1964 decision in the *New York Times* libel case as a repudiation, or a possible repudiation, of the "concept of seditious libel," a concept, he said, that "strikes at the very heart of democracy."

Political freedom ends when government can use its powers and its courts to silence its critics. My point is not the tepid one that there should be leeway for criticism of the government. It is rather that defamation of the government is an impossible notion for a democracy. In brief, I suggest, that the presence or absence in the law of the concept of seditious libel defines the society. A society may or may not treat obscenity or contempt by publication as legal offenses without altering its basic nature. If, however, it makes seditious libel an offense, it is not a free society no matter what its other characteristics. [59]

Kalven may be right, but it ought to be remarked that no one, on either side of the congressional debate on the Sedition Law, would have agreed with him, even though it would have been convenient for the Republicans to have done so.

The Virginia and Kentucky Resolutions

The Alien and Sedition Laws were soon denounced in resolutions adopted by the Virginia and Kentucky legislatures; these were written by Madison and Jefferson, respectively. Jefferson is said to have acted in order to preserve "human rights" and as a "sincere champion of the highest practicable degree of human liberty in all fields."[60] It is acknowledged that the resolutions are remembered primarily for the constitutional doctrine they expound, but it is insisted nevertheless that they were "intended *primarily* as a defense, practical and spirited, of civil liberties." The Alien and Sedition Laws are seen today as among "the most severe infringements" upon civil liberties "ever to be sanctioned by an American Congress."[61] This is not, however, the position adopted in the resolutions. It was not the power asserted but the fact that the power was being asserted *by the national government* that alarmed Virginia and Kentucky or, more precisely, the legislative majorities in Virginia and Kentucky. They advanced an extreme states' rights view of the Constitution, and Jefferson was prepared to dissolve the Union if this should prove necessary. This would depend, in part, on the response of the other states to the resolutions.

From his point of view, that response was not encouraging—not one other state joined Virginia and Kentucky in what was understood to be their extreme position—and in a letter to Madison the following year, Jefferson proposed a resumption of their efforts. More resolutions should be adopted, he said, resolutions expressing "in affectionate & conciliatory language our warm attachment to union with our sister-states," but also stating the condition of this attachment, which was that the "American people... rally with us round the true principles of our federal compact." If this did not occur, if he and Madison were "to be disappointed in this," the new resolutions must express the determination of Kentucky and Virginia, at least, "to sever ourselves from that union we so much value, rather than give up the rights of self government which we have reserved, & in which alone we see liberty, safety & happiness."[62]

Shortly after receiving this letter, Madison visited Jefferson at

Monticello, and the result of that visit is reflected in a letter Jefferson wrote to Wilson Cary Nicholas on September 5. He repeated the proposals he had made two weeks earlier to Madison, and in identical language—except that he omitted any expression of his willingness to sever the union.[63] Surely Koch and Ammon are correct in seeing this sentence as the "most extreme statement that Jefferson ever made concerning the meaning and intent of the Kentucky Resolutions," and the circumstances, plus a sentence in the letter to Nicholas, support their view that it was Madison's influence that led Jefferson to exclude the culpable sentence from the letter going to Kentucky. "Had Madison failed to argue as he did," they write, "the contention that the Virginia and Kentucky Resolutions contained in germinal form the later doctrines of nullification and secession would have rested upon firmer ground."[64] What this means is that if Madison had not persuaded his more impetuous and less politic colleague to be circumspect in what he committed to a letter that was likely to be seen by a number of people, Jefferson's name would have been linked with that of Calhoun's and Jefferson Davis's. But why not? Even the resolutions as they were published were sufficient to provoke the response that Kentucky was intending to dissolve the Union,[65] and it was public knowledge that, in 1797, Kentucky was engaged in negotiations with Spain concerning the navigation of the Mississippi.[66]

Jefferson's authorship of the resolutions, rumored at the time and admitted by him in 1821, has long since been confirmed by the publication of his writings. The second of his two drafts of the resolutions, the so-called fair copy, speaks of "nullification" and the "natural right" of each state "to nullify" acts of the national government that, in the judgment of the state, exceed the constitutional authority "delegated" to it; the fair copy even calls upon the states to declare the Alien and Sedition Laws "void, and no force," and to "take measures . . . for providing that neither these acts, nor any others of the General Government not plainly and intentionally authorized by the Constitution, shall be exercised within their respective territories."[67] It was Breckenridge who moderated Jefferson's language on this occasion by changing this call to civil disobedience into a call on Congress to repeal the laws with which the resolutions end.

But even the resolutions as Breckenridge moved them and as they were adopted by the legislature speak of "revolution and blood": "unless arrested on the threshold," these acts and others like them "may tend to drive these States into revolution and blood...." South Carolina's Ordinance of Nullification in 1832 merely did what Kentucky threatened (or resolved) to do, and what Jefferson wanted Kentucky and other states to do. And the South Carolina nullifiers recognized Jefferson as the source of their principle: "...we must come back to Mr. Jefferson's plain, practical and downright principle, as our 'rightful remedy'—a *nullification* by the state...of the 'unauthorized act.'"[68] Why, then, should he not be taxed with planting the nullification seed that germinated after his death and blossomed into the Civil War? Surely he was more moderate than John Taylor, whom he counseled against dissolution of the Union,[69] but this was mainly the counsel of patience. In November 1798, just after he had finished writing the fair copy of the resolutions, he wrote Taylor again, saying: *"For the present,* I should be for resolving the alien & sedition laws to be against the constitution & merely void, and for addressing the other States to obtain similar declarations; and I would not do anything *at this moment* which should commit us further, but reserve ourselves to shape our future measures or no measures, by the events which may happen."[70] It was eight months later that he wrote Madison calling for new resolutions threatening to dissolve the Union.

In the abstract there is no reason to be shocked by such sentiments. After all, Jefferson had already played the leading role in the dissolution of one union, a role for which he has been justly praised by his countrymen. Certainly Koch and Ammon are not shocked by that sentence in the letter to Madison:

By his willingness to consider the grave possibility of separation from the Union, Jefferson showed that he placed no absolute value upon "Union." Compared to the *extreme* evil of ruthless violation of liberty, a destruction of the compact which bound the states together was the *lesser* evil.[71]

But the Kentucky Resolutions themselves do not support this interpretation. They complain of the Sedition Act as a violation of the Constitution *because* the Constitution manifested the determination of the states and the people thereof "to retain to themselves the right of judging how far the licentiousness of speech and of the press may be abridged without lessening their useful freedom, and how far those abuses which cannot be separated from their use should be tolerated rather than the use be destroyed...." And the Kentucky Resolutions themselves say, not that aliens should not be banished, but "that alien friends are under the jurisdiction and protection of the laws of the State wherein they are...." According to the resolutions, the trouble with the Alien and Sedition Laws was that in enacting them, the United States was assuming powers that were reserved to the states. This, Jefferson and his friends could not permit. Rather than submit to this exercise of political power or concede the constitutional theory on which it was based, they would declare the laws null and void; failing of support in this, they would dissolve the Union. To preserve the liberty that was threatened by the Alien and Sedition Laws? Not so. Rather, to preserve the right of the states to enact and enforce their own alien and sedition laws—a right they were exercising.

The Virginia Resolutions drafted by Madison were more moderate than those of Kentucky, but the principle for which they contended, state sovereignty, was the same. In the address that accompanied them, this principle is clearly stated:

The sedition act presents a scene, which was never expected by the early friends of the constitution. It was then admitted, that the state sovereignties were only diminished, by powers specifically enumerated, or necessary to carry the specified powers into effect. Now, federal authority is deduced from implication, and from the existence of state law, it is inferred, that congress possesses a similar power of legislation; whence congress will be endowed with a power of legislation, in all cases whatsoever, and the states will be stript of every right reserved, by the concurrent claims of a paramount legislature.*

In what, then, does the evil of the Sedition Act consist? In the next and summary sentence the Virginia legislature leaves no doubt of its view: "The sedition act is the offspring of these tremendous pretentions, which inflict a death wound on the sovereignty of the states."[72]

The debates on the resolutions confirm this interpretation. In the first place, and somewhat unexpectedly for the modern reader who is accustomed to reading of the resolutions as a defense of civil liberties, the Virginia House of Delegates devoted the greater part of its time to the Alien Friends Act, not the Sedition Act. The arguments against it were familiar by this time. Mr. Mercer contended that "the federal government possessed no power over Aliens in time of peace; and therefore whatever power a sovereign state could exercise with respect to them, under the general law of nations, that power belonged to the state, and not to the general government...."[73] Only "specifically enumerated" powers may be exercised by the federal government, said Mr. Barbour, and no power over aliens is specifically enumerated;[74] the Alien Law represents central government usurpation. Mr. Foushee defied anyone to put his finger on any clause of the Constitution "which had taken away their [the states'] sovereignty," and, apparently, no one bothered to put his finger on the second clause of Article VI of Mr.

*This is not to deny the subtle, yet significant, differences between the Virginia and Kentucky Resolutions. These have to do with the difference in the manner in which the term "states" is used in the two documents and the difference in the manner of enforcement of the state claim. In 1830, during the South Carolina nullification crisis, Madison disavowed any responsibility for the nullification principle, and his argument is not mainly disingenuous. He could not so readily exculpate his colleague Jefferson. See his letter to Edward Everett of August 28, 1830, in *Writings,* vol. 9, pp. 383-403. In this Madison acknowledges the right of the Supreme Court to decide constitutional questions, with an appeal only to the sovereign people exercising their amendment power.

Madison's Constitution; Madison himself, of course, had he been present instead of working behind the scene, would have been too embarrassed to do so. The state, Foushee went on, "and [the] state only, had a right to pass" an alien law.[75] States are sovereign with respect to "strangers," insisted Mr. Daniel.[76] And so it went.

Virginia had an alien friends law indistinguishable in its essential provisions from the federal law; Virginia could not, then, consistently protest against the provisions of the federal law. Virginia was not acting out of a concern for aliens (the exclusion of which Jefferson had argued for in his *Notes on Virginia,* first published in 1784); instead, Virginia was contending against a reading of the commerce clause that permitted Congress to regulate the movement of aliens and slaves and, more generally, a reading of the Constitution that in wide areas would permit a constitutional majority in the country to govern the country.

The case against the Sedition Law was stated at the outset of the debates by John Taylor of Caroline County, and, with a single exception, later speakers in favor of the resolutions were content to state their opposition to the Sedition Law by referring to Taylor's argument.[77] Taylor made the familiar points against the law: that it was a clear violation of the First Amendment, that men tend to label speech false and licentious simply because they disagree with it, and that the law prohibited the criticism of officials essential to republican government. But he made all these points within the familiar context of a defense of state sovereignty. "If Congress should undertake to regulate public opinion, they would be sure to regulate it so as to detach the people from the state governments, and attach them to the General Government."[78] This law, like the Alien Friends Law, tended to concentrate power in Congress, he said, and such a concentration "would operate to the destruction of the state governments"; this would be despotism and would precipitate "revolution."[79]

As in the case of the Alien Law, the states' sovereignty argument was the only one that could consistently be adopted by Taylor and his fellow Jeffersonians, for just as Virginia had an alien law, it also had a sedition law. They were attacked on this ground by George K. Taylor in the course of a spirited defense of the national law:

In England...the laying [of] no *previous* restraints upon publications, is *freedom of the press*. In every one of the United States the laying [of] no *previous* restraints upon publications hath always been and still is deemed *freedom of the press*. In England notwithstanding the freedom of the press, the publication of false scandalous and malicious writings is punishable by fine and imprisonment. In every one of the United States, notwithstanding the freedom of the press, the publication of false scandalous and malicious writings is punishable in the same manner. If the freedom of the press be not therefore abridged in the government of any particular state, by the punishment of false scandalous and malicious writings, how could it be said to be abridged when the same punishment is inflicted on the same offence by the government of the whole people. [80]

After referring to the twelfth article of the Virginia bill of rights ("That the freedom of the press is one of the great bulwarks of liberty, and can never be restrained but by despotic governments"), he went on to argue that the "legislature of Virginia...could no more pass a law *restraining* the freedom of the press, than Congress could pass a law *abridging* the freedom of the press!...Yet it had never been doubted that false, scandalous and malicious writings are punishable in Virginia." He referred specifically to a 1792 law punishing "divulgers of false news," but he could have cited others.[81] If Virginia could do this without violating its bill of rights, Congress, he said, could enact the Sedition Law without violating the First Amendment.

There is no reason to believe that George Taylor did not hope to persuade his colleagues with this argument, but he was not unaware of the sense in which it was irrelevant.[82] He knew that the Jeffersonians were contending primarily for state sovereignty, and he knew what they intended, if necessary, to do for it; hence, he ended with a prayer for union and a love of it among Virginians. As General Henry (Light-Horse Harry) Lee had said during the previous day's debate, the real object of the resolutions was not repeal of the Alien and Sedition Laws, but rather the "Promotion of disunion and separation of the States...."[83]

The resolutions were adopted by a vote of 100-63 (and in the Virginia Senate, 14-3). In an effort to justify its conduct—and justification was certainly required—the majority drew up its "Address of the General Assembly of the People of...Virginia" and voted to circulate it, along with the resolutions, at public expense. This caused the minority, led in the House of Delegates by General Lee, to draw up a "counter address," which they sought to have subjoined to the other papers. Failing in this, they published it privately. It is said by his biographer to be the work of John Marshall,[84] and while there is no proof of its authorship, there is no doubt that it constitutes the best statement from the Federalist side of the Alien and Sedition Laws and of the Virginia Resolutions. It begins by deploring the resolutions and "the system of which they form a conspicuous feature"—that is, the plan to dissolve the Union—and speaks of "the happiness united America enjoys" and "the evils which disunited America must inevitably suffer." It then recounts, at some length, the difficulties America had encountered in its relations with Britain and France, justifying the attempts of Washington and Adams to maintain peace "without dishonor," continues by denying that an army led by "your Washington" can "be called mercenary," and then enters into a detailed defense of the Alien and Sedition Laws. Contrary to the view held by the Jeffersonians, "America is one nation," and the "power of protecting the nation from the intrigues and conspiracies of dangerous aliens who may have introduced themselves into the bosom of your country" belongs necessarily to the general government. The minority then refers to Virginia's alien law and concludes as follows:

That this measure should originally have been suggested as necessary for national safety, that it should have been preserved through a long course of reflection, that it should be deemed free from the objection of uniting the powers of different departments in the executive, as also of depriving an alien from his residence without a trial by jury, and yet that it should for the same causes produce a ferment in some states, as soon as the principle was adopted by Congress, might warrant reflections which we will not permit ourselves to express.

As for the Sedition Law, to "contend that there does not exist a power to punish writings coming within the description of this law, would be to assert the inability of our nation to preserve its own peace, and to protect themselves from the attempt of wicked citizens, who incapable of quiet themselves, are incessantly employed in devising means to disturb the public repose." Every state, either by statute or by common law, claims the right to punish such utterances, and prior to the passage of the Sedition Law, the general government could have punished them in its courts, for the "judicial power of the United States ... extended to the punishment of libels against the government, as a common law offence." Nor does the First Amendment forbid such laws, as a "punishment of the licentiousness is not ... a restriction of the freedom of the press." "If by freedom of the press is meant a perfect exemption from all punishment for whatever may be published, that freedom never has, and most probably never will exist."[85] Here, not in a judicial opinion—for he never had the opportunity to write one on this subject—but in a report written for the Virginia legislature, Marshall makes it clear that in his considered opinion, contrary to modern libertarianism and, specifically, to the assertion of Professor Kalven quoted above (see p. 101), a free society could indeed punish libels directed against itself and its officers.

The Address concludes with praise of the Union and a call for its defense against its enemies, and in this respect only did it differ from the various documents written by the Jeffersonians. For they did not deny the necessity of alien laws; they did not contend that libels could not be punished civilly or criminally; on the whole, they did not at this time insist on denying that distinction between the liberty and the licentiousness of the press. They merely denied an attribute of sovereignty to the United States. Jefferson, in that previously quoted letter to Abigail Adams, was emphatic on this point:

Nor does the opinion of the unconstitutionality, and consequent nullity of that law, remove all restraint from the overwhelming torrent of slander, which is confounding all vice and virtue, all truth and false-hood, in the United States. The power to do that is fully possessed by the several State Legislatures. It was reserved to them, and was denied to the General Government, by the Constitution, according to our con-struction of it. While we deny that Congress have a right to control the freedom of the press, we have ever asserted the right of the States, and their exclusive right, to do so.

It was only after their failure to provoke a favorable response to their resolutions from the other states that the Jeffersonians (but not Jefferson) began seriously to contend against the principle of a seditious libel law. Frustrated in their attempt to change the character of the Constitution into one of states' sovereignty, and unable to persuade the other states to join them in declaring the Alien and Sedition Laws null and void, though not yet deter-mined to force the issue by seceding from the Union (the size of the opposition in Virginia itself probably had something to do with this*), some of Jefferson's followers began to direct their attention to the nature of free speech and press instead of the nature of the Union, and began to attack the Sedition Law rather than the government that enacted it. It was in the course of doing this that they began to question whether the Blackston-ian view of free press as merely an uncensored press was com-patible with republican government, either state or national; and it was in the course of doing this that they developed what Leonard Levy has called "the new theory of First Amendment

---

*"There are many considerations dehors of the State, which will occur to you without enumeration. I should not apprehend them, if all was sound within. But there is a most respectable part of our State who have been enveloped in the X.Y.Z. delusion, and who destroy our unanimity for the present moment" (Jefferson to John Taylor, November 26, 1798, in *Works* [Federal ed., 1905], vol. 8, p. 480). This is the same letter, quoted above (see text at note 70), where he advised against secession "for the present."

freedoms." But even then, they were a great deal less "libertarian" than the modern champions of that cause.

The New "Libertarianism"

It was not Thomas Jefferson who led the attack on the restrictive view of freedom of speech and press. According to Levy, he proved to be "unreflective and uninventive as a theorist," continuing to speak only in "tired cliches."[86] The honor of developing the new libertarian theory of freedom of speech and press is accorded by Levy to Madison, St. George Tucker, and Tunis Wortman, among others; but, as I have argued elsewhere at some length,[87] this new "libertarianism" contains a considerable admixture of the familiar Jeffersonian states' rights theory of the Constitution. Even so, if freedom of speech "could not become a civil liberty until the truth of men's opinions...was regarded as relative rather than absolute,"[88] then certainly these men did not espouse a libertarianism that would be so designated today.

To cast doubt on the extent to which these Republican writers were "libertarian" in the modern sense is not, however, to deny Levy's main point—namely, that the passage of the Sedition Law in 1798 provoked some Americans to begin thinking about the meaning of free speech and press and their place in republican government. Prior to the introduction of the question as a political issue, that generation of Americans, however often they had spoken of the importance of freedom of speech and press, had not had the occasion to delineate with any precision what they meant by those words. Blackstone's definition was part of their legal inheritance, and until the Sedition Law they had had no occasion to wonder about its adequacy in a republican context. The Federalists were not being disingenuous when they pointed to the fact that the Sedition Law—by allowing the defendant to give in evidence the truth of the matter charged as libelous, and by empowering the jury to determine the law and the fact—was a liberalization of the traditional common law of seditious libel, reforms for which Englishmen had long been contending.[89] And they insisted, not without supporting evidence, that the federal courts were intended to exercise a common law jurisdiction.

Even as liberalized, however, the Sedition Law was still a law punishing seditious libels, and it was necessary to inquire whether such a law was compatible with republican government. The Jeffersonians began this necessary inquiry. The result was not, by modern standards, a "broad definition of the meaning and scope of liberty of expression,"[90] but it was a broader definition than the one that preceded it. The Jeffersonians did not repudiate the whole of criminal libel—for example, all of them, including Madison, would have allowed the states to punish libels and even libels of public men—but they did repudiate the idea of punishment of written censure upon government itself. In doing so, they repudiated one aspect of the 1798 Sedition Law and, as well, one part of the law of seditious libel as it stood in England at the end of the eighteenth century. (Sir James Fitz-james Stephen defined this as "written censure upon public men for their conduct as such [as well as] upon the laws, or upon the institutions of the country."[91])

According to Levy, the man who "contributed pre-eminently to the emergence of an American libertarianism" was a New York lawyer named Tunis Wortman, whose 1800 book was, in a sense, "the book that Jefferson did not write but should have."[92] But, as I have shown in detail elsewhere,[93] Wortman's position was essentially Jefferson's. He insisted that the powers of the national government did not "extend to the coercion of Libel," but he did not say this respecting the states. On the contrary:

The coercion of Libel is rather a subject of domestic superintendance than an object which properly relates to the general interests of the Union. Wherever such Coercion is proper or necessary our State *legisla-*

tures and tribunals are possessed of sufficient authority to remedy the evil. It is, therefore, to be presumed to have been intended that the States respectively should solely exercise the power of controlling the conduct of their own citizens in such cases....[94]

It should come as no surprise to learn that Wortman saw the federal Constitution as a "compact of union between the States," each state retaining its "sovereignty."[95]

The position of St. George Tucker was similar to Wortman's. He was professor of law at William and Mary, and his exposition of freedom of speech and press is said by Levy to have been "enormously important to the emergence of an American libertarianism because his absolutist theory of freedom of discussion appeared in his scholarly edition of Blackstone, for many years the standard edition used by the American bench and bar."[96] In it we find an argument against Blackstone's limited view of the privilege and, as is usual in these Jeffersonian statements, an argument that Congress had no authority to enact laws against the licentiousness of the press; but we do not find an "absolutist theory of freedom of discussion." True, Tucker did defend the "absolute and unrestrained exercise of our religious opinions," but so did everyone else, Federalist or Jeffersonian; and he did contend for an "absolute freedom of the press, and its total exemption from all restraint, control, or jurisdiction of the federal government"; but he made no such statement about state authority. Instead, he said the following:

Whoever makes use of the press as the vehicle of his sentiments on any subject, ought to do it in such language as to show he has a deference for the sentiments of others; that while he asserts the right of expressing and vindicating his own judgment, he acknowledges the obligation to submit to the judgment of those whose authority he cannot legally, or constitutionally dispute. In his statement of facts he is bound to adhere strictly to the truth; for every deviation from the truth is both an imposition upon the public, and an injury to the individual whom it may respect. In his restrictures on the conduct of men, in public stations, he is bound to do justice to their characters, and not to criminate them without substantial reason. The right of character is a sacred and invaluable right, and is not forfeited by accepting a public employment.

Whoever knowingly departs from any of these maxims is guilty of a *crime against the community*, as well as against the person injured; and though both the letter and the spirit of our federal constitution wisely prohibit the Congress of the United States from making any law, by which the freedom of speech, or of the press, may be exposed to restraint or persecution under the authority of the federal government, yet for injuries done the reputation of any person, as *an individual*, the state-courts are always open, and may afford ample, and competent redress, as the records of the courts of this commonwealth [Virginia] abundantly testify. [97]

Like Wortman, Tucker regarded the states as the seat of sovereignty under the Constitution, and like many another Virginian in the years to come, he regarded the states as capable of carrying the sovereignty to the point of seceding from the union. Each state, he said, is "still a perfect state, still sovereign, still independent, and still capable, should the occasion require, to resume the exercise of its functions, in the most unlimited extent." [98] But neither he nor Wortman was able to explain why he was willing to trust the states, but not the federal government, to impose limits on the freedom of speech. This argument was supplied in the report on the resolutions submitted to the Virginia House of Delegates in 1799-1800 by a committee (headed by James Madison) charged with writing a response to the replies by the states to the 1798 resolutions. This report is, without question, a "brilliant exposition," as Levy characterizes it, and the most significant statement of the principles on the basis of which the new Republican Party was organizing itself. What is especially interesting is the difference between this report and the principles Madison expounded ten years earlier in the *Federalist Papers*.

In 1788, Madison had espoused the cause of the large commercial republic, arguing that whereas some of the states were at that time "little more than a society of husbandmen," with the passage of time, and under a Constitution designed to foster a large commercial nation, each state would become more diverse and, in the fact of this diversity, would come to resemble every other state. "The changes of time," he said in the 56th *Federalist,* would have an "assimilating effect"; or, as he put it in the 53rd *Federalist,* increased intercourse among the states would in time "contribute to a general assimilation of their manners and laws." Now, a decade later, he seems to have assumed that local peculiarities would in fact be preserved and that the assimilation he had expected would not take place. This led him to oppose a "consolidation of the states" and any national laws designed to promote that consolidation or which depended on such a consolidation or, especially, any national laws whose expedience required a nation that knew no significant sectional differences. His reasons were profoundly republican; a republican government is one that governs by and through law, but a nation that has not eradicated local peculiarities in important respects is not one that can be governed by one national law. "Even within the legislative limits properly defined by the Constitution, the difficulty of accommodating legal regulations to a country so great in extent and so various in its circumstances, has been much felt...."[99] A country fundamentally diverse in character could only be governed by executive prerogative, for only executive prerogative could take account of the differences, encompass the discretion that diversity requires, and speak in the many voices appropriate to that diversity. In short, given what he now saw as the ineradicable heterogeneity of the country, an active national government would inevitably require an enhancement of the executive at the expense of the legislative power, and to that extent would cease to be republican. This is the theme developed so powerfully by Jefferson in the election of 1800: he and his party intended to save the country from "monarchy" or "monocracy." Madison's opposition to the Sedition Law can only be understood in this context.

The *peculiar* magnitude of some of the powers necessarily committed to the Federal Government; the *peculiar* duration required for the functions of some of its departments; the *peculiar* distance of the seat of its proceedings from the great body of its constituents; and the *peculiar* difficulty of circulating an adequate knowledge of them through any other channel; will not these considerations, *some or other of which produced other exceptions from the powers of ordinary governments,* all together, account for the policy of binding the hand of the Federal Government from touching the channel which alone can give efficacy to its responsibility to its constituents, and of leaving those who administer it to a remedy, for their injured reputations, under the same laws, and in the same tribunals, which protect their lives, their liberties, and their properties? [100]

The report argues that the Sedition Law was unconstitutional, that the First Amendment deprives U.S. courts of all jurisdiction over common law crimes, that the freedom of the press must extend beyond "an exemption from previous restraint, to an exemption from subsequent penalties also," and that the freedom of speech and press guaranteed by the First Amendment was absolute, admitting no exceptions, at least so far as the national government was concerned. Thus, Blackstone's definition of this freedom is not appropriate to the United States; there is an essential difference between the British government and the American Constitution that necessitates "a different degree of freedom in the use of the press."[101] In Britain the constitutional protections, from Magna Carta to the Bill of Rights, are designed to limit the powers of the executive, whereas the legislature is understood to be omnipotent; but in the United States, the people, "not the Government, possess the absolute sovereignty," and it is therefore necessary to secure "the great and essential rights of the people . . . against legislative as well as against executive ambition." "They are secured, not by laws paramount to prerogative, but by constitutions paramount to laws."[102] Freedom of speech and press are accorded constitutional protection because they are essential elements of the process whereby the people choose the members of the government, and "the right of electing the members of the Government constitutes . . . the essence of a free and responsible government."[103]

May it not be asked of every intelligent friend to the liberties of his country, whether the power exercised in [the Sedition Law] ought not to

117

produce great and universal alarm? Whether a rigid execution of such an act, in time past, would not have repressed that information and communication among the people which is indispensable to the just exercise of their electoral rights? And whether such an act, if made perpetual, and enforced with rigor, would not, in time to come, either destroy our free system of government, or prepare a convulsion that might prove equally fatal to it? [104]

Thus, freedom of speech and press is a condition of *republican* government, and that purpose also serves as a limiting condition. Not all speech is appropriate to republican government, and the fact that the First Amendment has deprived the national government of all authority over speech does not answer the question of a state government's authority over speech. There are limits to this freedom. Or as Madison puts it, there is a "proper boundary" between liberty and licentiousness, and he is not unaware of the difficulty in tracing it. "Governments elective, limited, and responsible in all their branches, may well be supposed to require a greater freedom of animadversion than might be tolerated by the genius of such a government as that of Great Britain."[105] How much greater he leaves us to infer. The federal government, to repeat, is destitute of all authority "for restraining the licentiousness of the press, and for shielding itself against the libellous attacks which may be made on those who administer it."[106] However, Madison nowhere says this of the states. On the contrary, the states, which do not suffer from the "peculiar" disabilities of the national government, will be expected to punish libels on "those who administer" our republican governments. In the Address that accompanied the 1799 report, he said that "calumny is forbidden by the [state] laws" and that "every libellous writing or expression might receive its punishment in the State courts."[107] His conclusion, like Jefferson's, was that the states, the seat of free government in the United States, the "ordinary governments," possessed the authority to punish defamatory libels, including defamatory libels of public officials acting in their public capacity.

It is altogether proper that the passage of the Sedition Law, and especially the manner of the trials conducted under its authority, should have provoked Americans to initiate an inquiry into the relation of free speech and press to free government. After all, even Hamilton, whom Jefferson and his party regarded as the greatest enemy of the public good as they understood it, had reservations about the wisdom of employing such legislation. He, like Marshall, may have regarded the Sedition Law as constitutional, but he did not conceal from his Federalist colleagues his anxiety concerning such measures. Writing to Oliver Wolcott when the sedition bill was first introduced on the floor of the Senate, Hamilton said:

There are provisions in this bill, which...appear to me highly exceptionable, and such as, more than anything else, may endanger civil war....I hope sincerely the thing may not be hurried through. Let us not establish a tyranny. Energy is a very different thing from violence. If we make no false step, we shall be essentially united, but if we push things to an extreme, we shall then give to faction *body* and solidity. [108]

As we shall shortly see, moreover, it was Hamilton who was largely responsible for instituting the liberalizing reforms in the state libel trials, reforms that Madison could only have applauded. And it was not by chance that these reforms were instituted in the northern, rather than in the southern, states.

"Incendiary Publications"

In a 1788 letter to Jefferson, James Madison said that in Virginia he had "seen the bill of rights violated in every instance where it has been opposed to a popular current."[109] Thanks partly to their acts of commission and omission, a popular current grew in Virginia that made a mockery of the Virginia constitution's guarantees of free speech and press. For by insisting that the national government had no authority to legislate on the slavery issue, Madison and Jefferson contributed their great names to the cause of its perpetuation. Instead of

119

adopting policies and constitutional doctrines that would have looked upon slavery as only a temporary national evil to be kept in a place where, to use Lincoln's language, it would be "in course of ultimate extinction," they fostered a constitutional doctrine that made abolition impossible without war and, assuming a continuance of antislavery sentiment outside the South, a division of the nation inevitable. No conflict was ever more "irrepressible" than the American Civil War, for slavery is an issue on which no country can remain neutral. Slavery either had to be placed in a position that guaranteed its "ultimate extinction," or it would have to expand until it was adopted in every part of the country. When, after the passage of the Alien and Sedition Laws, the national government was captured by the Jeffersonian party, with its notions of the respective powers of the national and state governments, the southern states were free to govern the slavery issue themselves, the northern states were free to be antislavery, if they wished, and the national government was expected to remain neutral. No house thus divided could long stand. It was not without logic that the South, defeated by the success of a party sworn to prevent the expansion of slavery beyond the Missouri line, chose to secede from the Union; and it was not without logic that the extreme abolitionists preferred this secession to any continuance of the divided house: the alternative was clearly war. And it was not unreasonable for the South, despite Lincoln's protestations that neither he nor his party would interfere with the institution of slavery in the states where it already existed, to see in his election to the presidency a blow to slavery that would inevitably be fatal. It was a question of slavery or the Union, but the South's 1860 decision for slavery was merely the logical consequence of decisions made by Jefferson and Madison as far back as the first decade of the Union's existence.

Consider the problem strictly within the context of speech and press freedoms. The southern states, and not without reason, saw in antislavery speech a very clear and a very present danger to the institution of slavery, which they regarded, in the words of South Carolina's Governor McDuffie in 1835, as "the cornerstone of our republican edifice."[110] Given his premise that this "republican edifice" should stand, it becomes altogether reasonable to embark on a policy of suppressing antislavery speech. This is what the South did on a major scale, in which project they had the warm support of Jefferson's latter-day heir, President Andrew Jackson.

It was a relatively simple matter to deal with local agitators. The problem for the South arose precisely from the fact that it was a part of a larger union, a Union containing states that did not—or did not always—suppress their local antislavery agitators, a Union within which communication was deliberately facilitated by a department of the national government; and with the passage of time, much of the mail distributed by this department was deposited by the enemies of slavery. It must not be distributed. Antislavery newspapers must never leave their place of publication or, failing that, the post offices in the communities of their destination. State after southern state began modestly by requesting the northern states to enact penal laws "prohibiting," in the words of a resolution adopted by the North Carolina legislature in December 1835, "the printing, within their respective limits, *all* such publications as *may have a tendency* to make our slaves discontented."[111] Two months later, Virginia went further and requested, "respectfully," that the "non-slave holding States...adopt PENAL ENACTMENTS" to suppress the abolitionist societies themselves.[112] Because they were part of a larger Union, their peculiar institution could not be preserved without the cooperation of the other parts of that Union. Hence, when the nonslaveholding states refused to comply with this request to adopt the nonrepublican policy of suppressing speech in order to preserve what the South regarded as the "cornerstone" of its so-called "republican edifice," some communities in the South (Charleston, South Carolina, among them) adopted the simple, if illegal, expedient of persuading the local postmasters

121

to refuse to deliver abolitionist mail and antislavery newspapers. Then, in order to gain the sanction of the law, they called upon the assistance of the national government; and in his annual message of December 7, 1835, President Jackson responded to the best of his ability. He too called upon the nonslaveholding states to suppress abolitionist agitation, and he went on to ask the Congress to enact a law prohibiting, "under severe penalties, the circulation in the Southern States, through the mail, of incendiary publications intended to instigate the slaves to insurrection."[113] Upon the motion of John C. Calhoun, this proposal was referred to a select committee of the Senate, rather than to the Post Office Committee, because, as one member put it, the latter "was composed, in a large proportion [four out of five], of gentlemen from non-slaveholding States." The select committee was composed of five members: Calhoun as chairman, King of Georgia, Mangum of North Carolina, Linn of Missouri, and Davis of Massachusetts, the only member to represent a non-slaveholding state.

President Jackson's message, Calhoun said, however friendly to the slave states in its intention, proposed congressional legislation that would constitute a palpable violation of the Constitution's guarantee of freedom of the press. Indeed, according to Calhoun, it was identical in principle with the odious Sedition Law of 1798, for although the latter prohibited the publication of certain materials, and Jackson's bill would have prohibited merely the circulation of materials, this difference was immaterial, for the purpose of publication is circulation. The object of each is the same: "the communication of sentiments and opinions to the public." Whatever difference there was between the two measures revealed Jackson's proposal to be the more invidious, because it constituted, or would constitute, a prior censorship insofar as readers in southern states were concerned:

It would indeed have been a poor triumph for the cause of liberty, in the great contest of 1799, had the sedition law been put down on principles that would have left Congress free to suppress the circulation, through the mail, of the very publication which that odious act was intended to prohibit. The authors of that memorable achievement would have had but slender claims on the gratitude of posterity, if their victory over the encroachment of power had been left so imperfect. [114]

Because, therefore, seen in the light of the principles of the Constitution, the President's proposal was at least as odious as the hated Sedition Law, Calhoun recommended to the Senate that it be rejected out of hand—but not without a ringing of the changes on the principles of free government.

Up to this point in this affair of "incendiary publications," the reader, following Koch and Ammon's appraisal of the Virginia and Kentucky Resolutions, might be tempted to see Calhoun, as Koch and Ammon see Jefferson and Madison, as a great defender of civil liberties, and specifically of the right of free speech and press. Here was the great Democrat Jackson proposing a censorship of the mails, a censorship that would have required postmasters to examine publications to ascertain whether they contained sentiments anathema to the slave states; and here was the great Democrat Calhoun, whose heroes were Jefferson and Madison, protecting free government against this onslaught and appealing to the memory of the victory over the earlier "odious" law. And, indeed, this was precisely how Mr. Justice Brennan, in *New York Times* v. *Sullivan,* chose to interpret Calhoun's action: "Calhoun, reporting to the Senate on February 4, 1836, assumed that its invalidity was a matter 'which no one now doubts.'"[115] But Calhoun was no more willing than Jackson to permit "incendiary publications" to circulate in southern states; like Jefferson and Madison before him, he too appealed to the right of the states to suppress, a fact Brennan did not deign to mention. Jackson's proposal was a violation of the First Amendment, but even more so of the very nature of the Constitution, for it assumed a national power that in fact, Calhoun insisted, was reserved to the states. On behalf of his select committee—but not, as it turned out in the ensuing debates, with the consent of a unanimous committee—Calhoun then proposed a substitute measure and urged its adoption. This substitute deserves to be quoted at length.

SEC. 1. Be it enacted, etc., That it shall not be lawful for any deputy postmaster, in any State, Territory, or District, knowingly to receive and put into the mail, any pamphlet, newspaper, handbill, or other paper, printed or written, or pictorial representation, touching the subject of slavery, addressed to any person or post office in any State, Territory, or District, where by the laws of the said State, Territory, or District, their circulation is prohibited. Nor shall it be lawful for any deputy postmaster in said State, Territory, or District, knowingly to deliver to any person any such pamphlet [etc.], to any person whatever, except to such person or persons as are duly authorized by the proper authority of such State, Territory, or District, to receive the same. [116]

Where Jackson had called for the suppression merely of publications, Calhoun called for the suppression of "any paper, printed or written...touching the subject of slavery," a category broad enough to include private letters. From the point of view of freedom of the press, his bill was certainly more odious than Jackson's, yet he attacked the latter in the name of the Constitution and the principles of free government. The only possible conclusion is that he saw the great "triumph for the cause of liberty, in the great contest of 1799," as a triumph for states' rights, not freedom of the press.

Calhoun left no doubt as to this. The President's proposed bill assumed the right of the national government to determine what papers were incendiary. To admit such a right "would be fatal to [the slaveholding] States," for the national government would then have the right to determine what is *not* incendiary. Such a power could not be lodged in the hands of officials of the national government—they, and this included the congressmen who enact laws as well as the postmasters who in this case would administer them, could not be trusted. Only the slaveholding states themselves could be trusted to govern this and any other aspect of the slavery issue. A national power to determine what is and what is not an incendiary publication would constitute "the

124

power to abolish slavery, [for it would give Congress] the means of breaking down all the barriers which the slaveholding states have erected for the protection of their lives and property."[117] The Sedition Law was "odious" because Congress assumed a power belonging to the states; Jackson's measure for dealing with the problem of antislavery agitation was "odious" because, once again, it assumed a power in the national government that had been reserved to the states.

Calhoun's bill did not make this constitutional mistake: the states would define (and had in fact already defined) what is incendiary, and the national government, working with those definitions, would cooperate with the states by excluding from the mails what the states wanted to be excluded. By so doing, the national government would help protect the "republican edifice" in the southern states—that is, slavery. Thus, the true definition of the First Amendment was, as one of Calhoun's colleagues on the select committee, Senator King of Georgia, said, "the right to print and publish whatever might be permitted by the laws of the state";[118] and, according to Calhoun, the states might "prohibit the introduction or circulation of any paper or publication which may, in their opinion, disturb or endanger the institution [of slavery]."[119] This is certainly not a civil liberties argument, although it is consistent with what southerners had said a generation earlier in the alien and sedition controversy. And like his mentor Jefferson, Calhoun too was unwilling to confine his resistance to protests uttered on the floor of Congress. Whether the bill passed or failed, he said, the slaveholding states would not permit antislavery publications to circulate among them. "It [was] a case of life and death with them...."[120] Nor, as he and his friends read the Constitution, would this be a defiance of the law:

But I must tell the Senate, be your decision what it may, the South will never abandon the principles of this bill. If you refuse co-operation with our laws, and conflict should ensue between your and our laws, the southern States will never yield to the superiority of yours. We have a

125

remedy in our hands, which, in such event, we shall not fail to apply. We have high authority for asserting that, in such cases, "State interposition is the rightful remedy"—a doctrine first announced by Jefferson—adopted by the patriotic and republican State of Kentucky by a solemn resolution, in 1798, and finally carried out into successful practice on a recent occasion [i.e., nullification] by the gallant State which I, in part, have the honor to represent. [121]

In the event, the Senate substituted a modified bill for Calhoun's and then rejected that modified bill by a vote of 19-25, a vote in which with very few exceptions, free states were aligned against slave states. But Calhoun was as good as his word, and despite the fact that the Congress, as part of a general statute respecting the organization of the post office, shortly thereafter provided for the punishment of any postmaster who failed to deliver any "letter, package, pamphlet, or newspaper," [122] postmasters in the South refused to deliver antislavery papers. Not even Horace Greeley could get his paper, the *New York Tribune,* delivered in Lynchburg, Virginia. [123]

In the light of these facts, it was disingenuous in the extreme for Brennan to cite Calhoun in the course of declaring Alabama's libel law to be constitutionally deficient. And it was no less disingenuous for Brennan to think he could dispose of his difficulties by simply saying there was no force in the "argument that the constitutional limitations implicit in the history of the Sedition Act apply only to Congress and not the States . . . . this distinction was eliminated with the adoption of the Fourteenth Amendment and the application to the States of the First Amendment's restrictions." [124] This is a case of robbing Peter to pay Paul; or better, of robbing Peter in order to rob Paul. The constitutional distinction may have been eliminated in this manner, but not the distinction insisted upon by Jefferson and Calhoun. The question of the original understanding of freedom of speech and press cannot be answered in this fashion.

If we ignore the institution for which Calhoun and his colleagues fought, we can say that there was nothing unreasonable about their choice of weapons. Abolitionist literature was indeed incendiary in the South; its circulation did indeed threaten the preservation of slavery and therewith of the very regimes erected in the slave states; or in Holmesian terms, it did present a very clear and a very present danger of bringing about what southern leaders regarded as an evil and what they were sworn to prevent. Although we can condemn southern leaders for their failure to adopt policies designed to put an end to slavery, it would be unreasonable to expect them to do what no leaders of any regime can do—namely, to remain indifferent to dangers to the regime itself. And speech, as the abolitionists and the friends of slavery both well knew, can endanger a regime. This was especially true of southern slavery, for the states that adopted and defended it were parts of a Union "dedicated to the proposition that all men are created equal," a Union that increasingly embraced men who were dedicated to the destruction of slavery—or failing that, the destruction of the Union that permitted it to exist in any of its parts.*

In the event, the southern states were more and more forced to promote conformity within their ranks, with test oaths that required state officers to swear "primary and paramount allegiance" to their "sovereign" states, by silencing even those who "espoused the old necessary-evil argument," by refusing to permit what in 1832 Virginia did permit: the publication of debates on the merits of slavery. To publish such debates was a policy "blended with...madness and fatality." One South Carolina paper even refused to print an essay *attacking* the policy of permitting a public discussion of the slavery question because " 'it is a subject that ought not to be agitated at all in this State.' "[125]

Eventually, as we have seen, the southern leaders came to realize that they could not permit free discussion of the slavery

---

*Hence, today there should be no *constitutional* obstacle to state legislation (or even federal legislation with respect to the mails and interstate commerce) forbidding proslavery propaganda; it is not difficult to imagine circumstances in which such publications and speech would constitute a clear and present danger to the well-being of states and nation. See *Beauharnais* v. *Illinois*, 343 U.S. 250 (1952).

issue even in the free states—and they had a number of northern allies with them on this at one time—or finally, the cruelest irony of all, in the Congress of the United States. The first of the so-called "gag rules," according to which the House resolved not to entertain any petition relating to the subject of slavery or to permit any discussion of such petitions, was adopted in 1836, and it was not until December 1845 that the last of them was rescinded, largely through the efforts of John Quincy Adams, who from the first had declared them to be "a direct violation of the constitution of the United States, the rules of this House, and the rights of [his] constituents."[126] By this time, however, whether it knew it or not, the nation had in effect decided that there should be freedom for antislavery speech everywhere, which means that it had decided that either slavery would end in the South or the nation would be divided. The divided house could no longer stand.

The States and the "Coercion" of Libels

It so happened that two of the principals in the alien and sedition controversy, Thomas Jefferson and Alexander Hamilton, were involved in a state seditious libel case that arose out of that controversy. The case serves to illustrate the sort of trials to be expected in the state courts to which the Jeffersonians consigned jurisdiction over libels.

Harry Croswell was the printer and, under a pseudonym, the editor of *The Wasp,* a Federalist newspaper published in the Republican state of New York. Shortly after Jefferson and his party had been swept into national office on their platform of saving the republic and states' rights, Croswell, in print, accused Jefferson of paying James Callender for "calling Washington a traitor, a robber, and a perjurer [and] for calling Adams a hoary-headed incendiary." He went on to say that no "democratic editor has yet dared, or ever will dare, to meet [these charges] in an open and manly discussion.'' He was probably right as to the editors—for Jefferson had indeed supported Callender with money—but if he expected the Republicans, who had so recently inveighed against the national Sedition Law, to remain indifferent to what was being said about them, he was quickly disabused. Two indictments were brought against him in the New York courts charging him with libeling Thomas Jefferson. Croswell, one indictment ran,

being a malicious and seditious man, of a depraved mind and wicked and diabolical disposition [intended with his words] to detract from, scandalize, traduce, vilify, and to represent him, the said Thomas Jefferson, as unworthy of the confidence, respect, and attachment of the people of the said United States, and to alienate and withdraw from the said Thomas Jefferson...the obedience, fidelity, and allegiance of the citizens of the state of New York, and also of the said United States; and wickedly and maliciously to disturb the peace.[127]

At the trial, Croswell sought the right to call witnesses on his behalf in order to prove the truth of the accusations he had made against Jefferson, but the trial judge denied him this. The truth or falsity of the words constituting the alleged libel was irrelevant, the judge ruled, as was Croswell's intent in publishing them. This left the jury with the task, first, of determining whether Croswell was responsible for publishing the words, and second, of determining the truth of the innuendoes (that is, whether the construction put upon the published words by the prosecution was fair). Under such conditions, and with a Republican judge presiding, it is not remarkable that Croswell was convicted. But he was not content to leave the matter there, and with the assistance of two of the leading Federalists in the country, his case was to assume a significance extending far into the future.

He petitioned for a new trial and, when this was denied as a matter of course, filed an appeal with the state supreme court. His principal defense attorney now became Alexander Hamilton, and the court before which Hamilton argued included

James Kent, later to become famous as Chancellor Kent and, after his retirement from the chancery bench, as the author of the extremely influential *Commentaries on American Law.* Kent's opinion in the case, built squarely and solidly on the arguments provided by Hamilton, may be said to constitute the foundation on which the state's law of freedom of the press was subsequently built. This is despite the fact that Kent's opinion was not controlling, since with only four of its five judges sitting, the court was evenly divided and Croswell's conviction was undisturbed.

It is striking that Hamilton should have agreed to be of counsel. Of course, as every schoolboy knows, he and Jefferson were not friends, but this fact does not suffice to explain the considerable attention he devoted to the case or what Thomas Reed Powell called "the wide range of [his] advocacy."[128] But the victim of the alleged libel was not simply Thomas Jefferson, Esq., he was Thomas Jefferson, President of the United States; and Croswell was accused of being a "malicious and seditious man" who published his words with a view to withdrawing "from the said Thomas Jefferson...the obedience, fidelity, and allegiance of the citizens of the state of New York, and also of the said United States...." Because of the repressive character of the common law as it was understood in New York, Croswell's case, even more than the trials of Callender and the other victims of the federal Sedition Law, presented the issue of the true meaning of free speech and press under a republican government.[129] The case, therefore, deserved Hamilton's time and energy, even if Croswell did not.

The precise question raised by the motion for a new trial was whether the trial judge had erred in denying Croswell the opportunity to prove the truth of his allegedly libelous statements and in restricting the jury to determining the fact of publication. Both Hamilton and Kent, of course, argued that he had erred, but their interpretation of the English precedents is not persuasive, and the reader is left with the impression that Chief

Justice Lewis, who filed an opinion denying the motion, was on sounder legal grounds. He insisted that Fox's Libel Act, which in 1792 settled the question of the role of the jury in English trials, was not, as Hamilton said it was, declaratory of the English law (and therefore a common law rule in New York), but was instead a revision of the law. In fact, although in form declaratory, "it was in substance a momentous change in the law of libel."[130] No more compelling is Hamilton's statement that the rule that truth is no defense in a libel action derives from a "polluted source," the Court of Star Chamber. Whatever its source, it had been firmly embraced by the common law.

A review of the common law of libel will serve to illuminate the issues at stake. Where the only damage done by a libel was to the reputation of the libeled party, there was no foundation for a criminal prosecution by the government, it being the policy of the law to leave the care of a man's reputation to himself and merely to provide the forum in which he might seek private remedy in a civil action against his libelers. When, however, the offense was of a public nature, there was a foundation for criminal prosecution. When, for example, the intent of a libel was to defame the government or its ministers or to cause disaffection with it or them or to bring it or them into hatred or contempt, the action might be punished as a seditious libel; or when the tendency of a libel (against either a private or a public man) was to cause a breach of the peace, it might be punished as a defamatory libel.* Leaving out of the account the history of *scandalum magnatum,* which had its beginnings in a statute of 1275,[131] the first English libel case of any importance was the case *De Libellis Famosis,* which Coke, as attorney general, prosecuted

*The fact that the rationale for punishing defamatory libels is their tendency to cause breaches of the peace did not mean that this tendency played any part in the trial. Apparently courts "have never required a factual showing of violence, either actual or potential." "Constitutionality of the Law of Criminal Libel," *Columbia Law Review* 52 (1952): 527. Nor has the unlikelihood of a breach of the peace been allowed as a defense. See Mason H. Newall, *Law of Slander and Libel in Civil and Criminal Cases,* 4th ed. (Chicago: Callaghan, 1924) pp. 934-935. 934-935.

before the Star Chamber in 1605. In Stephen's account of it, the case lays down the following points, among others:

It distinguishes libels made against a private person, and libels made against magistrates or public persons. In reference to libels against public persons it says: "If it be against a magistrate or other public person it is a greater offence" (than if against a private person) "for it concerns not only the breach of the peace, but also the scandal of government: for what greater scandal of government can there be than to have corrupt or wicked magistrates to be appointed and constituted by the king to govern his subjects under him? and greater imputation to the State cannot be than to suffer such corrupt men to sit in the sacred seat of justice, or to have any meddling in or concerning the administration of justice." It is said...that a libeller may be punished at indictment at common law or *"ore tenus* on his confession in the Star Chamber" by fine and imprisonment....It adds, that "it is not material whether the libel be true or whether the party against whom it is made be of good or ill fame, for in a settled state of government the party grieved ought to complain for every injury done him in any ordinary course of law, and not by any means to revenge himself either by the odious course of libelling or otherwise." It mentions various forms of libel, as writings, emblems, and pictures, and it says that when a man finds a private libel he should either burn it or give it to a magistrate, and when he finds a public libel give it to a magistrate that the author may be discovered....

The inference from all this seems to be that Coke's idea of a libel was, speaking generally, written blame, true or false, of any man public or private, the blame of public men being a more serious matter than the blame of a private man. [132]

The great—or perhaps better, the infamous—cases best known to the generation of the American Founders from their study of the common law, cases decided after the fall of the Star Chamber in 1641 and after the expiration of the last press licensing act in 1694, were those involving seditious libels, the libels of government or its ministers: *Tutchins* in 1704, for example, and the *Dean of St. Asaph's* case in 1783, and the *Tom Paine* case in 1792, in which it was held that the publication in England of the *Rights of Man* was a seditious libel. [133] It was in these trials, and especially in that of the Dean of St. Asaph's, that the great battle for liberty of the press was carried on in England. The issue was not whether libels could be punished without abridging the liberty of the press, but whether the procedure for trying libels was compatible with liberty of the press. Specifically, the issues concerned the role to be played by the jury in the determination of law and fact and, closely related to this, the question of the determination of the mischievous intent of the author or publisher. It was in the trial of the Dean of St. Asaph's that Erskine, as defense counsel, made his celebrated argument in favor of an enlarged role for the jury in the trial of libels, an argument he lost in the trial before Lord Mansfield but won nine years later when Parliament adopted Fox's Libel Act. The issue deserves some elaboration here because of the importance attached to it by advocates of the liberty of the press.

The criminality of any act rests on a judgment of the law upon a state of facts; and questions of law being for the judge to decide and questions of fact for the jury, "the judge's duty must be to tell the jury what judgment the law would pass upon a given state of facts...."[134] In England before Fox's Libel Act of 1792—and, as we shall see, in some jurisdictions in America even after 1792—in the trial of a libel the jury's role was limited to determining whether the defendant did indeed write or publish the libel and whether the construction put upon the published words by the prosecution was fair and acceptable. These were understood to be questions of fact. The judge determined whether the words were libelous, which was understood to be a question of law. Whether Shipley, the Dean of St. Asaph's, published the pamphlet entitled *A Dialogue Between a Gentleman and a Farmer* was a question of fact to be determined by the jury. Whether certain words contained therein were given a fair interpretation by the prosecution was also a question of fact to be determined by the jury. But whether the publication of these words, so understood, constituted a libel was a question of law to be determined by the judge. Erskine argued at considerable length and with great power that the criminality of any act depends upon a criminal intention, and that the question of intention is a question of fact to be determined by the jury.

It is possible, however, to agree with Erskine on this point without joining in his conclusion that the jury ought to be charged with determining the libelous character of the publication. It depends on the definition of the crime. In Stephen's words, "what is the intention which makes the act of publishing criminal? Is it the mere intention to publish written blame, or is it an intention to produce by such a publication some particular evil effect?"[135] In fact, at that time, seditious libel was defined as written blame of public men and institutions; this being so, the jury had only to decide the question of whether the defendant intended to publish the words containing the blame (or whether, for example, he had accidentally dropped the paper containing them out of his pocket). If, however, the crime had been defined as publication with the mischievous intent to cause disaffection, it would have been open to the jury to consider whether the defendant, in fact, intended to cause disaffection with his publication. But this was not the law at this time, although the typical indictments accused the defendants with a long list of evil intentions, perhaps because the men who drafted these indictments were paid by the page.* The crime consisted in the intentional publication only, and this was true for both seditious and defamatory libels. Nor was it necessary, except in cases where the alleged libel was privileged

---

*Consider the indictment against the Dean of St. Asaph's: *"The jurors, etc., present that W.D.S., etc.,* being a person of a wicked and turbulent disposition, and maliciously designing and intending to excite and diffuse among the subjects of this realm, discontents, jealousies, and suspicions of our lord the king and his government, and disaffection and disloyalty to the person and government of our lord the king, and to raise very dangerous seditions and tumults within this kingdom, and to draw the government of this kingdom into great scandal, infamy, and disgrace, and to incite the subjects of our lord the king to attempt by force and violence, and with arms, to make alteration in the government, state and constitution of the kingdom, *on* etc., *at,* etc., wickedly and seditiously *published, and caused and procured to be published, a certain* false, wicked, malicious, *seditious,* and scandalous *libel of and concerning our said lord the king, and the government of this realm,* in the form of a supposed dialogue (because of the occasion on which or the circumstances under which it was published), to prove malice in any criminal proceeding.[136] And, finally, whereas the truth of the matters charged in a libel was a sufficient defense in a civil action (the plaintiff not being entitled to "recover damages for an injury done to a reputation to which he had no right"),[137] in all criminal proceedings the truth of the published words constituted no defense, nor was it admitted in evidence even in mitigation of punishment. The maxim "the greater the truth, the greater the libel" was based on the theory that the libel was more likely to cause disaffection or a breach of the peace if it were true than if it were false, because in the latter case the victim of the libel could refute the charges leveled against him. This, very briefly, is how the criminal law of libel stood in England when the American Constitution, including the First Amendment, was being written.[138]

Fox's Libel Act in 1792 provided a means by which the intolerable harshness of this law first came to be mitigated, although it did not prevent numerous convictions during the stormy years immediately after its passage, which were the years of the French revolutionary wars. (It did not, for example, prevent the conviction of Tom Paine within the first year after its passage.) The act, after referring at the outset to the doubts respecting the function of juries in the trial of any libel (seditious, defamatory, blasphemous, or even, presumably, obscene), provided that the jury may "give a general verdict of guilty or not guilty upon the whole matter put in issue upon [the] indictment and information; and shall not be required or directed by the court or judge before whom such indictment or information shall be tried to

---

between a supposed gentleman and a supposed farmer, wherein the part of the supposed gentleman is denoted by the letter G., and the part of the supposed farmer in such supposed dialogue is denoted by the letter F., entitled, etc., *in which* said *libel is* [sic] *contained the* false, wicked, malicious, *seditious,* and scandalous *matters* following, to wit," etc. Stephen suggests that this indictment would have been good if it had consisted only in the matter printed in italics, and that all the rest is surplusage (ibid., p. 354).

find the defendant guilty merely on the proof of the publication by such defendant or defendants of the paper charged to be a libel, and of the sense ascribed to the same in such indictment or information.'' This seems clear enough, but the act then confused the matter to some extent by providing that the court or judge shall, ''according to their or his discretion, give their or his opinion and directions to the jury on the matter in issue...as in other criminal cases.''[139] The act assigned to the jury the right to give a general verdict ''upon the whole matter put in issue,'' and then became more specific by flatly providing that the jury should not be required to find the defendant guilty merely on proof of the publication of the libel and of the fairness of the interpretation of the innuendoes. But what, at that time, was the ''whole matter put in issue''? Did it comprise the intentions of the libeler to cause disaffection or a breach of the peace? The act does not say so, but, in the course of time, the effect of the act was the same as if it had. In Stephen's words, the Libel Act ''enlarged the old definition of a...libel by the addition of a reference to the specific intentions of the libeler—to the purpose for which he wrote.''[140] This was accomplished in part by the jury's habit of confusing intentions and motives; while perhaps agreeing that an intention to produce disaffection was illegal, jurors might refuse to bring in a verdict of guilty against a defendant with whose motives for causing disaffection they agreed.

The next significant event in the history of the English law of libel was the passage in 1843, long after Croswell's case in New York, of Lord Campbell's Libel Act. Among other reforms, it made truth a defense if it could be shown that publication was for a public benefit.[141] Even so, this privilege was restricted to cases of private defamatory libels and specifically held to be unavailable in prosecutions of seditious and blasphemous libels.*

---

*In 1846 an Irish newspaper publisher was prosecuted in the Court of Queen's Bench, Ireland, for publishing a seditious libel. He contended that he was permitted by Lord Campbell's Act to plead the truth of the matters charged as

The common law of libel inherited by the American states, therefore, unaffected as it was by the statutory revisions of 1792 and 1843, was by a considerable margin less liberal than the federal Sedition Law of 1798. The Sedition Law incorporated Fox's reform and, by allowing the truth to be pleaded in defense even in cases of seditious libel, accomplished something left undone by Lord Campbell's Act. Hence, when Madison, Tucker, and Wortman said that calumny and invective directed against federal officers could be punished in the state courts, they were not—except to the extent to which this common law had been modified by state statutes*—offering much by way of an enlarged understanding of liberty of the press.

In their treatment of Croswell's case, Hamilton and Kent reached the decisive issue of freedom in a republican regime. By rejecting the authority of Blackstone and Lord Mansfield, they themselves became the authorities in America. To both of them—for Kent accepted Hamilton's formulation without alteration or addition—the liberty of the press "consisted in publishing with impunity, truth with good motives, and for justifiable ends, whether it related to men or to measures."[142] This became the basis of the law in almost every American jurisdiction, the basis of what Justice Frankfurter was to call many years later the "common sense" of American libel law.[143]

This new law was not libertarian in the modern sense—neither Hamilton nor Kent advocated a law that would permit everyone

---

libelous; but the court, per Blackburn, C.J., held that the privilege was allowed only "where it is for the public benefit that the facts should be published," and that no one could contend that a seditious libel could be for the public benefit (*The Queen* v. *Duffy,* 2 Cox's C.C. 45 [1846]).

*Connecticut did precisely this in 1804 when it adopted, in almost identical language, Section 3 of the federal Sedition Law, making truth a defense and allowing the jury to "determine the law and the fact, under the direction of the court, as in other cases." Anastaplo is altogether correct in insisting that this statute was intended as a liberalization of the preexisting law and that, since there was no statute on the subject, the preexisting law was the common law of libel. See George Anastaplo, *The Constitutionalist: Notes on the First Amendment* (Dallas: Southern Methodist University Press, 1971), pp. 138-139.

to say anything at any time[144]—but it was surely more consonant with republican government, both because it permitted truth as a defense in a trial of public libels (when the allegations were published with good motives and for justifiable ends) and because it enlarged the role of the jury in the determination of the intent and tendency of the publication. In all criminal law, Hamilton argued, the intent constitutes the crime—homicide is not, of itself, murder. Whether intent and tendency are viewed as questions of fact, as Hamilton argued, or of law, or of a "compound of law and fact," as Kent put it, what is important in the law of criminal libel is that the determination of malice and tendency not be entrusted solely to the judges who, as Hamilton said and as history confirms, "might be tempted to enter into the views of government." *

A role for the jury does not by itself assure impartial trials; the experience under the Sedition Law was sufficient to prove this. But it would seem to be a prerequisite in criminal trials of what is alleged to be seditious behavior. The government must be able "to control the governed," as Madison said in the 51st

---

*It was precisely this temptation, notably in those trials conducted before Judge Samuel Chase, that had made the Sedition Law cases notorious in their time and infamous in the annals of American criminal trials. Nor does the relevance of the example of Chase end with his conduct on the bench. There is evidence in Hamilton's defense of Croswell that he had Chase and the subsequent events provoked by Chase's conduct very much in mind as he reflected on the freedom of the press and the trials for its abuse. At the beginning of the year of Croswell's trial, the House of Representatives had appointed a committee "to enquire into the judicial conduct of Samuel Chase," and two months later the House voted the impeachment by a strictly partisan vote of 73-32. He was to be acquitted in the Senate the following year, but the issue was pending and still in doubt during the Croswell appeal. Since it was common knowledge that if the Republicans succeeded in removing Chase from the federal bench, they would then proceed against other Federalist judges, a fair-minded man was entitled to be apprehensive for the future of an independent judiciary in America. Hence Hamilton, in what seems an obvious reference to these events, said in his closing argument in Croswell's case that he feared that "any political tenet or indiscretion might be made a crime or pretext to impeach, convict and remove from office, the judges of the federal courts" (3 Johns. at 358). Chase was an extreme Federalist, and the Sedition Law trials he conducted were travesties of justice. But it is extremely doubtful that his removal and replacement by a Republican judge would have buttressed the independence of the judiciary.

Federalist, and the law, including the law limiting the freedom of the press, is one of the means, and in a republic the most appropriate means, of doing this. But the government must also be obliged "to control itself" or to be controlled, and the requirement that the "trial of all crimes except in cases of impeachment shall be by jury" is a recognition of this necessity, especially in the absence of a truly independent judiciary. Hamilton in the 83rd *Federalist* was not prepared to say whether jury trials were more to be esteemed "as a defense against the oppressions of an hereditary monarch, than as a barrier to the tyranny of popular magistrates in a popular government," but essential they were. It is worth our attention to notice that while it was Jefferson who was responsible for the fact that the trials of seditious and other criminal libels would take place in state courts, it was Hamilton who was largely responsible for reforming the procedure in those state trials to make it conform more fully to the principles of republican government and, not accidentally, the federal Constitution.[145]

No less essential is the other major element in the law derived from the work of Hamilton and Kent in Croswell's case: the right to offer in evidence the truth of the allegedly libelous words. The maxim "the greater the truth, the greater the libel," or the more modest version in Chief Justice Lewis's opinion in *Croswell* that "truth may be as dangerous to society as falsehood," is not unreasonable in a hereditary monarchy or in any regime that, in Burke's words, finds its "sole authority" in the fact that "it has existed time out of mind." Speaking truth there may indeed be destructive of law and government, because the regime does not rest on true principles as such, but on historical principles. But both the federal Constitution and those of states were understood to rest on the laws of nature, on the self-evident truth that all men are created equal with respect to the natural rights of life, liberty, and the pursuit of happiness. Government is instituted among men to secure these rights and derives its just powers from the consent of the governed. No man is naturally

139

exalted over another, and public officers hold their temporarily exalted stations only at the pleasure of their fellow citizens. Given this foundation, speaking the truth concerning men and measures and, indeed, concerning the very basis of the regime cannot usually be "dangerous to society." Which means that the English law of libel, evolving in a different system, based on different principles, had to be reformed before it could be accepted in America. In Hamilton's words, "truth is [not only] a material ingredient in the evidence of intent," and must therefore be admissible on procedural grounds, but it is also "all-important to the liberties of the people [and] an ingredient in the eternal order of things."[146] Hamilton hoped to see the common law "applied to the United States," and his version of the common law, whatever the case with the English version, required the rule that the defendant be permitted to prove the truth of his allegedly libelous words. The common law was "principally the application of natural law to the state and condition of society," and without adherence to its principles "the constitution would be frittered away or borne down by factions, (the evil genii, the pests of republics)."[147] Thus, the natural law dictated the form of the Constitution and, through the vehicle of the common law, the manner in which government was to be administered under it: all men were to be free to publish opinions on public men and measures—the provisions respecting freedom of the press guaranteed this—but their publications were not to be maliciously false. The truth was to be the standard of political life.

A distinction drawn by Kent in his opinion serves to illustrate this role of truth. "There can be no doubt," he said "that it is competent for the defendant to rebut the presumption of malice, drawn from the fact of publication; and it is consonant to the general theory of evidence, and the dictates of justice, that the defendant should be allowed to avail himself of every fact and circumstance that may serve to repel that presumption."[148] He continued:

140

And what can be a more important circumstance than the truth of the charge, to determine the goodness of the motive in making it, if it be a charge against the competency or purity of a character in public trust, or of a candidate for public favor, or a charge of actions in which the community have an interest, and are deeply concerned? To shut out wholly the inquiry into the truth of the accusation, is to abridge essentially the means of defence. It is to weaken the arm of the defendant, and to convict him, by means of a presumption, which he might easily destroy by proof that the charge was true, and that, considering the nature of the accusation, the circumstances and the time under which it was made, and the situation of the person implicated, his motive could have been no other than a pure and disinterested regard for the public welfare. [149]

The conduct of public men must be measured by the highest standards of probity and their character by models of virtue and purity, and any published accusation of a failure on their part, measured by these standards and models, will not be punished under the law. On the contrary, it can be said that just as republican government requires public men of the highest character, it requires a press to point to the derelictions—that is, it requires a law which condones accusations of derelictions. But the law, being reasonable, will not presume that everyone must live according to these strict standards. Hence, the presumption of malicious intent in a libel of a *private* person cannot be rebutted by a showing of the truth of the charge—or in Kent's words, "this doctrine will not go to tolerate libels upon private character"—because no public good is served by revelations of the derelictions of private persons, the public being neither injured by these private vices nor otherwise concerned with them. [150] But that "falsehood is a material ingredient in a public libel" was a doctrine, Kent insisted, which even the English courts had occasionally admitted and which had taken firmer root in America. It is, he concluded, "the vital support of the liberty of the press." [151] Certainly it became firmly rooted after the advocacy of Hamilton and Kent.

In order to compare what are today held to be the true

principles of the liberty of the press in a democratic polity with the original understanding, it is important to remark that Hamilton and Kent did not advocate that the truth be a complete defense, even in a trial of a public libel. The malicious intent in a libel of a public person can be rebutted by a showing of the truth of the charges, but just as "this doctrine will not go to tolerate libels upon private character," so the showing of the truth will not alone justify "the circulation of charges for seditious and wicked ends."[152] For the truth, even in a republican polity, *can* be employed for "seditious and wicked ends." Hence the bill that was introduced in the State Assembly one year after *Croswell* by William Van Ness, who had been on the *Croswell* brief with Hamilton. It was unanimously enacted by both houses of the legislature, and in 1821 became part of the free speech and press section of the state constitution. The bill made it proper for the defendent in the trials of a criminal libel to give in evidence the truth of the matter charged as libelous, provided it be shown in the trial that the words were "published with good motives and for justifiable ends."[153]

Thus, the law of criminal libel was changed in two respects as a result of the *Croswell* case. The jury's role was enlarged significantly beyond the mere determination of fact of publication and truth of innuendoes, to embrace as well the determination of the criminality of the words. Second, the truth, provided good motives and justifiable ends could be shown, would be permitted in evidence to rebut the presumption of malice and, therefore, to acquit the defendant of the libel. Put differently, the law with respect to malice was changed, and the jury would thereafter play a major role in the application of the law. That this requirement that even the truth be spoken with good motives and justifiable ends was not retained inadvertently is proved by an event in the legislature. In April 1804, shortly before the opinions in the case were delivered, the legislature enacted a bill providing, in effect, that truth be a complete defense in the trial of a public libel; but the Council of Revision (which was composed of the governor and two judges of the Supreme Court and which could be overruled only by a two-thirds majority in both houses of the legislature) returned it, objecting that the proposed law "made no distinction between libels circulated from good motives and justifiable ends, and such as were circulated for seditious and wicked purposes, or to gratify individual malice or revenge."[154] Upon consideration of these objections in the Assembly, the bill "lost by a large majority." It was only two months later that this same Assembly, along with the Senate, adopted the Van Ness-Hamilton-Kent bill unanimously.

Conclusion

People v. *Croswell* began as an episode in the alien and sedition controversy. Croswell had accused Jefferson of paying Callender, a victim of the Sedition Law, to vilify Washington and Adams. But whereas the Sedition Law had provoked nullification and even disunion sentiments in Virginia, the indictment and trial of Croswell provoked the most thoughtful consideration of the meaning of freedom of speech and press that Americans had, to that time, ever engaged in. What began as a party matter ended in the unanimous adoption of a provision embodying the principles, here stated by the arch-Federalists Alexander Hamilton and James Kent, that can truly be said to have represented the considered opinion of the Americans of this time on the meaning of freedom of speech and press. *Croswell* came to be cited not just in New York but throughout the Union, even in the most Republican state of Pennsylvania, which had been the first state to adopt these principles in its constitution.*

---

*Justice Jackson, in *Beauharnais* v. *Illinois,* 343 U.S. 250, 295, 297 (1952), after reciting the history of the *Croswell* case and the influence of Hamilton and Kent, concluded that it "would not be an exaggeration to say that, basically, this provision of the New York Constitution states the common sense of American criminal libel law. Twenty-four States of the Union whose Constitutions were

These Americans of the founding generation were not libertarians, if we mean by that men who refuse to recognize a distinction between the liberty and the licentiousness of the press. On the one aspect of this general subject on which they expressed themselves at length, they were agreed concerning the authority of the states to punish public as well as private libels, whatever their disagreement concerning the authority of the federal government. Most of them would have agreed with Leonard Levy that "freedom of discussion and the law of libel [inherited from England] were simply incompatible,"[155] but they insisted that freedom of discussion and the law of libel as it was reformed by *Croswell* were not incompatible. The evidence is overwhelming on this point, despite Justice Brennan's assurances to the contrary. Take the example of Edward Livingston, who was one of the principal Jeffersonian spokesmen against the sedition bill when it was being discussed in the House of Representatives (see pp. 97-98). He later moved from New York to Louisiana and in 1821 was empowered by the legislature of that state to prepare a criminal code. His draft System of Penal Law for Louisiana provides for a criminal law of defamation indistinguishable in its essential provisions from the New

---

framed later substantially adopted it." The Pennsylvania constitution of 1790, art. 9, sec. 7, provided that in "prosecutions for the publication of a paper investigating the official conduct of officers, or men in a public capacity, or where the matter published is proper for public information, the truth thereof may be given in evidence; and in all indictments for libels, the jury shall have a right to determine the law and the facts, under the direction of the court, as in other cases." This provision was a response to a case that, two years earlier, had given rise to a good deal of agitation, that of Eleazer Oswald, the publisher of the *Independent Gazetteer* (*Republica* v. *Oswald*, 1 Dallas 319 [1788]). Yet this did not prevent McKean in *Cobbett's* case (see note 18, p. 246) from insisting that this constitutional provision was merely declaratory of the common law. Then, in 1805, after *Croswell*, one Dennie was indicted for a seditious libel—he had published a diatribe against democracy—in the Mayor's Court in Philadelphia, and the case was removed to the Pennsylvania Supreme Court for trial. In his charge to the jury, Justice Yeates said that the "seventh section of the ninth article of the constitution of the State must be our guide" and, in the course of elaborating the meaning of the provision, twice quoted Hamilton in the *Croswell* case (*Republica* v. *Dennie*, 4 Yeates 267 [1805]). Dennie, incidentally, was acquitted by the jury.

York law after *Croswell.*[156] It made no provision for the punishment of seditious libels—the "undefined, and perhaps undefinable, offence of libelling the government, a court, or any aggregate body"—because, as he said in the report accompanying the draft code, such a power is "inconsistent with the spirit of the constitution,"[157] but it did provide for the punishment of libels of public officials, as did the common law even after the post-Sedition Law reforms.

In time, prosecutions for seditious libel lapsed because, as Cooley put it, they were "unsuited to the condition and circumstances of the people of America";[158] even prosecutions for defamatory libels fell into desuetude,[159] in part because of the political impossibility of restraining a mass press in a democracy in which political gossip mongering is a nationwide industry. It passes belief, for example, that even a Democratic administration would have tried to prosecute Jack Anderson for falsely accusing Senator Eagleton (at the time the Democratic candidate for Vice-President of the United States) of having been arrested a number of times for drunken driving.* The typical public official today is much too dependent on the press to risk offending it by calling for prosecutions or even by filing civil suits. It was otherwise at the beginning, when the Federalists and Republicans alike entertained what proved to be certain illusions concerning the quality of public discussion of public matters. Seeking to maintain a high level of discussion and to protect their reputations from a licentious press, they saw no contradiction between such a law and freedom of the press.

---

*In 1939, Senator Tydings of Maryland, who had been falsely charged over a national radio network by Jack Anderson's former employer, Drew Pearson, with having had the Work Projects Administration build a road and yacht basin on his own property, tried to persuade Attorney General Robert Jackson to file criminal charges against Pearson under a District of Columbia defamatory libel law. Jackson refused, saying he did not think "'we want to clutter up the courts with this sort of matter.'" Whereupon, in 1941, Tydings tried to block confirmation of Jackson's appointment to the Supreme Court. See Eugene C. Gerhart, *America's Advocate: Robert H. Jackson* (*New York:* Bobbs-Merrill, 1958), pp. 231-233.

Two misconceptions have led us to misread the evidence concerning the original understanding of the speech and press clause of the First Amendment. First, the Jeffersonians were opposed to the Sedition Law not because they opposed all limits on the freedom of political speech, but because the limits in the Sedition Law were imposed by the national government. Jefferson made this as clear as anything can be in his letter to Abigail Adams. Second, we today fail to appreciate the distinction the Founders drew between religious and political speech, a distinction that required them to accord absolute freedom to the one and to impose limits on the other. Thus, they would say that Leonard Levy is only half right when he argues that "freedom of speech could not become a civil liberty until the truth of men's opinions, especially their religious opinions, was regarded as relative rather than absolute...."[160] They were fully convinced that the Constitution of the United States derived from a "self-evident" truth respecting man's nature and the government appropriate to it. In fact, toleration of different religious opinions rests, and can only rest, on this political truth. Men are endowed with rights to life, liberty, and the pursuit of happiness, and they consent to government in order to secure these rights, and not to improve their souls. If this were merely an opinion, it would be necessary to hold as legitimate the claim of a Charles I to suppress religious freedom and replace it with an established church. Or, as Professor Mansfield puts it, if this "truth were but an opinion, it could not protect free inquiry into other opinions."[161] The idea that religious and political opinions are to be treated alike, as if entitled to equal protection, derives from the gradual acceptance of the view, first expressed on the Court by Holmes in his *Gitlow* dissent in 1925, that the Constitution rests on nothing at all—or rather, on no principle immune from the whims of transient majorities.

CHAPTER 4

The Supreme Court
and the
Disarming of Freedom

The First Cases

IT is unfortunate that no speech and press case reached the Supreme Court before the twentieth century. Had an appeal been taken in one of the Sedition Law cases, for instance, we might then have had an authoritative statement from this early period of the meaning and purpose of the First Amendment. Especially if the opinion in such a case—say, Matthew Lyon or James Callender versus the United States—had been written by John Marshall, that case might then stand in relation to free speech and free government as *Gibbons* v. *Ogden* stands in relation to the power to regulate commerce or *Dartmouth College* v. *Woodward* to the impairment of contractual obligations. We would then have had an official statement of the principles of free speech in a republican regime, a statement written by a man firmly attached to republican principles and with a demonstrated and unequaled capacity to expound and defend them. *People* v. *Croswell* could, and did, serve as a model for the states in the trial of criminal libels, but there had been no federal libel statute since 1801, when the Sedition Law expired, and no federal trial since 1812, when the Supreme Court settled the question of whether federal courts have jurisdiction over common law crimes.[1] (They do not.) Then, in 1919, when the first speech case reached the Supreme Court, it bore little resemblance to *Croswell* or the Sedition Law trials.

Congress, in 1917, had enacted a law forbidding anyone to cause, or to attempt to cause, insubordination in the armed forces or to obstruct the recruitment services; and Charles Schenck and Elizabeth Baer were convicted for distributing leaflets whose purpose was obviously to accomplish what the law forbade. Rather than *Croswell* or the Sedition Law trials, this case resembled that of Clement L. Vallandigham, the "Copperhead" who proved so troublesome to Lincoln during the Civil War. Vallandigham, like Schenck but for different reasons, opposed the war of his time and the raising of troops by the government, and was arrested on the orders of General Burnside during a time when the privilege of the writ of habeas corpus was suspended. This arrest caused a furor, especially in Ohio and especially among Democrats, some of whom solemnly and vigorously protested to Lincoln, asserting that Vallandigham, although a civilian, had been seized and tried in a military court for no other reason than that he had addressed words "to a public meeting, in criticism of the course of the administration, and in condemnation of the military orders of that general." Lincoln's response should be pondered by anyone who insists that a republican government may never punish speech, even speech that falls in the general category of seditious speech.

Now, if there be no mistake about this—if this assertion is the truth and the whole truth—if there was no other reason for the arrest, then I concede that the arrest was wrong. But the arrest, as I understand, was made for a very different reason. Mr. Vallandigham avows his hostility to the war on the part of the Union; and his arrest was made because he was laboring, with some effect, to prevent the raising of troops, to encourage desertions from the army, and to leave the rebellion without an adequate military force to suppress it. He was not arrested because he was damaging the political prospects of the administration, or the personal interests of the commanding general; but because he was damaging the army, upon the existence, and vigor of which, the life of the nation depends. He was warring upon the military; and this gave the military constitutional jurisdiction to lay hands upon him. If Mr. Vallandigham was not damaging the military power of the country, then his arrest was made on mistake of fact, which I would be glad to correct, on reasonably satisfactory evidence.

I understand the meeting, whose resolutions I am considering, to be in favor of suppressing the rebellion by military force—by armies. Long experience has shown that armies can not be maintained unless desertion shall be punished by the severe penalty of death. The case requires, and the law and the constitution, sanction this punishment. Must I shoot a simple-minded soldier boy who deserts, while I must not touch a hair of a wiley agitator who induces him to desert? This is none the less injurious when effected by getting a father, or brother, or friend, into a public meeting, and there working upon his feelings, till he is persuaded to write the soldier boy, that he is fighting in a bad cause, for a wicked administration of a contemptable (*sic*) government, too weak to arrest and punish him if he shall desert. I think that in such a case, to silence the agitator, and save the boy, is not only constitutional, but, withal, a great mercy. [2]

In *Schenck,* the Court, in an opinion written by Justice Holmes, took it for granted that Congress not only had the authority but the duty to protect the integrity of the military and naval services—insubordination and obstruction were "substantive evils that Congress has a right to prevent." The only question of interest here is whether the conviction of these two defendants under this statute violated the First Amendment. Holmes conceded that in other circumstances their anticonscription leaflets would have been protected, but the "character of every act depends upon the circumstances in which it is done," and Schenck and Baer had acted during wartime. "The most stringent protection of free speech would not protect a man in falsely shouting fire in a theater, and causing a panic,"[3] Holmes said, though he did not explain whether this was so because the man shouted falsely or simply because his shout, whatever his intention, was instrumental in causing a panic.

In fact, Holmes left several questions unanswered. Schenck and Baer had not been indicted for causing insubordination or for obstructing the draft, for unlike Vallandigham's case, evidence of this having occurred was not available here. Instead, they had been indicted for *conspiring* to cause insubordination and *conspiring* to obstruct the draft, and the leaflet was offered as evidence of the illegality of their speech. As is usually true in cases where the conspiracy consists in an agreement to speak, the leaflet, with the allegedly illegal words, was also offered as evidence of the agreement. This raises a difficult question: by what standards is it determined that the speech may be attributed to the various defendants in a conspiracy trial? Holmes ignored this question, although the evidence of Baer's involvement in the printing and distribution of the leaflet was tangential at best. (The question was of decisive importance here because, there being only two defendants, there could not have been a conspiracy without Baer.) That having been settled, Holmes rushed to his conclusion. "It was not argued," he said, "that a conspiracy to obstruct the draft was not within the words of the Act of 1917." In fact, this case was disposed of by a previous conspiracy case, *Goldman* v. *United States,*[4] and he "thought fit to add a few words [only because] the right of free speech was not referred to specially [in *Goldman*]." Thus, all we really learn from this first case about the right of free speech is that it depends on the circumstances, so to speak, with the judicial formulation being Holmes's famous danger test: "The question in every case is whether the words used are used in such circumstances and are of such a nature as to create a clear and present danger that they will bring about the substantive evils that Congress has a right to prevent."[5] Because Schenck and Baer had been convicted of conspiracy, Holmes saw fit to ignore altogether the question of whether their leaflet had in fact created a clear and present danger, although without evidence of that, their speech was not illegal, and if their speech was not illegal, their agreement was not a conspiracy.

Schenck lacked the elements of a great case, the sort of case whose solution requires the Court to expound the fundamental principles of the Constitution and thereby to provide the rule by which public life is to be measured. Perhaps the outcome in *Schenck,* unlike, say, in *Fletcher* v. *Peck,*[6] was never in question; for this reason, perhaps not even Marshall would have been inspired to do much with it, although the example of *Marbury* v. *Madison* shows how much he could do with so little. Nevertheless, *Schenck* bequeathed us the clear-and-present-danger formula, which was soon to become the clear-and-present-danger test,[7] and that test was to play a prominent role in the disposition of subsequent cases, and especially in the free speech literature built up around these cases. In *Schenck* it served to remind us, as Lincoln's Vallandigham statement had already reminded us, that while freedom of speech is the rule, there are exceptions to the rule—and war is a prolific generator of exceptions to rules. The exceptions are based on an appreciation of the importance and power of speech, as well as on the knowledge that the exercise of this power is not always compatible with ends the government is entitled and sometimes required to pursue, such as victory in a war which will determine the fate of republican government itself. This was clearly Lincoln's view, and had it been his fate to serve on the Court instead of in the Presidency, he surely would have fashioned a law of the First Amendment that takes this into account. Thus, despite the argument that Justice Black was later to make famous, not all speech is protected, even though the First Amendment specifically says Congress shall make *no* law abridging the freedom of speech.

Within a few months of its decision in *Schenck,* the Court was given the opportunity to decide a case involving an authentic sedition law, a law enacted in 1918 as an amendment to the 1917 Espionage Act, under which Schenck had been convicted. This amendment forbade, when the United States was at war with Germany, the uttering or publishing of "disloyal, scurrilous and abusive language about the form of government of the United States, or language intended to bring the form of government of the United States into contempt, scorn, contumely and disrepute, or intended to incite [etc.] resistance to the United States in said war...." Five self-styled "rebels," "revolutionists," "anarchists," or "socialists" were convicted of having conspired to violate the provisions of this law by printing pamphlets attacking the sending of American forces to Russia and calling upon the "Workers of the World" to rise against the "capitalist" enemy, who was accused of fighting not only Imperial Germany but the "Workers Soviets of Russia." The Court, in a majority opinion written by Justice Clarke, devoted most of its attention to the question of whether there was sufficient evidence to support the jury's guilty verdicts, and dismissed the First Amendment defense in a one-sentence reference to *Schenck* (and a lesser-known case following *Schenck*). As to whether anyone could be punished for publishing abusive language about the "form of government," as opposed to language intended to provoke resistance to the war effort, the Court found it unnecessary to say. The distinction may be "vital or merely formal," but in either case it was irrelevant here, Clarke said, because the defendants had clearly intended to provoke a general strike and thereby to curtail production of war material.[8] One could not know from this opinion that the case presented questions that concern fundamental principles of republican government. But such questions were present, and if they were to receive the careful consideration they deserve, it would have to be in the dissent that Holmes wrote for himself and Brandeis.

Holmes's dissenting opinion has been called "the most eloquent and moving defense of free speech since Milton's *Areopagitica*"[9] and praised for putting the case against suppression of opinion in "perhaps its most perfect literary form for modern times."[10] He doubted that the pamphlets involved, which he referred to as "silly" and as "puny anonymities [unable] to turn the color of legal litmus paper," came close to creating a clear and present danger of disrupting the war effort; and in the absence of such a danger, there could be no exception to the First Amendment's guarantee of freedom of speech. And he now addressed himself seriously to the question of the intent of the utterances, saying that, strictly speaking, "a deed is not done with intent to produce a consequence unless that consequence is the aim of the deed." He concluded with the eloquent statement that has made his *Abrams* dissent perhaps the most celebrated of his judicial opinions:

Persecution for the expression of opinions seems to me perfectly logical. If you have no doubt of your premises or your power and want a certain result with all your heart you naturally express your wishes in law and sweep away all opposition. To allow opposition by speech seems to indicate that you think the speech impotent, as when a man says that he has squared the circle, or that you do not care wholeheartedly for the result, or that you doubt either your power or your premises. But when men have realized that time has upset many fighting faiths, they may come to believe even more than they believe the very foundations of their own conduct that the ultimate good desired is better reached by free trade in ideas,—that the best test of truth is the power of the thought to get itself accepted in the competition of the market; and that truth is the only ground upon which their wishes safely can be carried out. That, at any rate, is the theory of our Constitution. [11]

What he here refers to as persecution is said to be "logical" if one can be certain about the "premises" on which one acts. But, he suggests, any certainty of this sort is ill-founded, or founded only on an opinion that has no status other than what social science would call a value judgment. "Persecution" can, therefore, never be "logical." Instead of attempting to suppress the obnoxious opinions, they should be allowed to compete in the marketplace of ideas along with all "fighting faiths," including one's own. This is more than an argument for toleration, because Holmes does not leave it by saying that these ideas neither pick his pocket nor break his leg; he says the market is the best test of truth. And he suggests that the truth of the marketplace is the only basis on which men can safely fulfill their wishes. In any case, it is "the theory of our Constitution."

With all respect for those who have praised this statement, it is not at all evident that it can provide a sound foundation for the law of the First Amendment. In the first place, it is by no means clear, especially in its implications. Does it mean that the "thought" that wins acceptance in the market will, whatever its substance, be labeled the truth? Or, on the contrary, that the truth has an advantage that enables it to win in any competition? If the latter, then of course persecution is illogical because it is unnecessary. But since Holmes has suggested that there can never be any basis for certainty and that all "fighting faiths" come and go in the seasons of history, he must mean that the thought that wins is a relative "truth," not a truth strictly so-called. If this is what he means, it does not follow that other doctrines may not logically be suppressed. By the only relevant criteria—those supplied by the marketplace—they are false and, to say the same thing, unpopular; and to the extent that they are unpopular, they can be "safely" suppressed. The more obnoxious they are held to be, the more unpopular they will be; and the more unpopular they are, the more safely those who hold them may be persecuted. It would seem, therefore, that the "truth" that wins in the market provides a very good ground indeed upon which those who subscribe to it can "safely" carry out their wishes, including a wish to extirpate the last vestiges of what the market has characterized as obnoxious "thought." Instead of issuing in a rule of "freedom for the thought that we hate"—or as Holmes puts it in *Abrams,* loathe—it seems to permit suppression of that thought. On what possible basis may one complain if one's own opinion is no longer tolerated by those who speak in the name of the truth and are entitled so to speak because they won the competition? Unlike Jefferson's argument for toleration of all religious opinions, Holmes's argument for toleration collapses under analysis. Jefferson was able to tolerate all religious opinions because, kept in their proper place, they were all politically irrelevant; and their proper place was defined by a political doctrine that he held to be self-evidently true.

154

Still, the *Abrams* dissent was Holmes's first attempt to elaborate a theory of the First Amendment—if we ignore his somewhat casual treatment of the issue as it appeared in *Schenck*—and it was not to be his last. Within six years the Court had the case that foreshadowed the most troubling cases of the modern era, and Holmes's dissent in it was destined to be accepted by the foremost libertarians of our day as the basis on which they would build the law.

Gitlow v. *New York* was significantly different from *Schenck;* here the offense was specified in terms of speech, political speech, and, much more clearly than in *Abrams*, political speech concerning the "form of government," or better, the very basis of the regime. Gitlow, an American disciple of Stalin,[12] had been convicted under a New York statute that made it a criminal offense for anyone to advocate, advise, or teach, or to publish a paper that advocated, advised, or taught, that government should be overthrown by force or violence. Students of constitutional law will recognize it as the model for the Smith Act enacted by Congress in 1940. A divided Supreme Court affirmed Gitlow's conviction on the grounds that a state may punish "utterances endangering the foundation of organized government by unlawful means, and may regard utterances advocating the forceful overthrow of government as among those that endanger the foundation of organized government."[13] Furthermore, by way of emphasizing the intrinsic illegality of some speech—that is, its illegality irrespective of the circumstances in which it is uttered—the Court went on to stress that the Constitution does not require the state to wait until the "revolutionary utterances lead to actual disturbances of the public peace or imminent and immediate danger of its own destruction." On the contrary, it may punish "every utterance—not too trivial to be below the notice of the law—which is of such a character and used with such intent and purpose as to bring it within the prohibition of the statute."[14] The difference between the Espionage Act of 1917, under which Schenck had been convicted, and this

New York Criminal Anarchy Act consisted in the difference between the substantive evils they sought to prevent; the former sought to prevent insubordination in the armed forces (to state it simply), while the latter sought to prevent the utterances themselves (and, thereby, to protect organized, constitutional government). There was, so far as the Court was concerned, no question present in *Gitlow* the answer to which required the use of the danger test:

In other words, when the legislative body has determined generally, in the constitutional exercise of its discretion, that utterances of a certain kind involve such danger of substantive evil that they may be punished, the question whether any specific utterance coming within the prohibited class is likely, in and of itself, to bring about the substantive evil, is not open to consideration. It is sufficient that the statute itself be constitutional, and that the use of the language comes within its prohibition. [15]

What this means, among other things, is that Gitlow's political purpose was an illegal purpose, and that the law may take cognizance of the illegality of certain political purposes and may punish utterances made with the intent to effect these purposes. It may do this because, unlike the case of religious doctrines—which may be freely espoused—some political doctrines are incompatible with the principles upon which the country is built. It was with this last proposition especially that Holmes disagreed.

The organization to which Gitlow belonged (the precursor of the American Communist Party) was surely not a political party in the ordinary American sense. The argument of its "Left Wing Manifesto" was precisely that socialism could not be introduced by ordinary political action. It was "necessary to destroy the parliamentary state" by the use of such means as *"the political mass strike"* against the state itself, and to "overthrow...the political organization upon which capitalistic exploitation depends." "Revolutionary socialism does not propose to 'capture' the bourgeois parliamentary state, but to conquer and destroy it ... by means of political action ... in the revolutionary Marxian sense [which means] the *class action* of the proletariat *in any form* having as its objective the conquest of the power of the state" and its replacement by a new state "functioning as a dictatorship of the proletariat."[16] Gitlow and his associates in the United States in 1919 were no more reticent in expressing their contempt for the institutions of constitutional government than are some of the spokesmen of radical movements, left and right, in our own day.

There is probably no question, even among the most devoted followers of Holmes, that the American government has the authority to punish anyone who acts along the lines advocated by Gitlow's manifesto. Indeed, not even Gitlow argued, or would argue, that the Constitution required the government to remain indifferent to his *attempts* to overthrow constitutional government. As Lincoln said in his First Inaugural, it is "safe to assert that no government ... ever had a provision in its organic law for its own termination." In fact, Article IV, Section 4 of the Constitution requires the national government to guarantee New York and every other state "a republican form of government." But the fact that the government of New York, as well as of the United States, has the authority to prevent Gitlow from destroying the republican form of government in New York, as well as the authority to punish his attempts to do so, does not settle the constitutional question raised in this case, which is whether New York, or any government subject to the restrictions of the First Amendment, may punish words expressing the intent to destroy the republican form of government. The Court answered this by quoting a passage from an earlier state case: "If the state were compelled to wait until the apprehended danger became certain, then its right to protect itself would come into being simultaneously with the overthrow of the government, when there would be neither prosecuting officers nor courts for the enforcement of the law."[17] But of course, no one—at least, no one at that time—was insisting that the law

157

restrain itself until the revolution began; for example, in his dissent Holmes reasserted the relevance of the danger test and insisted, correctly, that there was no evidence that Gitlow's "redundant discourse" had any chance of "starting a present conflagration." The issue, he said, was whether the government may punish "publication and nothing more," and he denied any such authority.[18] The government may, he conceded, punish attempts to overthrow by force and violence, it may even punish speech that presents a real danger of such attempts, but it may not punish speech that is not discernibly connected in space and time with such attempts.

It is commonly held, and with good reason, that the opinion of the Court in this case is not, to say the least, fully satisfactory. Whatever has been said by others, it seems clear that the Court failed fully to appreciate the extent to which the power it left in the hands of the state is a power that lends itself readily to abuse, and that the Court failed in making no effort to delineate constitutional restrictions designed to prevent that abuse. In this respect, Holmes's opinion was clearly better. Properly applied, the danger test reduces, even if it does not eliminate, the possibilities of such abuse; and to the extent that it accomplishes this end, it is an appropriate rule of the First Amendment, a rule that we might expect Marshall to have formulated, in substance if not in form, had he been given the opportunity. Yet Sanford's opinion for the Court has the merit of never losing sight of the connection between freedom of speech and republican government, and in this respect it is defensible. The same cannot be said of Holmes's. In one of his most frequently cited statements, he made explicit what he had implied in *Abrams*—namely, that freedom of speech has no necessary connection with republican government.

If, in the long run, the beliefs expressed in proletarian dictatorship are destined to be accepted by the dominant forces of the community the only meaning of free speech is that they should be given their chance and have their way. [19]

This well-known statement makes clear what his *Abrams* dissent had left in some doubt: the First Amendment, in his view, protects the expression of all political doctrines, and leaves to the marketplace of ideas alone the determination of the winner. In the long run, the advocates of proletarian dictatorship may win; in the short run, they must be allowed to compete freely and thereby be given the chance to become the dominant force of the community and "have their way." But the dominant forces in the New York community of 1925 may not have *their* way, because their way, embodied in the Criminal Anarchy Act under which Gitlow was convicted, is incompatible with "the only meaning of free speech."

Holmes took no cognizance of the obvious and awkward question this poses: on what basis can freedom of speech be granted to those who would deny freedom of speech to others? Or to state this in its traditional form, does it make sense to tolerate the intolerant? And the traditional answer was that it did not. Before religious toleration could be established, religion had to be reformed, subordinated (as we saw in Chapter 1), and made politically irrelevant. Each sect had to be willing to live in peace with the others, and the basis of that agreement to live in peace was the common political doctrine to which they all subscribed and deferred. This is what the subordination of religion meant in practice, and it implied that each sect could trust the others to allow it to live in peace—so long as it obeyed the laws that applied to all. It is quite clear that the Republicans and Democrats and Socialists and Progressives and Populists and Whigs, and all the rest, cannot trust Gitlow's party to allow them to live in peace; they have Gitlow's word for that. He would "conquer and destroy" them. The only basis on which he and his friends can be tolerated is their weakness, but this is not Holmes's argument. One of his admirers, Professor Thomas I. Emerson, makes this clear:

The view that democratic rights should be denied to groups which repudiate democratic principles—that toleration is not owed to the intolerant—has always possessed considerable appeal. . . . Nevertheless the prevailing view of modern theorists has been that freedom of expression should be afforded all groups, even those which seek to destroy it. The classic statement of this view is that of Justice Holmes: "If in the long run the beliefs expressed in proletarian dictatorship are destined to be accepted by the dominant forces of the community, the only meaning of free speech is that they should be given their chance and have their way." [20]

Judging by the acclaim with which this book has been greeted by the civil libertarian community, I would agree that Emerson is right to call this "the prevailing view of modern theorists," and also right to attribute its origins to Holmes; it surely could not have originated in the First Amendment written by the men of the First Congress. This can be demonstrated—or, if not demonstrated, then affirmed—by a simple elaboration of Holmes's assertion: "If, in the long run, the beliefs expressed in [republican government] are destined to be accepted by the dominant forces of the community," that is all right with Madison and his colleagues. If, on the other hand, "the beliefs expressed in proletarian [or a Fascist, etc.] dictatorship are destined to be accepted by the dominant forces," that, too, is all right with Madison and his colleagues. We are asked to believe that by adding the First Amendment to the Constitution, they intended to establish a free marketplace of ideas, even at the price of republican government. One can agree that in the generally free marketplace that has prevailed in the United States, republican government has not generally required the suppression of unrepublican groups, but Holmes and his followers are not resting their case for toleration on this prudential argument. As Justice Black said in 1961, in another expression of the prevailing view, "education and contrary argument" may provide an adequate defense against Communist (or Fascist) speech, but if that "remedy is not sufficient," he said, echoing Holmes, "the only meaning of free speech must be that the revolutionary ideas will be allowed to prevail." [21] The only meaning of free speech turns out to mean that it is worse to suppress the advocacy of Stalinism or Hitlerism than to be ruled by Stalin or Hitler. The reasons for this are not, one might say, readily apparent.

The Strange Case of Oliver Wendell Holmes, Jr.·

All this would be unimportant were it not for the esteem in which Holmes is held, and the fact that such esteem reflects the extent to which his opinions have been accepted by "the dominant forces" of the constitutional law community. Felix Frankfurter, who certainly did not always agree with or follow Holmes's opinions, nevertheless said that Holmes was the exemplar who had built himself "into the structure of our national life and [had] written himself into the slender volume of the literature of all time.[22] For Benjamin Cardozo, his successor on the Court, Holmes was "for all students of the law and for students of human society the philosopher and the seer, the greatest of our age in the domain of jurisprudence, and one of the greatest of the ages."[23] And for Harold Laski, the English political scientist and frequent commentator on American affairs, Holmes was a great judge "because he...never ceased to be a philosopher."[24]

It is significant that unlike others who have gained fame as judges, Holmes is so frequently praised for his theoretical understanding as well as for his practical work on the Court. John Marshall was a great American judge, and to the extent that he is remembered at all in other places, it is solely for his services to his own country. Holmes, unlike Marshall and the others, occupied a place in a larger world, drawing his friends from the world of ideas: Laski, William James, Leslie Stephen, Sir Frederick Pollock, Henry and Brooks Adams. Holmes was—or was said to be—a philosopher, and his work on the Supreme Court reflects this detachment from the affairs of the world around him.*

*In fact, Holmes was a dilettante who dabbled in philosophy. There is no record of his ever having engaged in a serious philosophic discussion, or even a serious

The question is whether Holmes's was an appropriate "philosophy" to be expounded from the Supreme Court of the United States. In answering this question, one is required to pay tribute to his "wit, eloquence, and a certain grandeur of manner that captured for him the loyalty of many admirable men of the law," as Robert K. Faulkner put it in the course of answering this very question.[25] The men who praised him were no mean judges of either men or public affairs, including the work of the Court, and their judgment must be given weight. One must also acknowledge that much of Holmes's fame as a judge is richly deserved: he led the attack on the doctrinaire jurisprudence that had captured the Court of his day and had fashioned, largely from the due process clauses, a property right that sometimes threatened the very possibility of state or national government. And without doubt Holmes was wise in the law; his book on *The Common Law* alone is testimony of this. But the Supreme Court of the United States is not simply a court of law—its principal task is to expound the Constitution, to paraphrase one of Marshall's most famous statements. If it can be said that Holmes's conservative colleagues took too absolute a view of the rights accorded property by this Constitution, it must also be said that they were correct in seeing that the Constitution is one of rights as well as of powers. These are civil rights, but what are civil rights except natural rights modified, or "civilized," in order to make them applicable "to the state and condition of society," as Hamilton put it.[26] To Holmes, however, there was "no meaning in the rights of men except what the crowd will fight for,"[27] the way a "dog will fight for his bone."[28] He could

---

discussion of a philosophic work. References to philosophers abound in his correspondence with Laski, for example, published in two volumes and 1,481 pages, but what is said can only be described as chitchat. Readers are invited to test this judgment by consulting the index entries under Hobbes, of which there are some 79, or under the name of any other philosopher. A typical reference by Holmes reads as follows: John M. Zane "thinks Bentham, Austin, and Hobbes little better than asses" (Holmes to Laski, January 25, 1919, in *Holmes-Laski Letters,* ed. Mark DeWolfe Howe [Cambridge: Harvard University Press, 1953], vol. 1, p. 180).

say this because his studies had convinced him that there was "no reason for attributing to man a significance different in kind from that which belongs to a baboon or to a grain of sand."[29]

Holmes achieved fame as a judge not because of these opinions but despite them. He owes his fame partly to his good fortune in serving on the Court at a time when his views on the judicial power happened to be compatible with the political interests of the common man and happened to correspond to the views of the academic constitutional lawyers and the others who wrote the histories of the period. Holmes was no reformer—in fact, he was contemptuous of the efforts of the reformers, with their "tinkering with the institution of property," and said that "social regeneration" could be effected "only by taking in hand life and trying to build a race"[30]—but his view of the Constitution and of the role of the Court allowed him to write those famous dissenting opinions upholding legislation establishing maximum hours of labor, for example, or outlawing "yellow-dog" contracts, opinions cited in preference to those of other justices. Brandeis, Butler, and Stone may have written dissenting opinions in the first wiretapping case, with Brandeis's being what even Holmes referred to as an exhaustive examination of the problem; but it is Holmes's that is remembered. He called wiretapping in violation of law a "dirty business,"[31] and many a text has quoted that phrase. In *Buck* v. *Bell* he said "three generations of imbeciles are enough," and thereby delighted many a reader who overlooked the monstrous thing accomplished with these words.[32] Holmes wrote memorable opinions ("To quote from Mr. Justice Holmes' opinions," Frankfurter once said, "is to string pearls"),[33] and when he said that "if there is any principle of the Constitution that more imperatively calls for attachment than any other it is the principle of free thought—not free thought for those who agree with us but freedom for the thought that we hate,"[34] it did not matter that he said it in a dissenting opinion, and it did not matter that he cited no authority and provided no argument: his words carried weight. Justice Murphy cited them four times in a later naturalization case (this time actually a denaturalization case) and made of them a principle giving rise to a rule of constitutional law.[35] And it is his dissent in *Lochner* v. *New York,* rather than the carefully modulated dissent of Justice Harlan's, that is the one usually printed in the casebooks, picked up by the commentators, and thereby transmitted to succeeding generations. The Founders to the contrary notwithstanding, it became the accepted view that the Constitution, as Holmes put it in *Lochner,* was made "for people of fundamentally differing views."[36] The Constitution is here, as in *Abrams* and *Gitlow,* understood to be essentially a set of rules for a game open not merely to all religious players but to all political players as well, and it has no interest in the outcome of the competition among them—even if the winner promises to abolish the rules of the game.

This view of the Constitution is not readily reconciled with Holmes's denial of the rights of man. If men do not possess rights, or if there is no foundation for the rights they claim to possess, it would seem to follow that justice is merely the right of the stronger, and Holmes in fact says this in one of his legal papers:

What proximate test of excellence can be found except correspondence to the actual equilibrium of force in the community—that is, conformity to the wishes of the dominant power? Of course, such conformity may lead to destruction, and it is desirable that the dominant power should be wise. But wise or not, the proximate test of a good government is that the dominant power has its way. [37]

And if justice is the rule of the stronger, or the "dominant power," there is no basis for what might be called his unlimited pluralism, according to which all groups are entitled to play the political game—no basis, that is, except a First Amendment that constitutes nothing more than a trick played at the beginning by the numerically weaker, whereby the numerically stronger were induced to limit their power. There is, of course, an element of truth to this; the Constitution as a whole is, and was openly said to be, "a republican remedy for the diseases most incident to republican government,"[38] and these diseases were defined as abuses of the power that the majority would otherwise exercise by right. The problem is nowhere better stated than by Madison in the speech he made in the First Congress when he introduced the amendments that were to become the Bill of Rights:

But whatever may be the form which the several States have adopted in making declarations in favor of particular rights, the great object in view is to limit and qualify the powers of Government, by excepting out of the grant of power those cases in which the Government ought not to act, or to act only in a particular mode. They point these exceptions sometimes against the abuse of the executive power, sometimes against the legislative, and, in some cases, against the community itself; or, in other words, against the majority in favor of the minority.

In our Government it is, perhaps, less necessary to guard against the abuse in the executive department than any other; because it is not the stronger branch of the system, but the weaker. It therefore must be levelled against the legislative, for it is the most powerful, and most likely to be abused, because it is under the least control. Hence, so far as a declaration of rights can tend to prevent the exercise of undue power, it cannot be doubted but such declaration is proper. But I confess that I do conceive, that in a Government modified like this of the United States, the great danger lies rather in the abuse of the community than in the legislative body. The prescriptions in favor of liberty ought to be levelled against that quarter where the greatest danger lies, namely, that which possesses the highest prerogative of power. But it is not found in either the executive or legislative departments of Government, but in the body of the people, operating by the majority against the minority. [39]

Madison could justify the Bill of Rights, and all the other constitutional devices for limiting the power of the majority, potentially the stronger power, only insofar as it could be shown that these provisions were calculated to protect not only minority interests but also minority rights, rights for which there was some foundation other than the desires of the minor party. Without such a foundation, the constitutional restrictions on majority rule would indeed have been a trick played by the clever few on the sleeping or stupid many. By denying a foundation for rights, Holmes deprived civil liberty of its only firm foundation. Strangely, however, this did not prevent his interpretation of the First Amendment from being accepted as the "prevailing view," or his *Gitlow* formulation from being considered the "classic statement" of that view.

The fact that his *Gitlow* statement has come to be accepted as the correct formulation of the meaning of the First Amendment was undoubtedly assisted by the fact that *Gitlow* was, for another and unrelated reason, an unusually significant case. It was here that the Court took the radical step of nationalizing the law of freedom of speech and press by "incorporating" the First Amendment's provisions into the world "liberty" of the Fourteenth Amendment, thereby making them apply to the states as well as to the national government. This had the effect of bringing to the Supreme Court cases that earlier had been decided finally in the courts of the various states, and these now number in the hundreds. *Gitlow* was not a run-of-the-mill case, and what was done there proved to be of great consequence to the nation; and because Holmes was not a run-of-the-mill Supreme Court justice, what he said there proved to be more memorable than the opinion of the Court, even though what he said there cannot provide a sound foundation for the law of the First Amendment. What he said there, as well as in *Abrams,* was, in effect, that freedom of speech is absolute but that it does not matter if freedom of speech is abolished (by a "proletarian dictatorship"). This is, of course, an untenable position.

Madison and Hamilton, as we saw in the preceding chapter, cared deeply about freedom of speech because they cared deeply about republican government, and they applied their considerable powers to the task of defining the place free speech should properly occupy in a republican regime; but Holmes was indifferent to these larger constitutional questions. The Constitution occupied no special place in his thoughts; he never wrote a significant article or delivered a significant speech on the Constitution or on any of its provisions. Instead of attempting to guide the development of American political life informed by the principles of the Constitution, he turned to the study of private law, and found the law of its development in something resembling history. "The Path of the Law," as he said in his famous article under that title, is described by a principle of "spontaneous growth," but the cause of this growth is the will of society; it is the job of the judge to convert that will into law. Hence, he saw himself as "the supple tool of power." "I always say...that if my fellow citizens want to go to Hell I will help them. It's my job."[40] He was indifferent, unconcerned with the substance or the consequences of the doctrines espoused. He could refer to *Gitlow* as a case involving the right "of an anarchist (so-called) to talk drool in favor of proletarian dictatorship."[41] And when Eugene Debs was sentenced under the Espionage Act to ten years imprisonment for making what was mainly a socialist speech to a Socialist Party audience, Holmes, who wrote the opinion of the Court sustaining the conviction, could dismiss Debs's First Amendment defense as having been "disposed of in Schenck v United States," and leave it at that;[42] then, with reference to the case, he could say in a letter to Pollock that "there was a lot of jaw about free speech."[43] It was in this same spirit that he wrote his *Abrams* and *Gitlow* dissents: the freedom of this kind of speech is absolute because this kind of speech is nothing but "drool" and "jaw."

Freedom of Speech and Association

The *Debs* case, decided one week after *Schenck,* ought to have given the Court, and especially Holmes who wrote the opinion, a good deal more pause than it did. Nothing Debs said was directed at soldiers or sailors or could be fairly interpreted as an incitement to resist the draft or as an attempt to cause

167

insubordination in the military or naval forces. As Holmes himself put it, the "main theme of his speech was socialism, its growth, and a prophecy of its ultimate success"; yet Debs was convicted under the Espionage Act and sentenced to ten years' imprisonment largely because the trial judge's charge was so vague with respect to intent that the jury might have concluded that his exposition of socialism alone had "some tendency to bring about resistance to the draft."[44] Thus, the Court was squarely presented with the question of whether the advocacy of socialism and the making of general accusations respecting capitalism could, under the First Amendment, constitute criminal matter. *Debs,* in short, by resembling a seditious speech case in the traditional sense, possessed the elements from which the Court might have constructed an opinion expounding the fundamental principles of republican government. Rather than even attempting this, Holmes disposed of the First Amendment issue in that one-sentence reference to *Schenck,* and Debs's conviction was sustained. (President Harding pardoned him in 1921, after Debs, as Socialist candidate for President, polled almost a million votes in the 1920 election.) It was not until *Abrams,* eight months later, that Holmes chose to address himself to the fundamental issue. Then, writing under the immunity afforded by a dissenting opinion, he defined a freedom of speech that bore no necessary relation to republican government, and republican government itself became merely one of those "fighting faiths" to which men, in some mysterious fashion, became attached. So it came about that with respect to seditious speech properly so called, as opposed to Schenck's incitement, Holmes's legacy to the Court, and through the Court to the country, was the *Abrams* and *Gitlow* dissents, according to which all political doctrines, like all religious doctrines, are equal in the eyes of the Constitution. On the basis of this doctrine, the modern libertarians have attempted to build the law of the First Amendment. Holmes's view is thus said to be the only meaning of free speech.

Of course, it is not the only meaning of free speech. It was not Milton's or Blackstone's or Mill's; nor, with reference to the First Amendment itself, was it Marshall's or Madison's or Hamilton's or Jefferson's. Nor is its adoption necessary to protect civil liberty, as Tocqueville, probably the most sober and profound analyst of democracy ever to write, makes clear.

Tocqueville is not best known to us for his defense of freedom of discussion or freedom of the press. He wrote such a defense, but it is too subtle, too lacking in the resounding phrases that are picked up in judicial opinions and the anthologies devoted to the subject. In the one chapter devoted to freedom of the press in his justly famous study *Democracy in America*,[45] he argued that the sovereignty of the people and the liberty of the press are "correlative," because—at least in theory—it must be presumed that every citizen is capable of weighing arguments and making intelligent choices on the basis of these arguments. Yet he also confessed that he knew "of no country in which there is so little independence of mind and real freedom of discussion as in America."[46] On the one hand, censorship in a democracy is "absurd"[47] and "irreconcilably opposed" to universal suffrage; on the other hand, it would be desirable to limit the licentiousness of the press.[48] The difficulty presented to us in this chapter is resolved only when we remember what he considered to be the principal threat to liberty in a democracy—namely, equality and what goes with it, the sovereignty of public opinion. It was in this context that he wrote that "the liberty of the press . . . is the only cure for the evils that equality may produce."[49] This means that what is today thought to be an essential democratic institution (protecting the many from the few)[50] was valued by Tocqueville—as it was valued by Mill in *On Liberty*—as a means of protecting the talented few in an age of equality. Even so, he valued it more for the evils it prevented than for the advantages it ensured.

The liberty of the press must be unlimited, Tocqueville argued in the next chapter, at least with respect to politics, because an independent press is the "constitutive element of liberty." Whatever the vulgarity of the American press, or the extent to which it is given over to "trivia" and commercial advertising, the press is the cause of the dissemination, or circulation, of political life throughout the length and breadth of the country; it detects and publicizes "the secret springs of political designs," summons the politicians "to the bar of public opinion," and, by affording a means of communication between people who do not come into physical contact with each other, it even "draws up the creed of every party."

Tocqueville knew the difference between liberty and licentiousness, and would have favored the suppression of the latter, except for the fact that, in a democracy, there is no institutional means of suppressing licentiousness without destroying liberty. If anyone "could point out an intermediate and yet a tenable position between the complete independence and the entire servitude of opinion, [he would] perhaps be inclined to adopt it." Unfortunately, one begins by intending to correct the abuses of liberty and ends by being "brought to the feet of a despot."[51] Hence, toward the beginning of the next chapter he drew his conclusion:

> The more I consider the independence of the press in its principal consequences, the more I am convinced that in the modern world it is the chief and, so to speak, the constitutive element of liberty. A nation that is determined to remain free is therefore right in demanding, at any price, the exercise of this independence.

But this appears in the chapter on "Political Associations," and although these associations are constituted by speech, as it were, or by "the public assent which a number of individuals give to certain doctrines," it did not follow for Tocqueville that freedom of association is as complete as freedom of the press. On the contrary, as he continued in the immediate sequel,

> ...the *unlimited* liberty of political association cannot be entirely assimilated to the liberty of the press. The one is at the same time less necessary and more dangerous than the other. A nation may confine it

170

within certain limits without forfeiting any part of its self-directing power; and it may be obliged to do so in order to maintain its own authority. [52]

The difference between an expression of an opinion in the press and an association organized on that opinion consists in the strength of the latter, and it is this strength or power that ought to promote a degree of circumspection on the part of the law. But the limits within which the law should "confine" the freedom of association are themselves defined by the purposes or opinions of the groups, not by their strength. So long as "the differences of opinion are mere differences of hue," as Tocqueville observed them to be in the United States at that time, "the right of association may remain unrestrained without evil consequences."[53] Under such conditions, freedom of association can be as complete as freedom of the press, which, for reasons of expedience, is absolute. More harm than good will be accomplished should the law intervene at this stage against even the most "licentious" or outrageous opinion. But add the power of numbers, and especially of well-organized numbers, to that opinion and it becomes dangerous; and it may be necessary for the law to take cognizance of it and to act against the group that is prepared to act on its basis. In fact, "it may be obliged to do so in order to maintain its own authority."

Applied to the problems of our day, this means that Communist (or Fascist or Ku Klux Klan) doctrine may be freely expressed, not because it is not erroneous (if it were not erroneous, there would be no reason ever to act against its organized form, no matter how strong it became), but because it is both expedient to allow an unlimited liberty of political speech and inexpedient to attempt to place limits on it. Furthermore, in the United States it is safe to allow even erroneous doctrine to be expressed. This is what Jefferson meant when, in his First Inaugural, he described antirepublican opinion as "error," but urged that it be tolerated as impotent error: those who held it might "stand undisturbed as monuments" of the very strength of republican government. But just as he advised against the free immigration of monarchists and anarchists* (thus, contrary to Holmes, a constitution is not made "for people of fundamentally differing views"), the time came when he changed his mind about the impotence of the antirepublican forces in America and called for prosecutions under the sedition laws of the states.[54] This is precisely the opposite of Holmes's theory of the First Amendment; Holmes refused to accept the principle of allowing "opposition by speech" because "you think the speech impotent,"[55] and offered instead the principle that no speech is erroneous. This has two consequences: if no speech or doctrine is erroneous, then there is no reason for the law to be concerned, and no logical basis on which it may be concerned, when to advocacy is added the strength of organization. Second, and of much greater significance, if the official view of the Constitution is that all political doctrines must be tolerated because all are equal and none is erroneous, this seems certain, in the course of time, to undermine the attachment of Americans to republican government. It is, therefore, doubly important to know that on the basis of the Declaration of Independence, Communist doctrine is erroneous.

This is not because only one form of government is compatible with the principles of the Declaration; on the contrary, that document itself, as well as the text from which it is so largely

---

*"Every species of government has its specific principles. Ours perhaps are more peculiar than those of any other in the universe. It is a composition of the freest principles of the English constitution, with others derived from natural right and natural reason. To these nothing can be more opposed than the maxims of absolute monarchies. Yet from such we are to expect the greatest number of emigrants. They will bring with them the principles of the governments they leave, imbibed in their early youth; or, if able to throw them off, it will be in exchange for an unbounded licentiousness, passing, as is usual, from one extreme to another. It would be a miracle were they to stop precisely at the point of temperate liberty. These principles, with their language, they will transmit to their children. In proportion to their numbers, they will share with us the legislation. They will infuse into it their spirit, and warp and bias its directions, and render it a heterogeneous, incoherent, distracted mass." Jefferson, *Notes on the State of Virginia* in *Works* (Federal ed. New York: Putnam, 1904-05), vol. 3, pp. 487-488.

taken—namely, Locke's *Second Treatise of Civil Government*—acknowledges that enlightened men may give their consent to any one of a variety of forms of government. At the beginning, "upon men's first uniting into society," the whole power is in the hands of the majority, which may, Locke says, decide to form a government in which political power is placed in the hands of the many, the few, or even the one;[56] the form of government "instituted among men," or to which men give their consent, will depend on their view of which form will, under the circumstances, best secure their rights. Whenever *any* form of government—be it democracy or even monarchy—does not secure these rights (when it "becomes destructive of these ends," as the Declaration puts it), "it is the right of the people to alter or to abolish it, and to institute new government...." But the question of which form of government is instituted is a question to be answered on the basis of one man, one vote, because all men are equal by nature and, therefore, no man may govern another without his consent. This means that the right to decide the form of government cannot be usurped by a king, even George III, or by any part of the people, even the proletariat.

A rational people may decide that their rights may be best secured by a king, and even by a proletariat; but no rational people will consent to be governed by a king who claims to rule by divine right and refuses to acknowledge that men have rights and that the purpose of government is to secure these rights; and no rational people will consent to be governed by a proletariat that promises (and, as all history since 1917 attests, fulfills that promise) to institute a dictatorship. If any people should freely decide to be so governed, that would be an indication of a willingness to exchange its natural freedom for a conventional slavery, and any people doing that has demonstrated its lack of capacity for self-government or civil liberty.

Doctrines advocating government on the basis of the divine right of kings or the historical right of proletariats are, then, erroneous in the light of the self-evident truths acknowledged at our beginning in 1776. The nation, conceived in liberty and dedicated to the proposition that all men are created equal, is a nation that may not—as do, for example, Canadians—inscribe their coins with the words *Dei Gratia Regina* (Queen by the grace of God), let alone with the words *Historiae Gratia Dictator.* There may be kings or queens, but not by the grace of God or of history—not in the United States—because according to the laws of nature and nature's God, no man or woman is appointed to rule another; and a "proletarian dictatorship" (Holmes's term) was conceived and in practice has proved emphatically to be government imposed on, rather than with the consent of, the governed.

In principle, it is not difficult to accept Tocqueville's formulation of the problem and to build on it the law of the First Amendment. There should be no restrictions on political speech or press; even erroneous doctrines may be freely espoused. But the liberty of political association is not coextensive with this un-limited liberty of speech and press. Governments, defining the erroneous by the self-evident truths acknowledged at our begin-ning, may take cognizance of associations organized to translate the erroneous doctrine into practice. At a certain point, such associations become dangerous. It scarcely needs to be demonstrated, however, that elected governments, and especial-ly elected state governments, cannot always be trusted to delineate that point fairly or with due respect for the benefits of freedom of speech and press. *De Jonge* v. *Oregon* provides an example of the problem, but it is not for this that the case is noteworthy. It is noteworthy because of the opinion that Chief Justice Hughes wrote for a unanimous Court. This was a Court that comprised, in addition to Brandeis, Roberts, Cardozo, and Stone (who took no part in the case), those staunch "conserva-tives" Van Devanter, McReynolds, Sutherland, and Butler. The case was this: Oregon, in a fit of misguided passion, had convicted De Jonge under its Criminal Syndicalism Law and sentenced him to seven years' imprisonment, even though all he had done, or was charged with having done, was to have taken part in a public meeting called under the auspices of the Communist Party to protest police action in a labor dispute. The Court reversed the conviction. De Jonge, Hughes pointed out, had been convicted merely for participating in a meeting, regardless "of what was said or done at the meeting." "His sole offense as charged . . . was that he had assisted in the conduct of a public meeting, albeit otherwise lawful, which was held under the auspices of the Communist Party." In effect, he was convicted for being a member of the Communist Party. But he was not charged with being a member of the Communist Party, and conviction upon a charge not made is "sheer denial of due process."[57] The Communist Party, too, enjoys the right of peaceable assembly—when the purpose of that assembly is otherwise lawful. "Peaceable assembly for *lawful* discussion cannot be made a crime."[58] What Hughes does *not* say is that all discussion under the auspices of the Communist Party is lawful, and he cites the majority opinion in the *Gitlow* case in support of this distinction.

Of course, not every law directed at political associations will violate due process in this traditional sense. And given the occasionally demonstrated capacity of legislatures and executives to act as those of Oregon had acted here, there is good reason to doubt that the institutional safeguards built into our constitutions—even Madison's "auxiliary precautions" built into the federal Constitution—will guarantee that officials exercise the requisite care in defining the point where an association becomes dangerous. The constitutional question, then, and the question to which the *Gitlow* majority paid too little attention, is the extent to which, and the basis on which, a government's judgment that an association constitutes a danger should be reviewed in the courts. Brandeis undertook to answer this question in his concurring opinion in the 1927 case *Whitney* v. *California*.

The statute under which Miss Whitney had been convicted was

very similar to the New York statute involved in *Gitlow* v. *New York*. Brandeis acknowledged the possibility that the Communist Labor Party, to which she belonged, constituted a danger, and acknowledged as well the need for the political authorities to protect the state against that danger; what he refused to concede was that the First Amendment allows the political authorities to decide with finality that the danger exists and, consequently, that the power may be used. The legislature must decide "in the first instance," but the Court must also play a role in the decision; it has the task of fixing the standard "by which to determine" when a danger is clear or remote and whether the evil threatened is sufficiently serious to justify the repression of the group advocating the "noxious doctrine."[59] In this fashion, Holmes's clear-and-present-danger formula was made into a judicial rule whereby executives and legislatures were required to be prudent, to exercise this power only when to the advocacy of the antirepublican doctrine was added the danger that comes with organizational strength. Decisions to act against antirepublican groups were now reviewable by courts because the political branches of government could not be fully trusted to exercise the prudence required by the Constitution. "To reach sound conclusions on these matters," Brandeis wrote, "we must bear in mind why a state is, ordinarily, denied the power to prohibit dissemination of social, economic and political doctrines which a vast majority of its citizens believes to be false and fraught with evil consequences."[60] The difficulty the Court faced was in translating "ordinarily" into a rule of constitutional law.

A President, having been armed by Congress with the Smith Act, may decide that the Communist Party, however revolutionary its purposes and whatever its known associations with Moscow, is, under the prevailing circumstances, more of a nuisance than a threat to the nation's well-being, and that, under these circumstances, more harm than good would be accomplished by prosecuting its members. Or, perhaps because he is being subjected to strident charges of being "soft on

Communism,'' he may decide to bring prosecutions under the act. In either case, while we may ask him for an account of his reasons, we do not ask him to explain the standard "by which to determine" whether the danger is sufficient to justify his actions. We ask more of a court when it reviews convictions under the act. A court, playing the role Brandeis called for, must not only determine whether the President's decision was prudent but, precisely because it is a court and not an administrative review board or a council of revision, must also fix—or ought to fix—the standard by which to determine whether the decision was prudent. This it cannot do; there can be no formulaic substitute for sound judgment. What the Supreme Court actually did in the leading Smith Act cases was, first, to accept a jury's verdict of the gravity (and not improbability) of the evil posed by Eugene Dennis and his colleagues among the leadership of the American Communist Party,[61] and second, by way of balancing the account, to reverse the convictions of Oleta Yates and her Communist Party colleagues by construing a key statutory word in a fashion making the indictments untenable and finding reversible error in the trial judge's charge to the jury.[62] The only strictly judicial judgment in this was the elaboration of the rule—and it is a rule of constitutional law—that juries must be instructed that they may convict only if they are convinced that an advocacy of forceful overthrow is not too remote from an attempt to overthrow, a rule presumably observed by the trial judge in *Dennis* and not observed by the trial judge in *Yates*.

In effect, if not in form, the outcome of these cases is compatible with Tocqueville's principles respecting freedom of the press and freedom of association. The advocacy of Communist doctrine is tolerated, but not because it is legitimate doctrine; but the party organized to advance the illegal purpose expressed in the doctrine may, at a certain point, be suppressed. At a certain point, the "nation...may be obliged to do so in order to maintain its own authority," and the Supreme Court will play a role in determining whether the point has been reached. (Unfortunately, however, the point itself cannot be defined with particularity in a rule of law.) The press remains free, with all the benefits to republican government that this provides, and republican government is protected against the dangers posed by antirepublican associations. One further benefit ensues: although tolerated, Communist doctrine bears the stigma of illegitimacy or, in Jefferson's term, of "error." For reasons to be elaborated below, it is important that the Constitution attach this stigma to it, as well as to all other antirepublican opinion.

No purpose would be served by reviewing the cases that followed *Dennis* and *Yates.* Until recently, the Court continued, however gropingly, to acknowledge that Communist opinion was not wholly legitimate opinion and, therefore, that the Communist Party was not like.other parties. For that reason it was willing, although not consistently willing, to accept the loyalty oaths designed to exclude Communists from public employment. In doing these things, however, it did not satisfy all its members, most evidently Justice Douglas, who complained that the Court was not being completely "faithful" to the "philosophy" of Holmes's *Gitlow* dissent.[63] Complete fidelity required the line to be drawn, and drawn even more emphatically, between "ideas and overt acts."[64] No speech that is not "brigaded" with a clearly illegal act can be held to be illegal or illegitimate. This is what Holmes required, and therefore what the First Amendment requires; this was the "only meaning of free speech." Yet by the time Douglas issued this complaint (1969), the Court had already gone a long way toward satisfying it. It had removed the stigma of Communist Party membership when it ruled in 1967 that party membership as such did not disqualify one to teach in the public schools;[65] and in 1974 it went the full distance required by the *Gitlow* "philosophy" when it held that the Communist Party of Indiana could not be kept off the ballot simply because its officers refused to file an affidavit that the party did not advocate the overthrow of government by force and violence. The proposition that "any group that advocates violent overthrow as abstract doctrine must be regarded as necessarily advocating unlawful action" has been "'thoroughly discredited,'" the Court said.[66]

There is, of course, reason to doubt the efficacy of disclaimer oaths, but inefficacy has nothing to do with unconstitutionality, and oaths as such are not unconstitutional. This one would seem to be merely the negative formulation, applied to candidates for public office, of the constitutional requirement that all state and federal officials take an oath "to support this Constitution," since the Constitution, in its amending article, prescribes the only legitimate ways of making changes in the form of government; and by prescribing the legitimate ways, it clearly proscribes other ways. This is indeed one of those cases that Marshall spoke of where affirmative words are, in their operation, "negative of other objects than those affirmed." To the Court, however, Indiana was "burdening access to the ballot"; to which it is proper to reply that the Constitution's requirement of an oath "burdens" access to the office itself. Even so, it cannot be argued that it would be unconstitutional to require a Communist elected to public office to take an oath to support the Constitution (an oath he could not honestly take); but from the point of view of republican government, the only difference between a Communist on the ballot and a Communist elected consists in the degree of danger he represents.

Despite what the Court said, we are not discussing abstract advocacy of Communist doctrine; we are discussing a political association organized on the basis of that doctrine. In the America observed by Tocqueville, there were "factions, but no conspiracies,"[67] and he attributed this in part to the prevailing freedom of association; but Indiana had sufficient reason to conclude that this is no longer the case, and that the Communist Party, an avowed enemy of republican government and somehow affiliated with an enemy of the United States, bears a closer resemblance to a conspiracy than to a faction. Tocqueville

179

also observed that political associations in the United States were "peaceable in their intentions and strictly legal in the means which they employ; and [that] they assert with perfect truth that they aim at success only by lawful expedients."[68] What Indiana was asking of its political parties was an assurance that they aimed at success "only by lawful expedients." Unlike Oregon, it was not forbidding Communist Party meetings called to protest police brutality or to advocate equal employment opportunities; it was not forbidding the vote to party members; it was not forbidding advocacy of violent overthrow; it was not even forbidding the party's candidates a place on the ballot. It was, however, insisting that all parties affirm that they do not advocate that the Constitution be violated. If the Communist Party cannot make that affirmation, that ought to be seen as an indication of its willingness to use unlawful expedients—and *that* ought to be seen as an index of its illegitimacy and, therefore, ineligibility, not an ineligibility of its members abstractly to advocate anything, but its ineligibility as a group to win a place on the ballot. Nothing in the Constitution ought to be understood to forbid Indiana to take cognizance of the difference between unorganized and organized opinion, or between unarmed and armed prophets, to use Machiavelli's metaphor, since organization is one stage in the process of becoming "armed." To quote Tocqueville once more, "we are not to believe that [the Communist Party] will long be content to speak without acting; or that it will always be restrained by the abstract consideration that associations are meant to direct opinions, but not to enforce them...."[69] But this idea has now been "'thoroughly discredited'"—discredited by the Supreme Court, if not by experience.

Again, there is reason to doubt the efficacy of disclaimer oaths, but one important thing can be said of Indiana's: through its oath, the state pinned the label of illegitimacy on a group that is, by American standards, truly illegitimate. This is an important function of the law, more important than the warnings on cigarette packages, for example. Unfortunately, Indiana also provided the Supreme Court with the opportunity to remove that label and to replace it with a label of legitimacy, and this the Court did. Much of the opprobrium that was formerly attached to Communist Party membership has been removed. Eugene Dennis and his associates were "miserable merchants of unwanted ideas" back in 1951—Mr. Justice Douglas said so[70]—but looking back from the perspective of 1969, he described Dennis and his associates as "mere teachers of Marxism."[71] And in the Indiana case the Communist Party became a party equal to any other. Its members, said Brennan for the Court, have a legitimate interest in "casting an effective ballot,"[72] which can only mean (since their right to cast a ballot was not contested), casting a Communist ballot. For all that appears in Brennan's opinions for the Court in these two cases, the Constitution also guarantees their equal entitlement to employment by the Central Intelligence Agency.

The Disarming of Freedom

What has happened represents a change not in Communism or the Communist Party but in the official understanding of the Constitution and the principles on which it rests. Twenty years ago, it was possible for constitutional lawyer Robert A. Horn to write that "American citizenship and Communist party membership are intellectually incompatible but physically possible."[73] This, he added, was "the shape of our dilemma." He could censure the clamorous "witch hunters" who saw only the incompatibility and failed to respect legal process in their attempts to put an end to the possibility, as it were, and he could forthrightly acknowledge and deplore the injury done to innocent persons; but he nevertheless insisted on that incompatibility, and he refused to look upon knowing Communist Party activity as innocent activity. It is extremely doubtful that the books today contain such statements. It is no longer respectable for academics and "intellectuals" to say such things. It is no longer respectable in the books because it is no longer respectable in the law of the Constitution. Republican government in the United States today is not even remotely endangered by the Communist Party as such—the party is probably weaker today than during the McCarthy era, and it was not strong then. Rather, republican government is endangered by the weakness of our attachment to its principles and by our inability to defend it, not so much on the battlegrounds as in the books, so to speak.

When Justice Douglas spoke in 1951, of "the ugliness of Communism," he expressed confidence that, if understood, it would be rejected by the American people. "Full and free discussion" can be relied on to keep them "from embracing what is cheap and false."[4] But it never occurred to him to wonder whether the law's labeling of it as "cheap and false" does not play a role in the people's rejection of it as "cheap and false." There is implicit in his opinions an extraordinary depreciation of the role of the law, and especially of the authority attached to the law of the Constitution and to the Court that expounds it.

Writing in the 49th *Federalist* in response to Jefferson's suggestion that constitutional questions be turned over to conventions elected by the people, Madison, acknowledging Jefferson's "fervent attachment to republican government" and the weight of authority all his opinions bore, set down what then seemed (and still seem) to be unanswerable objections to the proposal. Every appeal to the people would, he said, carry an implication of some defect in the government, and "frequent appeals would, in great measure, deprive the government of that veneration which time bestows on everything, and without which perhaps the wisest and freest governments would not possess the requisite stability." All governments, he continued, rest on opinion, and the strength of that opinion and its influence on conduct depend not only on the number of others which each man supposes to hold that opinion, but on its venerability. "When the examples which fortify opinion are *ancient* as well as *numerous,* they are known to have a double effect." It would be otherwise in a nation of philosophers—there a "reverence for the laws would be inculcated by the voice of enlightened reason"—but in the world of real instead of imagined politics, said Madison, "the most rational government will not find it a superfluous advantage to have the prejudices of the community on its side." The Constitution is venerable, the embodiment of legitimacy, as Charles Black has so well said,[75] and the people of the United States have been attached to it passionately as well as rationally. Though judges may occasionally complain of the public's habit of confusing constitutionality and wisdom,[76] the public persists in associating them, and it is both inevitable and, for the reasons Madison gave, proper for the public to do so. What the Constitution says on any subject carries weight. If, then, Douglas wanted Americans to reject Communism, he would have been well-advised to put the authority of the Constitution behind that decision. Instead, he deprived that decision of constitutional support.

Madison praised his friend Jefferson for his "fervent attachment to republican government"; until recently, it continued to be respectable to profess such an attachment. No longer; not in intellectual circles.[77] It is truer today than when Lincoln first said it that the United States is the last best hope of earth. Who else can defend liberal democracy in a world in which it is besieged and discredited even where it continues to exist? Yet this is a truth that cannot be openly expressed in the academy or in the press, not without the risk of ridicule. Except in the labor movement, such sentiments, if uttered at all, are uttered apologetically. It used to be respectable to refer to Communists as "miserable merchants of unwanted ideas" even as one insisted on their right to organize, but nothing of the sort appears in the Court's opinion in the Indiana ballot case. Nothing at all, and that omission speaks volumes. Again with the exception of the labor movement, it is no longer considered respectable to use the term Communist as a term of opprobrium; nor is there any necessity for individuals to conceal their party membership or their sympathy for its cause or, for that matter, for the cause of the Soviet Union. The film industry, ever alert to the forces of the market, reflects this shift of extremes, and some of those it once blacklisted are now the recipients of its awards. The academic world no longer argues the issue of whether Communists should be permitted to speak, or even to teach; the argument about who may speak or teach rages in the universities, but not about Communists. The change has been dramatic, but it is not a change that reflects a change in Communism or a difference between Stalin and Brezhnev. It is a change that reflects, instead, the fact that the Constitution is now held to stand for the equality of all ideas.

The Constitution is held to do this because of the importance of ideas, and it is interesting that Lincoln, beginning from the same premise respecting the importance of ideas, drew the opposite conclusion as to what would follow. The "idea" embodied in the Kansas-Nebraska Act was that slavery was neither good nor bad and could be established, or not established, in any territory on the vote of the people of that territory; which is to say that in the eyes of the Constitution, slavery was not illegitimate. Lincoln refused to tolerate this idea. He and the Republican Party were willing to tolerate slavery in the states where it already existed, but tolerate it only as an evil institution contrary to the Founding principle. What they were not willing to tolerate was the principle that slavery was not intrinsically evil—and this quite apart from the question of whether slavery in fact would be extended into territories from which it had been excluded by the Missouri Compromise. He was willing to lead the nation into a civil war rather than allow the Constitution to be understood as being neutral on the question of slavery. His reasons are worth recalling here:

The assertion that "all men are created equal" was of no practical use

184

in effecting our separation from Great Britain; and it was placed in the Declaration, not for that, but for future use. Its authors meant it to be, thank God, it is now proving itself, a stumbling block to those who in after times might seek to turn a free people back into the hateful paths of despotism. They knew the proneness of prosperity to breed tyrants, and they meant when such should re-appear in this fair land and commence their vocation they should find left for them at least one hard nut to crack. [78]

The world has not become a safer place for liberal democracy since Lincoln's day, and its survival, even in the United States, does not depend in any direct sense on the Supreme Court; but the capacity and the will to defend it does depend in part on what is understood to be at stake. We say we are for the Constitution, and for constitutional government, but the Constitution is held to be neutral between the idea of liberal democracy and the idea of despotism, just as the Kansas-Nebraska men said it was neutral between the idea of freedom and the idea of slavery. Such a constitution can place no "stumbling block" in the path of despots.

Conclusion

It is interesting—and it proved to be important—that Holmes, in his exposition of the First Amendment, should have used the term "fighting faiths." Men should realize, he said, that "time has upset many fighting faiths." But it was the specific purpose of the religious clauses of the First Amendment to cause the disappearance not of many but of *all* fighting faiths, the sort of religious faiths for which men in the past had demonstrated too great a willingness to fight. But since fighting faiths would not disappear of their own accord, they had to be superseded by a political truth. This truth, which was meant to endure, consigned all religious beliefs to a subordinate position where, having lost their militant proclivities, they could safely be ignored by the law. Religious beliefs and religious differences

185

would then be politically irrelevant. By speaking of fighting faiths in the context of the speech and press provisions of the First Amendment, Holmes consigned political doctrines to the same category of irrelevancy. Whether a person is a liberal democrat or a Communist is, according to Holmes, of no more concern to the law than whether a person is a Methodist or a Baptist. This, he said, is the "only meaning of free speech."

But those who are ruled by tyrants have no need to speak politically because they are permitted no opportunity to act politically. It is sufficient that they "express" themselves by their presence at Nuremberg rallies or in Red Square, by a shout of *Sieg Heil* or the raising of a clenched fist. It is probably not by chance that it was only after Holmes's became the "prevailing view" of the First Amendment that the term "freedom of expression" made its appearance in the literature. (Professor Emerson entitles his massive and widely acclaimed study *The System of Freedom of Expression.*) Freedom of expression is a commodious term, capable of encompassing not only speech but, as Emerson makes clear, all forms of communication, including those that have nothing whatever to do with self-government. The essential difference between the term "speech," the uniquely human capacity, and the term "expression" is that the former is connected to rationality, and it is man's rationality that makes him, unlike other animals, a being capable of governing himself. Speech makes possible the discussion and the reasoning requisite to the determination of how best to secure the rights with which men alone are endowed. Men may agree to be governed for self-interested reasons (to secure their rights), but it is the function of speech (of discussion, of reading, of thinking) to make known to men what is truly in their interests. It was only after a good deal of discussion that the Constitution was written and government instituted among Americans, and the form of government instituted requires discussion to continue—in Brandeis's words, "public discussion is a political duty"[79]—precisely to enable Americans to govern themselves. Speech is a condition of *republican* government, which is why the Founders accorded it constitutional protection. In Madison's words, freedom of speech is an essential element of the process whereby the people choose the members of the government, and "the right of electing the members of the Government constitutes...the essence of a free and responsible government."[80] The Founders' use of the phrase "freedom of *speech*" was not inadvertent, any more than Emerson's use of the word "expression" was inadvertent, although it probably was inadvertence that led him to remove the word speech from the First Amendment and put in its stead the word expression: "In construing specific legal doctrines which... will govern concrete issues, the main function of the courts is not to balance the interest in freedom of expression against other social interests but to define the key elements in the First Amendment: 'expression,' 'abridge,' and 'law.'"[81] He can be excused for this because, as we shall see in the following chapter especially, the term "expression" comes closer to describing the kinds of utterances the Court has brought within the range of the First Amendment's protection. The Court has done this without considering the consequences for republican government.

CHAPTER 5

Freedom of Expression and the Public Morality

IN 1971 the Supreme Court heard an appeal from California involving a person sentenced to thirty days' imprisonment for marching up and down a courthouse corridor wearing a jacket prominently displaying a political opinion in language considered offensive by many people. In reversing the conviction, the Court, through Justice Harlan, said that the "ability of government, consonant with the Constitution, to shut off discourse solely to protect others from hearing it is...dependent upon a showing that substantial privacy interests are being invaded in an essentially intolerable manner."[1] The problem thus identified is one frequently encountered by the courts, and over the course of many years the Supreme Court has produced a substantial body of constitutional law governing its various aspects. What is involved is speech uttered or printed outside the conventional media: in public parks, for example, or using sound trucks that cruise the public streets, or in public libraries, or outside a county jail, or by students in a school, or on grounds, public or private, adjacent to a school, or in the vehicles of a public transit system. These are public forum cases, and after a false start many years ago when it upheld Boston's right to restrict public addresses in the Boston Common,[2] the Court has made it clear that the states and municipalities may not absolutely forbid the use of public property for purposes of speaking or for the distribution of handbills and the like.[3] But they may place reasonable restrictions on this use of a public forum, restrictions taking into account what might be called, in the words of another part of the Constitution, the time, place, and manner of the speech. A group may communicate its message by parading in the streets, but a city may deny a permit to parade at a time when the streets are customarily jammed with other traffic.[4] So, too, a group may mount a demonstration across the street from a courthouse, but not on the grounds of a county jail, a constitutionally different kind of place.[5] And sound trucks may be used, but not in a "raucous" manner.[6] Some of these cases raise the question of the "captive audience," in which speech is directed to a public at least part of which may not want to hear it or, in the case of written material, see it, and the precise issue presented is the extent to which the state may, on behalf of an unwilling audience, place restrictions on the speaker. Hence, in *Cohen* v. *California,* the courthouse corridor case, the Court saw the issue as one involving the right of the state to "shut off discourse" when private interests were, allegedly, being invaded in an "intolerable manner."

This mode of analysis is altogether appropriate in the typical public forum case. Not everyone has access to the mass media, so a genuinely free exchange of political opinions, and the wide dissemination of information needed if government is to be responsible to the will of the people, requires the availability of other "media," or necessitates reasonable access to facilities that provide a substitute for the press as traditionally understood. On the other hand, some of the public facilities used by "speakers" are intended to serve other, wholly legitimate public purposes, such as the carrying of traffic or the conducting of legal trials or the detention of prisoners or the instruction of students. The balancing of these interests can best be

189

done by rules governing time, place, and manner; in effect, this is another version of Holmes's clear-and-present-danger test. In both lines of cases the Court focuses on the circumstances in which the speech is made. Thus, if Cohen had chosen to shout his message in a loud voice, or had used a bullhorn in that courthouse, this probably would have constituted an intolerable invasion of a "substantial" private—and even a public—interest. Or if he had marched in the courtroom itself, especially during a trial, the outcome of his case would have been different. But he was quiet, he did not block traffic, and he did not insist on communicating his message by marching in the corridor at a time when the building was normally not open to the public. Manner, place, and time were, then, in his favor, and the Court reversed his conviction. The constitutional right to freedom of expression depends on the circumstances of the speech, not its substance. Hence, there is a constitutional right to say "Fuck the Draft" in a courtroom corridor or, as the Court made clear, anywhere else within the constraints of the constitutional law of time, place, and manner.

Vulgar Speech and Public Good

Cohen's words are, of course, a far cry from the kinds of speech Milton, Mill, and Tocqueville were anxious to protect or the Founders thought they were protecting; and someone not familiar with the modern decisions of the Court might well wonder what purpose embodied in the First Amendment is served by his expression, or mode of expression, or what harm would be done or threatened by allowing the public authorities to punish those who use or adopt it. Indeed, until very recently it was assumed that such language is not part of the speech the Constitution protects. Only a month or so before the *Cohen* decision came down, the man who was shortly to become Solicitor General of the United States, Robert H. Bork, could tell a law school audience that not even "the most obsessed absolutist" would argue that the states are forbidden "to punish the shouting of obscenities in the streets."[7] And although California did argue that it was "reasonably foreseeable [that Cohen's] conduct might cause others to rise up to commit a violent act against the person of the defendant," it apparently proceeded primarily on the assumption that there are certain words, this one among them, whose public utterance ought to be forbidden, irrespective of time, place, or manner. California's premise was that within limits that were not exceeded in this case, the law may be used to enforce what another state was to call the conventions of decency. This is no longer true. Even "acting as guardians of public morality," the Court said, the state may not attempt to "remove this offensive word from the public vocabulary."[8] Is this because public morality is none of the state's business? Or because it needs no support from the law? Or because it is not harmed by the public use of indecent speech? Or because, whatever the consequences for public morality, it must yield to the prior claims of freedom of expression? The Court did not address itself to these questions. Cohen's conviction, said Justice Harlan for the Court, rested upon "the asserted offensiveness of the *words* used," not upon any conduct engaged in or any conduct incited or provoked by his words, and the states may not punish mere words.[9] Neither time nor place and manner "brigaded" this speech with an illegal act, and there was no other question to be decided. Four-letter words are words; words, "emotive" as well as "cognitive," are part of expression; and the Constitution protects expression.

Until recently, this was not true. The law that formerly governed this kind of speech had been set down in 1942 in the *Chaplinsky* case, in an opinion written by one of the Court's most celebrated civil libertarians, Frank Murphy. "There are," he said in a frequently quoted statement,

certain well-defined and narrowly limited classes of speech, the prevention and punishment of which has never been thought to raise any Constitutional problem. These include the lewd and obscene, the profane, the libelous, and the insulting or "fighting" words—those which by their very utterance inflict injury or tend to incite an immediate breach of the peace. [10]

Profanity was not considered to be speech in the constitutional sense, and it was therefore unnecessary to consider the time, place, or manner of its utterance. Merely the fact that it was publicly uttered caused an injury of some sort, and in those days it was not necessary for the Court to specify the nature of this injury, or even to indicate whether it was an injury suffered by individual persons or by the public collectively. The reason for this was that the Court began from the premise that the Constitution had some purpose in protecting speech, and that not all speech contributed to that purpose. "It has been well observed," Murphy continued, that Chaplinsky's insults, as well as the profane, libelous, lewd and obscene, "are no essential part of any exposition of ideas, and are of such slight social value as a step to truth that any benefit that might be derived from them is clearly outweighed by the social interest in order and morality."[11]

The contemporary Court acknowledges, at least formally, that the Founders had some purpose in protecting freedom of speech, but that purpose does not serve as a limiting principle for them, as it did for the *Chaplinsky* Court. In *Cohen,* Harlan stated this purpose as follows:

The constitutional right of free expression is powerful medicine in a society as diverse and populous as ours. It is designed and intended to remove governmental restraints from the arena of public discussion, putting the decision as to what views shall be voiced largely into the hands of each of us, in the hope that use of such freedom will ultimately produce a more capable citizenry and more perfect polity and in the belief that no other approach would comport with the premise of individual dignity and choice upon which our political system rests. [12]

An unlimited freedom of expression will, it is hoped, contribute to the development of a more capable citizenry and a more perfect polity, and any restrictions on this freedom are incompatible with individual dignity.

But the Court knows very well that not all speech contributes to a "more perfect polity"; it knows, for example, that speech uttered at certain times or in certain places or in a certain manner has consequences that, in fact, make it punishable or its restriction permissible. The question is, then, why speech may be limited with a view to protecting transit riders from political propaganda[13] or keeping the sidewalks free from obstructions,[14] but not with a view to protecting the conventions of decency. The Court's answer to this question is by no means clear.

Harlan admitted that he personally regarded Cohen's word as distasteful—"perhaps more distasteful than most others of its genre"—but he said he knew of no principle that would allow him to distinguish one offensive word from another, or offensive words generally from the inoffensive. More to the point, he denied that California could draw a principled distinction—it is often true, he said, "that one man's vulgarity is another's lyric"[15]—or rely on public opinion to supply the distinction. What he implied, however, was that the proscription of Cohen's word emanated from the benighted opinion of the "most squeamish among us," and surely, he said, the state has no right "to cleanse public debate to the point where it is grammatically palatable" to them.[16]

The relevance of this is not readily apparent. The people of California had drawn a distinction between decent and indecent speech, and the state had supported this distinction with its criminal law. It was not the task of the Court to determine whether a principled distinction could be drawn between the word here proscribed by custom and by law and some other word. Nor, assuming there is (or at that time was) such a thing as profanity, was there any necessity for the Court to decide whether Cohen's word was profane. (If it is not, what is?) The only question was whether the First Amendment forbids the proscription of the profane. That was the question the unanimous Court answered in *Chaplinsky* in 1942, and the distinction it drew was between speech that served a public purpose and speech that did not. The principle on the basis of which it drew that distinction was supplied by its understanding of the purpose of the First Amendment. The contemporary Court is of the opinion that all speech—not simply the freedom of all speech, but all speech itself—contributes to the end sought by the First Amendment. It arrived at this opinion by studying not the Founders' purpose in protecting speech but Cohen's purpose in speaking. His "linguistic expression," Harlan observed, "serves a dual communication function," one "emotive" and the other "cognitive," and the Court could not "sanction the view that the Constitution, while solicitous of the cognitive content of individual speech has little or no regard for that emotive function...."[17] The next year, by way of emphasizing the rights of emotive speech, the Court reversed the conviction of a person who had called a policeman a "son of a bitch" and threatened to kill him (but did not *try* to kill him). Even in this context the Court spoke of the "transcendent value to all society of constitutionally protected speech."[18] It would seem that the Constitution forbids *all* legally drawn distinctions among words, emotive or cognitive, decent or indecent, whether the distinctions are principled or arbitrary. It does this because all speech contributes to the advancement of the First Amendment's purpose—the "more perfect polity." But since different speeches have different consequences and different speakers aim at different ends, the only polity whose perfection can be fostered by allowing all speeches is Babel. Beyond that there would appear to be no substance to Harlan's idea of a "more perfect polity"; it is a polity with no other discernible feature, which is why all speech is appropriate to it. It is a polity without a public good. It follows that the states may not prohibit what they happen to regard as speech inappropriate to what they happen to regard as the public good. As for private citizens who find the speech offensive, they can close their ears or look another way, unless they are truly "captive."

We are in a position now to understand why, unlike Cohen's speech, political advertisements may be prohibited in public buses or picketing on the sidewalks. The explanation is that, through the nexus provided by time, place, and manner, these speeches are converted into acts, and no part of the Constitution guarantees complete freedom of action: these speeches have consequences that the states and municipalities "have a right to prevent," as Holmes put it in his danger test. These speeches become acts when they adversely affect the legitimate activities of other private persons. But is it really the case that the public use of indecent speech has no consequences to the public, no deleterious effect on the public good, that would permit the states and municipalities—and, indeed, the nation—to intervene?

The Court did not address itself to this question; but, then, neither did the *Chaplinsky* Court. That Court merely assumed that profanity had deleterious consequences for "order and morality." The Court's difficulty today derives in part from the fact that it has never before been necessary to demonstrate that vulgar speech is detrimental to the kind of government instituted in the United States. As with so many institutions and practices that have come under attack in recent years, we have forgotten the reasons for the "conventions of decency." To adapt Nathan Glazer's felicitous formulation, we no longer "remember the answers" to these questions, and we no longer remember the answers because, until recently, no one dared to ask the questions.[19] One looks in vain for a discussion of the problem of vulgar speech or of obscenity in the records of the Constitutional Convention of 1787 or in the *Federalist Papers* or in the debates in the First Congress on the First Amendment, which fact allowed Justice Douglas to jump to the conclusion that censorship of obscenity is a product of latter-day squeamishness,* but from which it is more reasonable to conclude that the

Roth v. *United States,* 354 U.S. 476, 514 (1957). Dissenting opinion. *Paris Adult Theatre I* v. *Slaton,* 413 U.S. 49, 70-71 (1973). Dissenting opinion. The argument that the First Amendment was intended to protect obscenity was ad-

Founders took it for granted that obscenity was not constitutionally protected speech. Tocqueville is interesting on this point. In the United States, he said, no one is punished for publishing licentious books because no one is induced to write them; and no one writes them, he added, "not because all the citizens are immaculate in conduct, but because the majority of the community is decent and orderly."[20] The Founders took it for granted that speech such as Cohen's was beyond the pale, just as they took it for granted that the laws would be enforced, the flag not spat upon, nor draft records burned with homemade napalm; until recently, we were all allowed to take these things for granted. Then, when the Court suddenly was challenged to state the reasons why the word "fuck" ought not to be publicly uttered, it found it was unable to supply a reason. In this posture, like many a university administrator, it found it easier to float along on what it understood to be the popular tide. It always is.

That tide had not run out with *Cohen,* and within two years the Court found it necessary to say that not even the schools may enforce the conventions that used to govern public speech and discourse. In 1972 the Court had a case, *Rosenfeld* v. *New Jersey,*[21] in which the state had punished a person for his repeated use of language more shocking than Cohen's in, of all places, a public school board meeting; and in a companion case, Oklahoma had punished the use of the same language in a speech delivered in the chapel of the University of Tulsa.[22] The Court, over the angry dissents of four justices, remanded both cases for reconsideration in the light of *Cohen.* Then, in 1973, came the case of Barbara Papish.

---

vanced at some length by Judge Frank in the appendix to his opinion in the Second Circuit's decision in the *Roth* case, but none of his evidence supports his argument. For example, as Leonard Levy subsequently proved, the Founders did *not* repudiate the "common law concerning freedom of expression"; and it is not relevant that Franklin published a *Letter of Advice* on the choosing of a mistress or that Hamilton carried on an adulterous relationship (*United States* v. *Roth,* 237 F2nd 796, 806ff [1956]).

Miss Papish was, nominally at least, a graduate student in journalism in the University of Missouri. She was expelled for distributing on campus a newspaper filled with the familiar vulgarities—all the four-letter words, plus cartoons that an earlier generation would have dared to circulate only surreptitiously—in violation of a bylaw promulgated by the university's Board of Curators. This sanction was applied not by the state courts but by the Student Conduct Committee of the university and affirmed first by the chancellor and then by the Board of Curators. It was Miss Papish who went to court; she sought, and was denied, injunctive relief in the federal district court, in a decision affirmed by an equally divided vote of all the judges in the Eighth Circuit Court of Appeals. She won, however, in the Supreme Court. Over the dissent of three justices, the Court, in a *per curiam* decision, held that Miss Papish's speech, because it expressed an "idea," was protected by the First Amendment. It is clear, the Court said, that "the mere dissemination of ideas—no matter how offensive to good taste—on a state university campus may not be shut off in the name alone of 'conventions of decency.' "[23] That is, such conventions may not be enforced by the criminal law. Nor may they be enforced by public school officials, even when they have been violated in a school by students of that school—not, at least, when the vulgarity is used to express an "idea." In effect, then, although the school may be a "place" constitutionally unlike a courthouse corridor or a roadside billboard, given the Court's generous notion of what constitutes an "idea,"[24] the law respecting vulgar speech is the same in both places. It would seem that the Constitution forbids the public enforcement of public morality whenever "expression" is involved. The question, again, is whether this is of any consequence.

Now the Constitution, in order to form a more perfect union, establish justice, secure the blessings of liberty and the rest, quite obviously forbids a number of things that the national and state governments might otherwise be inclined to do, and the First

Amendment occupies a prominent place among the constitutional prohibitions. In the manner of Milton, Mill, and Tocqueville, the First Amendment was intended to protect something, and, it is fair to assume, something that was understood to be worthy of protection. Its religion clauses especially were intended to protect a self-defined private life, insofar as they designated the relation between man and God as altogether a matter of no concern to government. It may even be true to say—and we shall have more to say about this shortly—that the speech and press provisions were also intended, in part at least, to protect this self-defined private life. Hence, for example, it is no proper concern of the state of Georgia if a man spends his time watching pornographic films in his own home.[25] The First Amendment was surely not written with this sort of man in mind, but the principle applies to him as well as to Thomas Jefferson, although it was the hope that men would avail themselves of the privacy thus afforded to become more like Jefferson and less like Stanley. But our cases involve public speech, not private life, and that inevitably involves other people and gives rise to other considerations. Public speech is a part of public life, and the sort of public life envisaged and *protected* by the Constitution requires a variety of restraints, self-imposed if possible but publicly imposed if necessary. It assumes a public good to which individuals must defer and by which their acts are judged, if need be.

Rosenfeld and Papish were in no position to deny this. They had spoken publicly, not indulged themselves privately, and had suffered publicly imposed penalties; the only argument they could make against the imposition of these penalties was one stated in terms of the alleged benefits to the public of their speech. By speaking publicly, that is, they took on a responsibility not borne by Stanley. If they had been so foolish as to argue that they should be permitted to speak publicly as they did simply because to speak in this fashion is good for themselves, they would have opened themselves to the reply that, however that might be, to speak publicly in this fashion is not, in the public's opinion, good for the public; and the law, including the law of the Constitution, defines what is good for the public. Therefore, to support the holdings in these cases, it must be argued that the public good is better served by allowing vulgar speech to be freely expressed than by allowing the law or the public schools to attempt to suppress it; or, stated otherwise, that more harm than good is done by punishing this form of "expression." It is possible, even probable, that this is sometimes true; but to demonstrate that it is either usually or always true would require an argument the Court has never been able to supply.

Rosenfeld had addressed a public school board meeting, as he was entitled to do, attended by approximately 150 persons, 40 of whom were children and 25 women; and in this setting he repeatedly criticized various teachers and board members, again as he was entitled to do. But he also repeatedly denounced them as "motherfuckers," and it seems almost supererogatory to have to argue that he was *not* entitled to do this, just as it seems almost irrelevant to have to make the argument in terms of the probable immediate effect of his speech on the private interests involved. Such incivility (to put it mildly) is surely a private wrong, an infringement, as Blackstone defines it, of the private rights "belonging to individuals, considered as individuals"; what the Court cannot see is that it is also a public wrong, a crime that affects "the whole community, considered as a community."[26] Rosenfeld's words are words calculated to provoke a violent response from the persons so addressed, yet the law expects them to restrain themselves and even threatens to punish them if they do not; but the law cannot reasonably expect them to exercise this restraint unless it can promise them that it will itself impose the necessary sanction by punishing the speaker. The law should not have to wait until the victims of these verbal assaults act or threaten to act against the speakers. But it can do this only if it is permitted to make a distinction between

199

protected and unprotected speech, a distinction based on the substance of speech rather than its time, place, or manner. Unprotected speech would be defined as speech that, by its very nature, is offensive and is likely to lead to a breach of the *public* peace. The principle here is the same as that underlying criminal libel laws: more is at stake than private reputation and private injury.

This country managed to live most of its years under rules, conventional and legal, that forbade the public use of profanity—in the press, in public forums, in films, on radio, in television; and it would be an abuse of language to say that its freedom was thereby restricted in any important respect. Now, suddenly, and for reasons that ought to persuade no one, we are told that it is a violation of the First Amendment for the law to enforce these rules; that however desirable it might be to see them preserved, there is no way for the law to do this except by threatening the freedom of all speech. The argument is almost jejune. Is it really impossible for law, especially law supervised by the Supreme Court, to embody standards according to which Rosenfeld's vile invective can be distinguished from, say, Martin Luther King's strictures? Is it true that Cohen's speech cannot be punished except on the basis of a rule, devised by the "most squeamish among us," that would endanger all "robust" speech? Do we really live in a world so incapable of communication that it can be said that "one man's vulgarity is another's lyric"? Cohen was not a wandering troubadour and did not pretend to be one, and surely it is disingenuous to insist that the law cannot draw a line between his vulgarity and the minstrelsies of a Walter von der Vogelweide, or that that line will not be visible to law enforcement agencies. To assert otherwise, as Harlan does and as the champions of freedom of expression typically do,[27] is to exaggerate the imprecision of language and the subjectivity of judgment. Of course there will be cases where the power to judge speech by its substance will be abused, but the answer to this is Supreme Court review; and of course there will be borderline cases, but the law faces that problem in many, if not all, areas.

What the modern civil libertarians leave out of the reckoning is the harmful consequences of not permitting the law to define some speech as unworthy of constitutional protection. Without this power, the law must wait upon the reactions of Rosenfeld's victims, as if the only wrong committed is the wrong done to them. When they react violently or threaten "to take the law into their own hands," then Rosenfeld may be stopped because then, and only then, will he have committed an offense. This is a rule of law more appropriate to the state of nature than civil society. It teaches that men must at least threaten the use of private force in order to vindicate their private rights, and that is a lesson the law ought not to teach. In fact, it is the opposite of what citizens should learn from the law: the law should teach civility, which it can do by announcing as one of its principles that incivility is a public offense punishable by the public authority. What Justice Murphy might have said in support of his altogether proper *Chaplinsky* judgment is that some speech in and of itself constitutes an offense against civilized society in the United States.

The Founders themselves taught the lesson needed by such a regime. The rules they adopted at the beginning of the Constitutional Convention of 1787 provided that a "member may be called to order by any other Member, as well as by the President [of the convention], and may be allowed to explain his conduct or expressions, supposed to be reprehensible," and there is no reason to suppose that they lacked confidence in their ability to recognize reprehensible speech. Nor did they overlook the necessity of other rules of propriety: they also provided that when "the House shall adjourn every Member shall stand in his place until the President shall pass him."[28] Elements of this are preserved in the parliamentary practice whereby members address each other as honorable members or gentlemen or distinguished colleagues, and not as Rosenfeld addressed the members of the school board. By so doing, they are only secondarily paying respect to the particular individuals they are addressing

201

(there are surely some in any assembly who are not worthy of it); they are primarily paying respect to the idea of republican government itself. Kings may speak haughtily and tyrants cruelly, insultingly, or even contemptuously, but men who share a legislative duty because they recognize the principle of the equality of all men must adopt a mode of address that reflects a disposition to respect the interests of others because, unless shown to be otherwise, they are equally respectable—that is, no less respectable than one's own interest. To speak politically is to speak politely, and to speak politely is to speak in a manner befitting free men because it disavows any claim of moral superiority.

Nor is this all. Republican government is government by consent; it assumes that the public business will be conducted only with the consent of the governed, and a polite mode of address is the appropriate mode of address because it is best calculated to elicit that consent or to maintain the conditions that make it possible. This is why the Constitution authorizes each House of Congress to "punish its Members for disorderly Behavior" (Article I, Section 5), and why, by providing that no member may "for any Speech or Debate in either House . . . be questioned in any other place" (Article I, Section 6), it authorizes each House itself to censor speakers who abuse the privilege. These provisions are an indication that the Founders did not assume that the conditions of government by consent could be left to chance. Government by consent requires a willingness on the part of everyone involved to be governed by a majority of which he may not form a part, and we know from experience, including our own experience, that this willingness rests on mutual trust and respect, which themselves rest on a common interest or bond stronger than anything that divides us. Only through mutual trust and respect can the people's representatives compromise their differences by accommodating each other's interests. On the one occasion when this willingness was conspicuously absent in this country, and when the country

202

divided as a result, Lincoln called upon his most sublime rhetoric to refashion the Union, which had to be not simply a reunion of the separated states but a union of the people of the United States.* Men so bound together can speak to each other and re- spect each other's rights and interests, accommodate each other, compromise with each other, and all this to make possible government by consent. They can share a common rule, whether of nation or of school district. Insults are inappropriate to this enterprise; Rosenfeld's ugly epithets make it impossible. In some way, he probably knew this. Like so much of the obscenity em- ployed by the denizens of the counterculture, his vulgarity was probably intended to serve a political purpose; his was not, however, a purpose shared by the men who wrote the Constitu- tion.

For all that appears in the majority opinions in these cases, rules of propriety or "good taste" or "conventions of decency" are merely arbitrary devices serving no purpose except to protect the prudish sensibilities of "the most squeamish among us," and certainly serving no public good. One wonders how the justices would react—or permit the Capitol Hill police to react— if Cohen were to appear in the corridors outside their courtroom wearing his jacket, or if members of the American Nazi Party were to march there brandishing their placards with their ugly racial epithets. Would they allow counsel in oral argument—per- haps Rosenfeld appearing *pro se*—to address them as Rosenfeld addressed the members of the school board or to decorate their written briefs with Papish's cartoons? If not, why not? Would they then see that the institution of the law and the majesty of the Court would be undermined by such speech in that place? Like Caligula's appointment of his horse to the office of consul,

*In addition to the Gettysburg Address, I have in mind the closing paragraph of his First Inaugural: "I am loth to close. We are not enemies, but friends, we must not be enemies. Though passion may have strained, it must not break our bonds of affection. The mystic chords of memory, stretching from every battlefield, and patriot grave, to every living heart and hearthstone, all over this broad land, will yet swell the chorus of the Union, when again touched, as surely they will be, by the better angels of our nature."

such speech is contemptuous and is intended to be contemptuous, and it is not for nothing that judges have been given the power to punish for contempt. At one point, Harlan hinted that a statute narrowly drawn to "preserve a decorous atmosphere in the courthouse" or in certain other places might survive constitutional challenge.[29] Very good, but what is a "decorous atmosphere," and how could he define indecorous speech except by employing some notion of the public good?

But more than a statute applicable to certain places will be required to preserve a decorous atmosphere in those places. What is required is a "citizenry" educated to regard indecorous speech as improper speech in any place; and if the justices think this education can take place without the assistance of the law, they are surely wrong, as anyone with an open eye and ear can now attest. The vulgarities expressed publicly by the defendants in these cases have now become an accepted mode of discourse. We have been taught by the law that they are not illegitimate, and the legitimacy followed as a matter of course. Harlan's narrowly drawn statute has no chance of preserving a decorous atmosphere in a courthouse set in a world that no longer knows the meaning of decorous.

Papish especially is an astonishing decision to come from a Court that would depend on the public schools, with their "secular means," to provide citizenship education. On this subject the Founders did have something to say. We know from the correspondence of Jefferson and Madison concerning the founding of the University of Virginia, for example, that public education does not consist solely, or even primarily, in the learning of a political catechism. It means studying the fundamental principles of free government, of course, and Jefferson and Madison thought the works of Sidney and Locke to be "admirably calculated to impress on young minds the right of Nations to establish their own Governments, and to inspire a love of free ones."[30] They thought students should also be required to study the Declaration of Independence, the *Federalist,* and other American works; but more generally, said Jefferson, students should have instilled into their minds "the first elements of morality,"[31] and according to the report written by Jefferson and endorsed by Madison and the other commissioners for the University of Virginia, the university should be devoted to the cultivation of morals among the youth of the state, instilling "in them the precepts of virtue and order."[32] Now we are asked by the Supreme Court to believe that Madison's First Amendment was intended to prevent state universities, Madison's University of Virginia among them, from expelling a Miss Barbara Papish. We do not believe it.

Obscenity and Public Morality

> As there is a degree of depravity in mankind which requires a certain degree of circumspection and distrust, so there are other qualities in human nature which justify a certain portion of esteem and confidence. Republican government presupposes the existence of these qualities in a higher degree than any other form. Were the pictures which have been drawn by the political jealousy of some among us faithful likenesses of the human character, the inference would be that there is not sufficient virtue among men for self-government; and that nothing less than the chains of despotism can restrain them from destroying and devouring one another.[33]

In his concurring opinion in *Abington School District* v. *Schempp,* where the Court invalidated a requirement that the public school day begin with the reading of Bible verses, Justice Brennan insisted that the Court be shown why it was necessary to resort to "religious means" to achieve "secular ends." Until that be done—and it was clear he was of the opinion it could not be done—the state legislatures and public schools authorities would have to make do with moments of "reverent silence" and such familiar practices as recitation of the Pledge of Allegiance and "readings from the speeches and messages of great Americans."[34] Neither he nor the typical state official who prescribes

school prayers or Bible readings (in addition to the strictly patriotic ceremonies) is very specific as to the ends being sought
here—presumably they are talking about civic education—but
that fact is itself a reflection of the problem they would solve,
albeit with sometimes different means. They can speak of civic
education, or even of the education of citizens, but such
old-fashioned terms as "moral education" or "the formation
of character" or "the cultivation of tastes" seem inappropriate
in the American setting, even though it might be agreed that
some characters and some tastes are not suited to citizenship in
America. At one time it was understood that it was precisely
the self-governing community that must impose on itself the
most severe restraints, and that it was a function of a public
moral education to inculcate the habits of restraint, but this was
a view of republican politics that did not survive the birth of the
modern liberal state. Because it aims to *liberate* men and thereby
to promote a privacy unknown in classical republics, the modern
liberal state is limited with respect to the means it may adopt to
achieve public ends. More than that, a government constituted
to secure the private rights of man is limited with respect to the
public ends themselves. It may not force its citizens to subscribe
to a particular religious creed or punish them for failing to subscribe to any; it may not preach; it may not, out of a desire to
protect articles of faith, forbid the dissemination of scientific
knowledge, nor, out of a desire to protect family life, forbid the
dissolution of marriages; and it may not, following Rousseau,
forbid the establishment of a theater, or, following Plato, banish
the poets from the city or, in the effort to encourage public
spiritedness, establish a community of wives and common tables
for meals, and so on. What, then, may the United States do in
order to promote good citizenship?

In the secular realm we have taught civics, waved and saluted
the flag, and sung *The Star-Spangled Banner* almost into the
ground. But we have also employed somewhat more subtle
means. Constituted by an eighteenth-century revolutionary

principle and war, and reconstituted after a terrible civil war, we found our heroes and models in our successful beginning and in our own history. Parson Weems's biography of Washington went through eighty editions, and its tales of young Washington's moral rectitude found their way into the 122 million copies of McGuffey's *Readers.* More recent generations were taught to love Lincoln, "the richest symbol in the American experience."[35] It is no exaggeration to say that we built a political religion out of these materials, and the schools have made much of it. Indeed, as Justice Brennan acknowledges at least indirectly, it is on the schools that we have traditionally placed much of the burden of inculcating the habits appropriate to our institutions, and the schools drew their canons from our own history. Without belaboring the point, we can say that the exemplary method of instruction can, in the proper setting and in appropriate conditions, accomplish what Brennan asks of it.

The Supreme Court's recent First Amendment decisions, however, can scarcely be said to have contributed to this instruction or to the conditions that make it possible. Schoolchildren may not, in fact, be required to recite the Pledge of Allegiance;[36] nor be forbidden to wear armbands by way of protesting a war;[37] nor be suspended for even gross misbehavior without being given elements of a due process hearing;[38] nor be expelled, even after a full due process hearing, for distributing grossly obscene newspapers on a state university campus.[39] A state may not refuse to hire or retain a teacher "who wilfully advocates, advises, or teaches the doctrine that the Government of the United States, or of any State...should be overthrown by force, violence, or any other unlawful means,"[40] or require him to certify that he is not presently engaged in any effort to overthrow the government by force or violence;[41] and no state has yet been able to devise a flag desecration statute capable of withstanding the Supreme Court's scrutiny.[42] In the light of these decisions, state legislators and school officials are entitled to a degree of skepticism respecting Brennan's reassurances concerning the efficacy of the "secular means" of promoting civic virtue.

Perhaps the least understood of these secular means is censorship, and especially the censorship of what are understood to be obscene materials. The argument against it is familiar enough, too familiar to justify any but the briefest of expositions from me. In what was essentially the first of its modern cases, *Roth* v. *United States,* the Supreme Court devised a rule according to which a jury composed of average persons, applying "contemporary community standards," was empowered to decide whether a work, taken as a whole, appealed to a "prurient interest."[43] If it did, it was obscene. The trouble with this rule is that many a literary and dramatic masterpiece could not survive an encounter with such a jury. That is the case against censorship. In fact, it is Milton's case, and Tocqueville's case, and John Stuart Mill's case.

Strangely, it is not the case the Court made as it moved away from its *Roth* decision. It had begun, in *Roth,* by agreeing with *Chaplinsky* that obscenity was not part of the speech protected by the First Amendment, thus, nominally at least, making one exception to the principle of freedom of expression whereby the Court will not judge the substance of "mere" speech. This required of the Court a rule or test of obscenity, and the Court saw soon enough that the rule it had elaborated in *Roth* was inadequate. It therefore said that in addition to prurient appeal, a work had to be "patently offensive" and to be *"utterly* without redeeming social value"—and the emphasis was the Court's.[44] In the determination of patent offensiveness and social value or social importance, the trial judges and ultimately the Supreme Court justices themselves would play a role. This proved to be a test of obscenity that no work, masterpiece or trash, could fail. All that was needed to save a work from the censor was some college professor to testify that he found it to possess a modicum of "social value," and the work has not been written, staged, or filmed that cannot find its champions among college professors.* Justice Douglas insisted the First Amendment forbade censorship of any materials, and offered the assurance that "people are mature enough to pick and choose, to recognize trash when they see it, to be attracted to the literature that satisfies their deepest need, and, hopefully, to move from plateau to plateau and finally to reach the world of enduring ideas." But a few pages earlier he had said there is no such thing as trash, and, therefore, no such thing as art. There is only one plateau: "Some like Chopin, others like 'rock and roll,' some are masochistic, some deviant in other respects...." In fact, there is no such thing as a work that does not have social importance:

Is it not important that [the masochists, fetishists, and other "deviants"] communicate with each other? Why is communication by the "written word" forbidden? If we were wise enough, we might know that communication may have greater therapeutical value than any sermon that those of the "normal" community can ever offer. But if the communication is of value to the masochistic community or to others of the deviant community, how can it be said to be "utterly without redeeming social importance"? "Redeeming" to whom? "Importance" to whom? [45]

Everything that anyone has a taste for has "social" importance.

---

*The *New York Times* of January 14, 1970, printed the following wire service dispatch:
  "LONG BEACH, CALIF. JAN. 13 [1970] (AP)—Four nude models—two male, two female—postured before the coeducational sociology class of 250 persons.
  "On movie screens, lesbian and heterosexual couples went through acts of lovemaking.
  "Sound systems blared recordings by the Beatles and from the rock musical 'Hair.'
  "Two hours after the class ended yesterday, California State College suspended its teachers, Marion Steele, 31 years old, and Dr. Donald Robertson, 29, for thirty days without pay. Further action was threatened.
  "Mrs. Steele and Dr. Robertson said they had staged the show to ridicule what they called America's prudishness about sex as contrasted with its toleration of what they considered such 'glaring obscenities' as the Vietnam War, violence on television and pollution of air and water.
  "'This produces hangups and keeps millions from enjoying genuine sexual pleasure and makes our entire world obscene,' Dr. Robertson told the class."

Douglas, of course, customarily adopted the most extreme position in First Amendment cases, and it should be mentioned that he was writing in dissent here. Still, the Court adopted the substance of his position in the *Fanny Hill* case, although it continued to accept censorship of obscenity in principle. It just turned out that nothing was obscene because there was always someone willing to testify that a work was not *"utterly"* without value or importance. But in a world where there is no difference between art and trash, but only a difference between someone's idiosyncratic taste and someone else's idiosyncratic taste, it would seem that the censor's taste is as good as anyone else's and, therefore, that he would be incapable of making a poor judgment. Which is to say, in a world of everyone doing "his own thing," the majority can do no wrong. There is, to repeat what I have said before, no ground on which to rest an objection to the majority's rule. The objection *"I* like it" is sufficiently rebutted by the democratic response *"We* don't." To put the case against censorship on the ground that freedom of expression should be granted to everything is to undermine the reason for granting freedom of expression to anything and, therefore, to undermine the case against censorship.

When, in the *Fanny Hill* case in 1966, the Court had arrived at the point where it could no longer give a reasonable argument against censorship of obscenity, it had done more than involve itself in a logical muddle; it had removed from the law the distinction between art and trash, and this played a role in the further vulgarization of American life. Like censors everywhere, presumably, American censors were capable of egregious errors: the benighted librarian who refused to shelve *The Scarlet Letter,* the insensitive customs official who seized *Ulysses,* or the Comstockian vigilante who glued together the pages of every copy of *A Farewell to Arms* she could find in her local bookstore. Anyone who advocates censorship while refusing to acknowledge the propensity of censors to act foolishly and sometimes maliciously is himself acting foolishly or maliciously.

210

Yet censorship, undertaken in order to maintain the distinction between the nonobscene and the obscene, has the perhaps unintended effect (unintended certainly by the typical censor) of helping to maintain the distinction between art and trash. At a minimum it requires a judgment of what is worthy of being enjoyed and what is unworthy of being enjoyed, and this has the effect of lending some support to the distinction and its importance.

The Court, implicitly, and Justice Douglas, explicitly and blatantly, denied this. Instead of saying that a work of literary merit ought not to be proscribed no matter how obscene it may appear to the "average person" with his "contemporary community standards," the Court said that a work which is not *"utterly* without redeeming social value" ought not to be proscribed. Thus, we were treated to the unedifying spectacle of professors of literature from Harvard and Williams testifying in favor of *Fanny Hill*. The censor's mistakes could sometimes be corrected—Judge Woolsey's celebrated action in the *Ulysses* case is proof of this—and, besides, the forbidden book was more than likely to be available to those who wanted it; being consigned to under-the-counter custom is not the worst fate to befall a book. (The worst fate is for no one to want it.) But there is no institutional solution to the problem caused in part by the ending of censorship, which has the effect of establishing the absolute sovereignty of the free and mass market, the market that refuses on principle to recognize the authority of critical judgment in the world of the arts. The distinction between trash and art disappeared into the distinction between that which is *"utterly"* worthless and that which is not *"utterly"* worthless, as if that distinction were of any importance, and as if *that* were a distinction to be made by members of the learned professions. The opponent of censorship is surely justified in his opinion that the typical censor in a democracy is a threat to the arts, but he might now be made to see that the ending of censorship has the effect of establishing the sovereignty of the free mass and commercial market, which is not a market where the arts flourish. With censorship there was at least one restraint on the commercial republic, and it was a moral restraint; the ending of censorship removes the restraint and thereby has the effect of creating or strengthening a public taste for works in which moral questions play no part. But great art deals with moral questions.

This point deserves some elaboration. The law does not permit sexual intercourse in public and, since the Court's 1973 decisions, it no longer seems likely that it will permit it. Why not? This being a free society where it is important for people to communicate with each other, why do we not permit this? If, in John Stuart Mill's famous words, "the sole end for which mankind are warranted, individually or collectively, in interfering with the liberty of action of any of their numbers, is self-protection [and if] the only purpose for which power can be rightfully exercised over any member of a civilized community, against his will, is to prevent harm to others,"[46] on what possible basis can it legitimately prevent public sexual intercourse? The police may have to ascertain that neither party is being raped (for that would come under the category of "harm to others"), but once reassured on that point, the role of the police would be to protect the copulating couple. (We assume, on time, place, and manner grounds, they are not blocking traffic.) Why, then, do we not permit this? We do not permit it precisely because it does, in a subtle way, cause harm to others. The law that permits it is a law that has forgotten altogether the distinction between human beings and other animals, the animals that know no shame; and it is a law that causes the public to forget the distinction. Sex can take place publicly, but it is not possible to make love in public, which insight led George Orwell in *1984* to portray the real horror of the totalitarian state to consist in the inability of the two lovers to find a place where they might be alone. So the law of a liberal society, the society that protects privacy because it is important for human beings to enjoy privacy, is permitted to censor at least to the extent of forbidding this kind of sex. It does so because privacy is needed for *human* sex, and this law has the function—and some would say that law generally has the duty—of pointing us in the direction of the human. Human sexuality needs the assistance of the law.

But what is the essential difference between public sexual intercourse and the public display, sale, or distribution of pornography? In terms of the effect on the viewing public, what, if anything, is the difference? If books are important, does that importance not consist in the fact that we are affected by them (the censors and their opponents seem to agree at least on this), and that we are affected by different books differently? If the censor knows what he is doing, he recognizes that it is not the fact that a book treats an erotic theme that makes it censorable or objectionable; some of the greatest works ever written deal with eroticism. What makes a particular book objectionable is the manner in which it treats that theme. The effect of a book on its readers is related to the manner in which it treats its subjects. In Stendhal's *The Red and the Black,* surely one of the greatest novels ever written, the young Julien Sorel seduces Madame de Rênal by taking her hand; and when, at first objecting, she allows her hand to be held in his, the reader knows the rest will follow in due course. When it does, when Julien makes his way surreptitiously to her bedroom, and when she, leaping out of bed and denouncing him for his boldness, nevertheless does not insist that he leave, the reader is told only that when, some hours later, Julien left her room, "there was nothing more for him to desire." It was not because he was squeamish that Stendhal chose to avoid a detailed description of the coupling that we know took place in that bedroom; he knew that he would lose the audience for which he was writing—and, like D. H. Lawrence, gain an audience for which he was not writing—if he provided that description. That description would destroy the art of the novel because it would, in its effects, make voyeurs of its readers, who would be drawn to that particular event as participants in it and away from the context in which that event has its meaning for Stendhal—and, of course, for Julien and Madame de Rênal. They would be drawn to that scene as thousands—indeed, probably hundreds of thousands—were drawn to *Lady Chatterley's Lover* by the promise of that once-forbidden four-letter verb printed out on the page.

The Red and the Black is not a novel about sex—although, sex plays an important role in it; it is a novel about heroic longings in a world where there can be no more Napoleons. The erotic relationship between Julien and Madame de Rênal takes place in the immediate context of the family to which Julien is attached only as tutor to her children; and their sexual union has its meaning only when measured against her attachment to her children and her husband and in the context of Julien's longings. Her infidelity is a terrible thing to her and a significant thing to Julien who, through it, not only wins her love but registers a triumph over M. de Rênal and what he represents. It was not squeamishness but his artistry that required Stendhal to forgo the description of their coupling.[47] To have portrayed it after the fashion of our books and magazines would have corrupted his readers, just as we would be corrupted by the sight of sexual intercourse in public areas.

A work of art exists only in re-creation: it requires the reader, or viewer, to engage himself in it, to become involved in it; his involvement in it is a necessary part of the re-creation, as Ian Robinson says in an uncommonly fine essay. But to involve oneself in the sexual union of others, either by watching it or reading about it, is to understand sex in the language of pornography: "To do so habitually and with delight is to demonstrate that one's passions find their home in the language of pornography."[48] The censor forbids pornography (literally, whores' writing) for the same reason the law forbids public sexual intercourse: involvement in such spectacles, as a reader or as a viewer, is corrupting because it reduces human sexuality to the kind of activity described, measured, and prescribed for by those newest of scientists, the sexologists. To look upon it in these terms is to see it in the language of Masters and Johnson, but lovers cannot perform for Masters and Johnson, allowing their pulses to be taken, their body temperatures to be gauged, and so on. Love needs privacy, which is one reason why the law forbids public sexual intercourse and forbade pornography. This is what it means to say that censorship, in trying to maintain the moral distinction between the nonobscene and the obscene, has the effect of maintaining the distinction between the human and the base, and therefore, as I argued above, between art and trash. A people that is told by the law, with the support of the learned professions, that it is not improper to satisfy its taste for pornography will come to understand sexual relations in the language of pornography and will lose sight of the moral setting in which human sexual relations exist. Such a people will have no taste for moral questions, and, therefore, no taste for the great art which deals with these questions. It will prefer *Fanny Hill* to *The Red and the Black,* ultimately because it is taught that there is no reason not to. This was one of Rousseau's arguments for censorship.[49]

We are often told that censorship is a legacy of Puritanism (there is an element of truth to this), and that its advocates display a morbid fear of sex and sexuality, sometimes bordering on, if not spilling over into, the psychopathic; the example of Anthony Comstock compels one to admit that there is some truth to this as well. But it is also said that censorship can be advocated only by someone insensitive to the beauty of the arts and the role they can play in the lives of men, and this is not true. Lessing, for example, was one of the greatest lovers of art ever to live and write, and he admitted the legitimacy and even necessity of censorship.[50] And Rousseau, in the very context of his attack on the theater, admitted that he never willingly missed a performance of any of Molière's plays. Like Plato, he would banish the poets from the good city, yet he was himself a poet, musician, opera composer, and novelist, and he demonstrated his love for and knowledge of the arts in his work and in his life.

These examples alone ought to convince us that the problem of censorship cannot be comprehended in simple disjunctions of art versus philistinism or enlightenment versus ignorance. Besides, who would be bold enough to suggest that the ending of censorship in the United States has led to the flourishing of the arts?

Rousseau's is not a familiar argument, and it is not one that the Supreme Court has ever made or even had to consider. For a long time, the Court was not required to consider any argument about censorship because, surprisingly, until recently it was not understood to raise any First Amendment problems. The so-called Comstock law, under which every "obscene, lewd, lascivious, or filthy" publication is banned from the mails, was enacted in 1873, and the first cases under it reached the Supreme Court in 1896. What is remarkable about those cases is what they do *not* contain: there is not even a trace of an argument that the law violated the First Amendment. Not even the defendants raised the point. Lew Rosen, in the first case, published a paper, "Broadway," showing pictures of "females in different attitudes of indecency," pictures partially covered with lampblack which, readers or "viewers" were advised, was easily erased with pieces of bread. Rosen, who was sentenced to thirteen months at hard labor and fined $1, raised a number of objections, the most interesting one being that the indictment was "fatally defective" in that it did not set out with reasonable particularity those parts of the paper relied on to support the charge of obscenity, but it apparently never occurred to him that the First Amendment protected him. As for the failure of the indictment to describe the allegedly obscene matter, that was held not to be error. On the contrary, the Court said, "'some respect [must be paid] to the chastity of our records.'"[51] A month or so later, the Court decided by the narrowest of margins that a newspaper article that was admittedly "exceedingly coarse and vulgar" was not, however, lewd, lascivious, or obscene; these terms, it said, "signify that form of immorality which has relation to sexual impurity," and the article in question had nothing to do with sex.[52] Four justices dissented on this issue of the scope of the statutory words, but once again, nobody said anything about freedom of the press. As late as 1932, a man with the improbable name of O. B. Limehouse was convicted under this statute for mailing "filthy" letters, and the opinion of the Court upholding the conviction was written by that famous libertarian, Justice Brandeis, and not even he thought it relevant to mention the First Amendment or freedom of the press.[53] In these circumstances, it is not remarkable that the justices found it unnecessary to make a case in favor of censorship. Marshall might have acted differently if his Court had had the opportunity to review the first of the *Fanny Hill* cases, which was decided in Massachusetts in 1821,[54] but state speech and press cases were then thought not to involve a federal question. Thus, for a long time, we were allowed to take it for granted that censorship of obscenity was, like the support of decency generally, a legitimate and necessary public policy. When that assumption was challenged, it turned out that we could no longer remember why this was so.

This may account for the Court's conspicuous failure in the recent cases to discuss the reasons in favor of censorship, even though it acknowledges a duty to weigh those in the balance with the reasons against it. There are occasional references, usually in separate and dissenting opinions, to the frequently made argument that obscene publications tend to induce criminal sexual behavior, but the justices are right to be suspicious of this; the evidence is not convincing. In *Jacobellis,* Brennan acknowledged, as did even the President's Commission on Obscenity and Pornography,[55] that it might be necessary to prevent the distribution of obscenity among children, and Brennan went so far as to speak of "the legitimate and indeed exigent interests of States and localities...in preventing the dissemination of material deemed harmful to children."[56] But he did not discuss the issue of whether obscenity was in fact harmful to children, and as far as we know from what he said, Brennan would be unprepared to meet the argument made in some quarters today that children actually benefit from it. A few years later, the Court upheld a conviction for the selling of obscenity to minors; although it acknowledged a state legislature's finding that obscenity is a "basic factor in impairing the ethical and moral development of our youth and a clear and present danger to the people of the state," the Court added its own doubt that "this finding expresses an accepted scientific fact."[57] Here, instead of having to rely on the studies of social scientists and the usually tendentious testimony of chiefs of police (as to whether obscenity causes sex crimes), the justices might have reflected on what must surely be visible to them as they drive or are driven through the streets of Washington or as they thumb through the daily newspapers. There is no way the "sexual revolution" can be confined to adults or its blatant manifestations concealed from children. Indeed, to judge by their tastes in entertainment, it would appear that the sexual revolution has had its most profound effects on the young. Every parent knows this, if he wants to know it. Children learn easily enough the differences between what the adult world says and what it does, what it honors in its exhortations and what it honors with its custom. It can learn some of this simply by observing the lurid movie advertisements combined with the designations, "Adults Only" or "X-rated."*

---

*A recent decision, *Erznoznik* v. *City of Jacksonville,* 95 S. Ct. 2268 (1975), illustrates the problem perfectly and, one might almost say, humorously. Jacksonville adopted an ordinance forbidding, as a public nuisance, the showing in drive-in theaters of motion pictures in which "the human male or female bare buttocks, human female bare breasts, or human bare pubic areas are shown." It conceded that the ordinance was aimed at films that, if shown in regular enclosed theaters, would not be obscene, even under the rule of *Miller* v. *California.* Erznoznik managed a drive-in theater whose screen measured 35 feet by 70 feet and stood 54 feet above the ground. It was clearly visible from "two adjacent public streets and a nearby church parking lot." The city supported the ordinance on "time, place, and manner" grounds, contending that the films on this drive-in screen invaded the privacy of those outside the theater. But the Court, scrupulously citing precedents, brushed this argument aside in a couple of paragraphs. The city also supported the ordinance as an exercise of its "undoubted police power to protect children" (the words are Justice Powell's in the majority opinion), but the Court emphasized that children have First Amendment rights too, and that this ordinance was "overbroad in its proscription" (p. 2275). The Court concluded by denying that the ordinance could be upheld even

Besides, the only reason to keep obscenity from the son is to prevent him from becoming like the father, and if there is nothing wrong in the father's taste for obscenity, there cannot be anything wrong in the son's. In any case, it was not until the 1973 cases, when the Court announced its retreat, that it addressed itself seriously to the question of why the law ought to discourage the public distribution and display of obscenity and pornography.[58] This failure was not, however, unique to the Court. In modern times there have been a number of powerful writings against censorship, but until Harry Clor's book in 1969[59] there was nothing of comparable weight written against obscenity. Rousseau's *Letter to M. d' Alembert on the Theatre* was published 200 years before the *Roth* case and appears to have been forgotten almost everywhere.

In addition to his concern for the health of the arts, Rousseau argued that there is a connection between self-restraint and self-government, or democracy; and it followed for him that democracy, more than any other form of government, would require citizens capable of forgoing the satisfaction of every passion or desire. According to Rousseau, if the citizens of a democracy are unable to restrain themselves by observing the rules they collectively give themselves and, through the inculcation of good habits, promote among themselves, they will have to have rule imposed on them by others. Tyranny, it used to be said, is the inevitable mode of government for a self-indulgent people who carry liberty to the point where it becomes license. It was the tyrant who could allow the people to indulge themselves even to satiety. Indulgence of the sort we are now witnessing did not threaten his rule, because his rule did not depend on a citizenry of good character. Anyone can be ruled by a tyrant, and the more debased his subjects, the safer his rule. A case can be made for complete freedom in the realm of public

as a traffic regulation; a wide variety of scenes from the typical film are probably just as "distracting to the passing motorist." And that was that. A *New Yorker* cartoon or perhaps a Woody Allen film might do justice to all this, except, of course, it is finally not funny.

amusements among such a people, whose pleasures are derived from activities wholly divorced from their labor and any duties associated with citizenship. Among them a theater, for example, can serve to divert the search for pleasure from what the tyrant regards as dangerous or pernicious pursuits;* but in a free self-governing community, not only must strict attention be paid to the manner of public amusements, but even the establishment of a theater must be discouraged. Thus, not only is the popularization of the arts bad for the arts themselves, but a strict censorship is also necessary to the political health of a democracy.

This, shorn of all its details and supporting analysis, was the argument made by Rousseau on the eve of the establishment of the modern liberal state. It is deliberately extreme, reminding us in the austerity of its prescriptions more of classical Sparta than of any country existing in the Western world he knew or we know; but this fact does not weaken the power of its analysis, precisely because that analysis is of a problem rooted in the very nature of things.

The tendency in modern times, a tendency dating from the Enlightenment and strengthened by that extremely influential book, John Stuart Mill's *On Liberty,* has been to deny the existence of the problem. In fact, modernity is founded on that denial. It was said—and said so powerfully that Mill in *On Liberty* was able to assume it—that freedom was good for the arts and sciences and was therefore good for civil society. We have begun

---

*The modern tyrant does not encourage passivity among his subjects. On the contrary, they are expected to be public-spirited: to work for the State, to exceed production schedules, to be citizen soldiers in the huge armies, and to love Big Brother. Indeed, in Nazi Germany and the Soviet Union alike, the private life was and is discouraged, and with it erotic love and the private attachments it fosters. Censorship in a modern tyrannical state is designed to abolish the private life to the extent that this is possible. George Orwell understood this perfectly. This severe censorship that characterizes modern tyranny, and distinguishes it sharply from premodern tyranny, derives from the basis of modern tyrannical rule: both Nazism and Communism have roots in a kind of utopian theory. The modern tyrant parades as a political philosopher, the heir of Nietzsche or Marx, with a historical mission to perform. He cannot leave his subjects alone.

to have our doubts about an uncontrolled science—first the atomic bomb and then pollution cast doubt on this proposition—and there is more than enough reason now to have doubts about the uncontrolled arts. The Court decontrolled the arts, so to speak, and the impact of that has been profound. It not only permitted the publication of sex but it *caused* the publication of sex—or, to coin a word, the "publification" of sex.

The ending of censorship brought out into the open an activity that had formerly, and for very good reasons, been confined to the private world. It emancipated sex, or so we are constantly being told; but not at all surprisingly, this emancipated sex turns out to be sex abstracted from its human setting.[60] The immediate and obvious consequence of this is that sex is now being made into the measure of existence, and such uniquely human qualities as modesty, fidelity, abstinence, chastity, delicacy, and shame, qualities that formerly provided the constraints on sexual activity and the setting within which the erotic passion was enjoyed, discussed, and evaluated, are today ridiculed as merely arbitrary interferences "with the health of the sexual parts."[61] Seemingly sober men and women, bearing the credentials of science, abstract from everything human to draw their picture of sexual man, the man seeking *The Joy of Sex* (whose author is quoted in the *New York Times* as telling us to reexamine fidelity with its "religio-social dogmas, personal feelings, fantasy needs, and the deeply proprietorial attitudes of one another enjoined on husband and wife by the priest, the neighbor, folklore and the attorney").[62] But sexual man is an abstraction, as much an abstraction as the "economic man" created by an earlier generation of scientists. In each case, the picture is drawn by abstracting from human nature. In each case, the only acknowledged basis of a human relationship is calculating self-interest, formerly monetary gain and now sexual fulfillment, and of a very narrow sort indeed. In each case, society is to be reconstituted on this one aspect in isolation from the whole human being. If this new breed of scientists succeeds, every enduring

221

human relationship will have disappeared with the qualities that made them possible: the modesty and delicacy needed for love, the fidelity needed for marriage and friendship, the bonds of affection needed for the family. They must disappear because they are constraints on sexual passion. With them will go the last possibility of constitutional government.

In the absence of authoritative direction by state or church, we Americans have relied to a considerable extent on the family not only to nurture the young but also to instill the habits required by citizenship in a self-governing community. We have relied on the family to teach us to care for others, to moderate the self-interest that in our time is not likely to be much moderated by love of God or love of country. Bernard Bailyn was speaking of colonial America when he said that the family not only introduced the child to the basic forms of civilized living, shaped his attitudes, and formed his patterns of behavior, but also "endowed him with manners and morals."[63] This familial function was only slowly changed by the passage of time. And what is it, or what has it been, that constitutes the family? The democratic family is not constituted by the laws that in aristocratic times prevented the subdividing of estates or recognized only the authority of the father, bestowing on him the political authority to command its other members. It is not constituted by the conventions under which marriages are arranged to the end of uniting property rather than persons, or according to which "men live more for the remembrance of what has been than for the care of what is." The democratic family is constituted by what Tocqueville calls natural ties rather than legal or social ties; it is characterized by a "familiar intimacy" bred by equality instead of a "filial obedience" resting on authority. "I think that in proportion as manners and laws become more democratic, the relation of father and son becomes more intimate and more affectionate; rules and authorities are less talked of, confidence and tenderness are often increased, and it would seem that the natural bond is drawn closer in proportion as the social bond is loosened."[64] But that natural

222

bond is not unbreakable, certainly not standing alone, and not under all conditions. It may be true, as Tocqueville says, that "filial love and fraternal affection...emanate spontaneously from human nature itself,"[65] but so too do all the passions, and not all of them are compatible with the life of the family. The case in point, of course, is the sexual passion.

Democracy began by freeing the desires, and whether it lives or dies depends on its ability somehow to domesticate them; not to suppress them, but so to arrange matters as to ensure that the freed desires are made compatible with civil society. The market economy promised to domesticate the desire for material well-being by making a virtue of acquisitiveness, and we express the principle of this in the familiar formula "private vice equals public virtue." The democratic family promised to domesticate the sexual desire: marriages would be entered into freely by the parties, instead of being arranged by parents or families; but they would be preceded, especially in the case of the young woman, by an education of a certain sort. According to Tocqueville, she was taught to believe that every girl could "become the wife of the man who loves her; and this renders all breaches of morality before marriage very uncommon [and] the same cause operates, though more indirectly, on married life. Nothing better serves to justify an illicit passion, either to the minds of those who have conceived it or to the world which looks on, than marriages made by compulsion or chance." Tocqueville continued:

In a country in which a woman is always free to exercise her choice, and where education has prepared her to choose rightly, public opinion is inexorable to her faults. The rigor of the Americans arises in part from this cause. They consider marriages as a covenant which is often onerous, but every condition of which the parties are strictly bound to fulfill, because they knew all those conditions beforehand, and were perfectly free not to have contracted them.

Thus, Tocqueville concluded, the "very circumstances which render matrimonial fidelity more obligatory, also render it more easy."⁶⁶ There was no disharmony between sexual desire (promiscuous by nature) and the family, and the family could perform the role required of it by democracy. In the America he observed, and continuing well into the twentieth century, sexual desire was domesticated, and this (as well as other reasons) allowed Tocqueville to be sanguine about the future of democracy in the United States.

But circumstances can change and, thanks partly to the Supreme Court, have changed radically. Then men were busy, now they have time on their hands; then the imagination was confined, now nothing limits it and everything excites it. Then public opinion censured, even condemned, infidelity, especially on the part of the wife; now infidelity is held to be a matter of little consequence, easily forgiven when weighed against the superior claims of sexual fulfillment. The America Tocqueville observed did not make sexual indulgence a virtue; it did not exalt sexual fulfillment by making it the measure of existence and even a constitutional right;* nor, in the guise of sex education, did it teach its young the physics of love and assume morality could take care of itself.

It would seem to follow that as the constitution of the family depends less on laws and authoritative conventions and more on the "natural bonds" or the affections it generates, the more vul-

---

*Walter Barnett, *Sexual Freedom and the Constitution: An Inquiry into the Constitutionality of Repressive Sex Laws* (Albuquerque: University of New Mexico Press, 1973). Professor Barnett argues that sexual fulfillment is a constitutional right because the Constitution guarantees freedom of expression, including sexual expression. Nothing must inhibit it, not even the laws prohibiting incest, because the family affords a full range of sexual opportunities: "Formerly, the prohibition on incest between blood relatives was thought to be justifiable on the genetic theory that sexual unions between individuals who were closely related would be more likely to produce defective offspring—a theory now rendered more debatable by modern genetic science and in any event made largely irrelevant by the availability of effective contraception....It seems clear that the incest taboo is not instinctive but the product of cultural conditioning, because no aversion to sexual intercourse between relatives exists in animals other than man" (p. 12). In this fashion he reduces human sexuality to animal sexuality, the model for man becoming "animals other than man." It is this sexual expression that is—if Barnett has his way—a constitutional right.

nerable it becomes. When those bonds are loosened and those affections allowed to languish—and the sexual revolution in all its aspects certainly contributes to that—the democratic family will prove a very fragile institution indeed. Anyone concerned about the future of constitutional democracy in the United States should ponder the consequences of this.

Conclusion

There was no illusion among thoughtful men that censorship laws would be easy to administer, and there was a recognition of the danger they presented. One obvious danger was that the lawmakers would demand too much, that zealots like Anthony Comstock, who always pose a threat to the liberal state, would become the agents of the law and demand more than they may, under liberal principles, legitimately demand. They might demand not merely decency, for example, but sanctity. Macaulay stated the problem in his essay on Restoration comedy (mild fare compared to that regularly exhibited in our day):

It must, indeed, be acknowledged, in justice to the writers of whom we have spoken thus severely, that they were to a great extent the creatures of their age. And if it be asked why that age encouraged immorality which no other age would have tolerated, we have no hesitation in answering that this great depravation of the national taste was the effect of the prevalence of Puritanism under the Commonwealth.

To punish public outrages on morals and religion is unquestionably within the competence of rulers. But when a government, not content with requiring decency, requires sanctity, it oversteps the bounds which mark its proper functions. And it may be laid down as a universal rule that a government which attempts more than it ought will perform less.... And so a government which, not content with repressing scandalous excesses, demands from its subjects fervent and austere piety, will soon discover that, while attempting to render an impossible service to the cause of virtue, it has in truth only promoted vice.[67]

The truth of this was amply demonstrated in the United States in

225

the Prohibition era, when the attempt was made to enforce abstemiousness and not, labels to the contrary, temperance. In a word, the principle that should guide the liberal state in this area of policy is not to seek to eradicate vice—the means to that end are incompatible with free government—but to make vice difficult, knowing that while it will continue to flourish covertly, it will not be openly exhibited or condoned. At a minimum—and the liberal state may properly concern itself only with the minimum—this requires a public labeling of vice as vice. Rousseau made this minimum prescription even in the context of his maximum argument that the decent self-governing community ought to ban the theater altogether:

Is our city so big, have vice and idleness already made such progress that it can henceforth no longer subsist without the theatre? [D'Alembert and Voltaire] tell us that it tolerates worse entertainments which shock both taste and morals-manners alike, but there is quite a difference between presenting bad morals-manners and attacking good ones; for this latter effect depends less on the qualities of the entertainment than on the impression it makes. In this sense, what relation is there between a few migratory farces and a resident drama, between the smutty talk of a charlatan and the regular performances of dramatic works, between the booths at the fair, built to divert the populace, and an esteemed theatre where the decent folk will think they are being instructed? One of these amusements is without consequence and stays forgotten the day after; but the other is an important affair which merits all the attention of the government.... Vice hardly insinuates itself by shocking decency but by taking on its likeness. [68]

What the Supreme Court has done in its obscenity decisions is to make it possible for vice to take on the likeness of decency, precisely because it may no longer be labeled as vice. Obscenity and pornography, once restricted to illegitimate theaters and peripheral bookstores, offering their wares furtively because they were occasionally raided by the police, are now exhibited in the legitimate theater and sold openly in every place where books or magazines are sold. What can be exhibited openly can, of course, be enjoyed openly and without shame, and that has had consequences apparent to everyone. The *New York Times,* the country's leading newspaper, complains bitterly and often about pornography and prostitution around Times Square, and calls upon the police, or the mayor, or somebody to do something about it.[69] But do what? The denizens of Times Square—and not merely the *Times* itself—are entitled to freedom of expression. The *Times,* after years spent attacking censorship, also complains about the pornographic condition of films, books, and the legitimate stage, calling upon "sophisticated critical judgment to do something about this."[70] But the critics are not adequate to this task, even if they were inclined, as those on the *Times* itself are not inclined, to undertake it. It was the law, not the critics, that formerly confined pornography to the illegitimate theater, and the Supreme Court removed the law. In so doing, it removed the stigma of illegitimacy, and pornography moved to the center of the city and to the prominent place it now occupies in our lives. Not even the 1973 decisions of the Court are likely to change that, although the Court deserves credit for making the effort.

An obscene work is now defined as a work that, taken as a whole, appeals to a prurient interest, portrays sexual conduct in a patently offensive manner, and—this is new since 1973—does not, when considered in its entirety, have "serious literary, artistic, political, or scientific value."[71] Thus, an otherwise obscene work must have some merit before it can escape proscription. This is surely a more workable and sensible rule than the one it replaced, according to which an obscene work had to be *"utterly"* worthless before it could be proscribed. In addition, the Court redefined—or defined more clearly—the community whose standards are to be applied in the determination of prurient appeal and patent offensiveness. At this writing it is not yet clear whether the community will be state or local; it is only clear that it need not be national, and it is therefore possible that a work will be forbidden in one place and permitted in another.

The reaction to this from what is usually denominated as "enlightened opinion" was that the country had taken, or had been forced to take, a backward step, or a step to the right. President Nixon was widely held to be ultimately responsible because he had appointed four of the five justices making up the majority in these 1973 cases (Mr. Justice White, a Kennedy appointee, provided the fifth vote), and even without Watergate that was sufficient to mark the decisions as wrong, to say the least. They were said to be an attempt to put down "the sexual revolution," and most commentators in the prestigious press were clearly in favor of that revolution, if not as actual participants then as sympathetic observers or putative participants.[72]

Despite the Court's more recent efforts, the sexual revolution will not be so easily put down. The Court can reverse its decisions, but it cannot so readily or simply undo the consequences of its decisions. Consequences of this sort "remain when their cause is removed," as Rousseau put it, and he added the somber thought that "as soon as they begin to be felt, they are irremediable."[73] Whether he was right about this we may soon be able to judge.

Morality cannot be legislated, we are told and have reason to believe, but the law can lend support to the moral dispositions of a people. Tocqueville had this in mind when he warned that the religion which had "struck its roots deep into a democracy" must be preserved, watched carefully "as the most precious bequest of aristocratic ages."[74] The principle can be generalized to apply to all those decent habits that are required for self-government. Liberal democracies especially are limited with respect to the means they may properly adopt to generate these habits or moral dispositions, and it is therefore especially important that ours preserve those with which it began. The Supreme Court has not appreciated the role that law must necessarily play in this project.

CHAPTER 6

The Supreme Court and American Democracy

IN his dissenting opinion in *Adamson* v. *California,* Justice Black said that the provisions of the Bill of Rights "may be thought outdated abstractions by some [and] it is true they were designed to meet ancient evils. But they are the same kinds of human evils that have emerged from century to century wherever excessive power is sought by the few at the expense of the many."[1] In this fashion, Black managed to evoke an image of George III imposing his rule on a body of reluctant colonists who then, having cast off the tyrant's yoke, guard themselves against his potential successors by denying them the powers they would use. It is an appealing formulation because it casts the Court in the role of defender of democracy, of the people. And the Bill of Rights does indeed speak of the people. The First Amendment protects the "right of the people peaceably to assemble," and the Second the "right of the people to keep and bear arms," and the Fourth the "right of the people to be secure in their persons, houses, papers, and effects, against unreasonable searches and seizures," and the Ninth the possession "by the people" of certain unenumerated rights. To secure these rights is to secure the rights of the people, and there are indeed

229

cases where the Court has, to the immense advantage of the people, secured these rights against local despots seeking excessive power in the fashion suggested by Black. It is sufficient to recall Jersey City Mayor Frank Hague, and what the Court prevented him from doing to the C.I.O.[2] Nevertheless, Black's formulation conceals more than it reveals: what it conceals is, in the first place, the nondemocratic character of judicial review. In so doing, it conceals a problem the Founders regarded as characteristic of popular government.

As we know from the *Federalist,* and especially from the 10th and 51st *Federalists,* the men who wrote the Constitution were concerned to inhibit the power of the people, who would rule by right but would misrule by inclination unless somehow prevented from doing so. In writing the Constitution, the Founders' task was to find "a republican remedy for the diseases most incident to republican government."[3] As they saw it, and as our experience on the whole confirms, the government of a democracy is not inclined to be undemocratic; it might be inclined, however, to deprive minorities of their rights. To guard these rights and, more specifically, the rights belonging to all men, the Constitution was made to embody "auxiliary precautions,"[4] and no reader of the 51st *Federalist* can be excused for failing to see that these "precautions" were designed especially with an eye to the power of the many, not the few. Judicial review, although not mentioned in this context, has proved to be not the least efficacious of these "auxiliary precautions." More to the point, in the typical First Amendment case the Court has not been confronted with a few seeking "excessive power" at the expense of the many. Most often, it has been confronted with the many seeking power, whether excessive or not, at the expense of the few: the few Communists, the few Klanists, the few (or the quondam few) pornographers, or in the religious cases, the relatively few Jehovah's Witnesses. As Alexander Bickel said, "judicial review is a counter-majoritarian force in our system."[5]

Despite isolated examples to the contrary, judicial review was not a majoritarian force in the past—for example, when it was used to strike down maximum-hours laws or laws prohibiting "yellow-dog" contracts—and it has not been a majoritarian force in the present. Who would be so bold as to say that public school segregation would have been struck down in a popular referendum, even a national referendum? Is it not clear (and the action taken by thirty-odd state legislatures since *Furman* v. *Georgia*[6] would so indicate) that a majority of the people are not opposed to capital punishment? Or to laws forbidding abortion?[7] And in the one case of legislative reapportionment where we are in a position to know, the Court had to impose its rule of one man, one equally weighted vote on an unwilling majority of the people of Colorado, and not merely a statewide majority but a majority within every county in the state.[8] Judicial review, as these famous recent examples show, is indeed a "counter-majoritarian force in our system," but it is not to be faulted for that alone. In its way, the Constitution is counter-majoritarian; legislative majorities are assumed capable of violating its provisions, and we have come to depend on the Supreme Court to keep them within constitutional bounds. We have done so, however, with the understanding that the Court will enforce the provisions of the Constitution, not its own idiosyncratic notions of how the country ought to be governed. We have done so with the confidence that the justices are not only better placed to respect constitutional principles but also better able to understand and explicate them.

Justice Black's formulation, according to which the Court protects the many from the few, also serves to conceal something else. It makes it appear as if popular government could be secured merely by enforcing checks on government itself, and in this it ignores the conditions, or what modern social science is inclined to call the sociological conditions, of a self-governing community. This social science is increasingly aware of the "social prerequisites" of the various forms of government, of the role of "personality structures," "belief systems," and the

231

"means of social training—the family and the school in particular."[9] It tends to err only insofar as it gives these "social factors" a life of their own, a life in which they are unaffected by the political or legal context in which they develop and manifest themselves to us. Professor Dahl, whose words were just quoted, criticizes Madison for stressing the importance of political institutions and, Dahl thinks, underestimating the importance of "inherent social checks and balances."[10] But what Dahl was describing in 1956 was, of course, the Madisonian system: the "pluralism" he found, to mention merely one example, is a product of the large commercial republic deliberately fostered by the Constitution, as well as of the constitutional ban on religious establishments. An American "belief system" that includes a significant degree of tolerance, to mention one more example, also finds its being in the absence of an official church, as well as in the principle of equality. The point is that these sociological factors are dependent on political factors, including, of course, the law, and they can be changed by changes in the law. Instead of Madison, Dahl and his social science colleagues should be criticizing Justice Black and his fellow members of the Court, who *do* underestimate the importance of social institutions. They do this when they hand down decisions calculated adversely to affect—if not to destroy—those institutions on which American democracy depends. Whether the protection of the many from the few will conduce to a decent self-governing country of the sort the Founders hoped for depends, as even modern social science knows, on the character of the people constituting the many; and that character depends on the condition of religion, the family, the schools, and on the strength of the people's attachment to republican principles. The Court in its First Amendment decisions has proceeded in blissful ignorance of this, promoting pornography in the name of freedom of expression; casting aside, as so many irrational encumbrances, the conventions of decency that used to govern public discourse; refusing to permit financial support to religious education; and

232

subtly undermining the venerable character of the Constitution itself. The Court owes its role as a "counter-majoritarian" force to the people's confidence in its ability to "remember the answers" that a self-governing country needs to remember, but in its First Amendment work it has not earned that confidence. Instead of remembering or conserving, the Court has been inclined to see its role as an innovator or pathfinder. Litigants representing today's fashionable causes know this very well indeed, which is why they are litigants in the courts rather than lobbyists before the legislatures.

Tocqueville saw the disposition of Americans to turn political questions into legal questions; he was of the opinion that this was, on the whole, a salutary practice. Does not law look to the past in its search for precedent, and is it therefore not well placed to find principle and to render principled decisions? There may once have been reason for thinking this, but the constitutional law of the First Amendment has not been built on the precedents and principles of the past. One looks almost in vain for references in the Court's opinions to what the great commentators—Story, Kent, and Cooley, for example—have written on freedom of speech and religion, or to what the Founders intended with the First Amendment. And in those exceptional cases where such guidance has been sought, it has been rejected or misunderstood. Madison's "Memorial and Remonstrance" is frequently cited in the religion cases, but not the Madison of the First Amendment debates in the First Congress, and no reference is made to the fact that Washington and Marshall, among others, opposed Madison's "Memorial and Remonstrance." Jefferson's words on toleration of erroneous opinion are used to support the proposition, itself erroneous, that the Constitution recognizes no truth, not even Jefferson's "self-evident" truths. Justice Brennan cited Jefferson and others in his opinion in *New York Times* v. *Sullivan,* and, having misunderstood them, came up with a "central meaning of the First Amendment" that Jefferson and the others would not have

233

recognized. Justice Douglas has looked to Popes and cardinals when it suited his purpose, and to some Colorado divine who thinks *Fanny Hill* a very moral work,[11] when that suited his purpose; but his purpose has borne little resemblance to the Founders'. Since it is the Constitution they are expounding, the very Constitution from which alone they derive their right to impose limits on the political branches of government, one might have supposed they would have been given pause by Leonard Levy's revelations—if revelations they were—concerning the original understanding of the First Amendment; but nothing of the sort has happened. The only explanation of this must be their opinion that they know better than the Founders, and this, presumably, entitles them to "strike out on new paths," to work their innovations and, generally, their new wonders to perform. Certainly, in the First Amendment cases, they have not been impelled in their new directions by the people.

On the contrary, a recent study found that more than two-thirds of those polled would not allow free speech to "people promoting Communist, racist or atheist causes," and the people and the legislators they elect still hold to the old-fashioned view that vulgar and obscene speech ought not to be accorded constitutional protection; 68 percent of the people, according to a 1972 poll, persist in the opinion that "exposure to pornography harms the morals of young people."[12] This is thought to be a function of their lack of appreciation for the arts. Perhaps. But are they not entitled to doubt the wisdom of a sophistication that sees value in practically anything written or produced, and even to despise a sophistication that looks upon tattooing—of all things—as an "art form" and therefore, in the view of the New York Civil Liberties Union, deserving of First Amendment protection?[13] They still cling to the old-fashioned view that the school books their children are required to read ought not to include works in praise of rape or in contempt of their religious beliefs ("Even hillbillies have civil rights," their placards say) and to wonder why their form of censorship is regarded so contemptuously when, at the same time, the Department of Health, Education, and Welfare can announce plans "to provide research, assistance, and guidance to local educational agencies in eliminating sex bias from curricula and educational material."[14] Outraged, they responded outrageously in Kanawha County, West Virginia, but they have a point. Among them the family is still a respected institution, and they continue to be suspicious of the fashionable idea that sexual fulfillment is the measure of a truly human life. Hence, they find it difficult to accept the related proposition that all the laws that somehow inhibit sexual fulfillment, or that channel it in the direction of marriage, are unconstitutional. They suspect this is not the Constitution they and their forbears have lived under, and of course they are right. Among them, patriotism continues to be honored, and they tend to hold the view—too simple, no doubt—that they should not be asked to make sacrifices to defeat Communism in the remote corners of the earth while protecting the right of Communists to run for public office in their own communities. They hold that Communism and what they call Americanism are incompatible, and of course they are right; but almost nothing in the wider context in which they live their lives supports them in this, now not even the Constitution. Unlike the situation in 1937, for example, when the Court was impelled by the people to forgo its doctrinairism of that day, the causes of "freedom of expression" are not to be found in anything fairly denominated as "the people." What is disquieting, however, is that public opinion is, inevitably, beginning to follow the Court and the "elites" the Court follows.[15]

In the beginning, the Supreme Court saw itself as "republican schoolmaster,"[16] and in its Marshallian role of expounding the law of the Constitution it can scarcely avoid being a teacher of some sort. This fact led one student of the early Court to speak of judicial review as an institution allowing philosophy to be brought to bear on action through the medium of law.[17] Unfortunately, the Court is also an institution that allows sophistry to be brought to bear on public law, and there is inevitably more sophistry than philosophy at large in the intellectual world. The typical legislator, being elected, listens more attentively to other voices, and what he hears is a public opinion that is not sophisticated or reflective or, in one sense, even rational; but precisely because it contains elements of a republican past, it also contains vestiges of a wisdom needed by republican government. But judicial review requires that legislator to listen as well to the Supreme Court. And when the justices who exercise this immense power look not to the Founders—or, generally, to a past that was republican in its thought and politics—but rather to the fashionable thought of the present day, which is anything but sympathetic to republicanism and its conditions, the effect can be devastating.

This is now recognized, even in the pages of one of the principal agents of fashion, the *New York Times.* In a recent column, William V. Shannon acknowledged the role played by political assassinations, the Vietnam war, racial and generational turmoil, and Watergate, as any observer must, but he quite properly recognized that even these factors cannot fully account for the present condition of the country:

Any recognition of the importance of privacy or of the need for self-discipline has almost vanished. Exhibitionism and voyeurism are mistakenly identified as civil liberties. Pornographers, publicity freaks, and manufactured "personalities" parade across the cultural scene, pop up on television, and haunt the fringes of politics.

These symptoms and others caused him to wonder whether democracy could survive "if common moral values are leached away by a popular culture that endorses violence and self-indulgence." Hence his conclusion:

It is on this deepest level that there is cause for pessimism. In our communities, in our schools, and most of all in our family life, we must renew the moral capital upon which freedom depends. If we are once again to have a politics of decency and generosity we must cultivate those virtues in every sphere. [18]

236

But the cultivation of those virtues is not readily accomplished in a liberal democracy, and it cannot even be attempted until the Supreme Court is persuaded to forgo its doctrinaire attachment to "freedom of expression" and to complete separation of religion and state. A First Amendment that guarantees "freedom of expression" and forbids assistance to the churches is not congenial to either the cultivation or the preservation of the virtues upon which democracy depends.

Why is free speech good? The Court doesn't know. Was free speech intended to serve republican government and only republican government? The Court doesn't care what the original intention was. Is there a connection between decent public discourse and decent government? The Court doesn't even bother to wonder. Is there a connection between the privacy of sexual behavior and the family and, therefore, with republican government? For a period that may prove to be decisive, the Court did not even acknowledge the relevance of the question. Is there a connection between morality and republican government—or, in Tocqueville's formulation, can liberty govern without religious faith? Whatever the answer, the Constitution is now said to have built an impregnable wall between church and state.

Philosophic men of the past addressed themselves to these questions and provided answers. But the Supreme Court no longer remembers those answers. The Founders, in their different ways, also provided answers, but the Court no longer remembers their answers either. Instead, it has allowed itself to be carried about on the wind of modern doctrine.

Notes

Chapter 1

1. *The Debates and Proceedings in the Congress of the United States* (cited hereafter as *Annals of Congress*), vol. 1, p. 759 (August 15, 1789).

2. *Everson* v. *Board of Education,* 330 U.S. 1, 15 (1947).

3. Edward S. Corwin, "The Supreme Court as National School Board," *Law and Contemporary Problems* 14 (Winter 1949); Mark DeWolfe Howe, *The Garden and the Wilderness: Religion and Government in American Constitutional History* (Chicago: University of Chicago Press, 1967).

4. *Walz* v. *Tax Commission,* 397 U.S. 664 (1970).

5. *Zorach* v. *Clauson,* 343 U.S. 306, 313 (1952); *Walz* v. *Tax Commission,* at 716. Dissenting opinion.

6. *Annals of Congress,* vol. 1, pp. 451 (June 8, 1789), and 757, 758 (August 15, 1789).

7. Ibid., p. 759 (August 15, 1789).

8. Ibid.

9. Merely as one example, consider the case of Connecticut, which was to some extent governed by the Congregational ministry, the so-called "Standing Order." See Anson Phelps Stokes and Leo Pfeffer, *Church and State in the United States* (New York: Harper & Row, 1964), p. 74.

10. *Annals of Congress,* vol. 1, p. 784 (August 17, 1789).

11. Ibid., p. 796 (August 20, 1789).

12. This read as follows: "No state shall infringe the right of trial by jury in criminal cases; nor the rights of conscience; nor the freedom of speech, or the press." Ibid., p. 452 (June 8, 1789).

13. Bernard Schwartz, *The Bill of Rights: A Documentary History* (New York: Chelsea House, 1971), vol. 2, p. 1153. I cite Schwartz on Senate action because his volume refers both to the *Annals of Congress* and the Senate *Journal,* neither of which, at this time, recorded the debates in the Senate.

14. Irving Brant, *James Madison: Father of the Constitution, 1787-1800* (Indianapolis: Bobbs-Merrill, 1950), pp. 271, 272.

15. Act of August 7, 1789, 1 *Statutes at Large* 50. The actual form of the action taken by the First Congress was to "adapt" the Ordinance to the new "Constitution of the United States."

16. *Annals of Congress,* vol. 1, p. 757 (August 15, 1789).

17. Ibid., p. 758 (August 15, 1789). Italics supplied.

18. Michael J. Malbin, "The Supreme Court and the Definition of Religion," Ph.D. dissertation, Cornell University (1973), p. 82.

19. *Engel* v. *Vitale,* 370 U.S. 421, 437 (1962). Concurring opinion.

20. *Walz* v. *Tax Commission,* 397 U.S. 664, 716 (1970). Dissenting opinion.

21. James Madison, *Writings,* ed. Gaillard Hunt (New York: Putnam, 1900-1910), vol. 2, p. 189.

22. Francis Newton Thorpe, *The Federal and State Constitutions...* (Washington: U.S. Govt. Printing Office, 1909), vol. 3, p. 1888.

23. *Annals of Congress,* vol. 1, p. 451 (June 8, 1789). This was dropped only because it was thought to be unnecessary: the Preamble to the Constitution already acknowledged the source of power to be in the people, and this acknowledgment was affirmed when the words "or to the people" were added to what we now know as the Tenth Amendment. (Ibid., p. 790.)

24. Thorpe, *The Federal and State Constitutions,* vol. 3, p. 1888.

25. Schwartz, *Bill of Rights,* vol. 2, p. 709.

26. Alexis de Tocqueville, *Democracy in America* (New York: Vintage, 1945), vol. 1, p. 316.

27. See, for example, Russell Kirk, *The Roots of American Order* (La Salle, Ill.: Open Court, 1974).

28. Thomas Jefferson, *Notes on the State of Virginia,* in *Works* (Federal ed., New York: Putnam, 1904-05), vol. 4, p. 83.

29. Ibid., p. 80.

30. Harvey C. Mansfield, Jr., "Thomas Jefferson," in *American Political Thought: The Philosophic Dimensions of American Statesmanship,* ed. Morton J. Frisch and Richard G. Stevens (New York: Scribner's, 1971), p. 38.

31. Tocqueville, *Democracy in America,* vol. 1, p. 316.

32. Ibid., p. 318. And see Jean-Jacques Rousseau, "Civil Religion," in *The Social Contract,* bk. 4, chap. 8.

33. Madison to Jefferson, Oct. 24, 1787, in Madison, *Writings,* ed. Hunt, vol. 5, pp. 28-29.

34. John Locke, *Second Treatise of Civil Government,* sec. 6.

35. Madison to Webster, March 15, 1833, in Madison, *Works* (Congressional ed., 1865), vol. 4, p. 294.

36. *Annals of Congress,* vol. 1, pp. 421-422.

37. Ibid., p. 423.

38. *Federalist* no. 9.

39. Jefferson, *Works* (Federal ed.), vol. 4, p. 78.

40. Ibid., p. 80.

41. Jefferson to Roger C. Weightman, June 24, 1826, in *Works* (Federal ed.), vol. 12, p. 477.

42. Locke, *Second Treatise,* chap. 1.

43. Jefferson, *Works* (Federal ed.), vol. 4, p. 76.

44. Mansfield, "Thomas Jefferson," p. 28.

45. Thomas Hobbes, *Leviathan,* bk. 3, chap. 37.

46. Spinoza, *Theologico-Political Treatise,* chap. 6; *Works of Spinoza* (Dover ed.), vol. 1, p. 87.

47. Jefferson to Benjamin Rush, April 21, 1803, in *Works* (Federal ed.), vol. 9, p. 457. Italics in original.

48. Jefferson, "Syllabus of an Estimate of the Merit of the Doctrine of Jesus, Compared with Those of Others," ibid., p. 461.

49. Ibid., p. 462.

50. Ibid., pp. 462-463.

51. See S. Gerald Sandler, "Lockean Ideas in Thomas Jefferson's 'Bill for Establishing Religious Freedom,'" *Journal of the History of Ideas* 21 (1960): 110-116. In three parallel columns, Sandler cites five ideas concerning toleration as they appear first in Locke's *Letter,* then in the notes Jefferson made on Locke's *Letter,* and finally in the "Bill for Establishing Religious Freedom." The similarity is remarkable. As Sandler says, "there can be little doubt of [Jefferson's] indebtedness to Locke for his ideas on religious toleration."

52. Thomas Paine, *Age of Reason* (New York: Willey, n.d.), p. 248.

53. Ibid., p. 88.

54. Jefferson, *Notes on the State of Virginia, Works* (Federal ed.), vol. 4, p. 79.

55. Paine, *Age of Reason,* p. 52.

56. Jefferson, "Syllabus," in *Works* (Federal ed.), vol. 9, p. 461.

57. Washington to the Hebrew Congregation of Newport, August 17, 1790, in *Writings,* vol. 31, p. 93*n*.

58. Tocqueville, *Democracy in America,* vol. 1, p. 45.

59. Thomas I. Pangle, *Montesquieu's Philosophy of Liberalism* (Chicago: University of Chicago Press, 1973), p. 257.

60. Montesquieu, *The Spirit of the Laws,* bk. 25, Chap. 12, as translated by Pangle in ibid., p. 256.

61. Pangle, *Montesquieu's Philosophy of Liberalism,* pp. 256-257.

62. *Federalist* no. 10.

63. Max Farrand, ed., *The Records of the Federal Convention* (New Haven: Yale University Press, 1911, 1937), vol. 1, pp. 134-136.

64. Locke, *Second Treatise,* esp. chap. 5; Adam Smith, *The Wealth of Nations* (New York: Modern Library, 1937), esp. pp. 753-755.

65. Jefferson, *Works* (Federal ed.), vol. 4, pp. 81-82.

66. Max Farrand, ed., *Records of the Federal Convention,* vol. 1, pp. 134-135. See also *Federalist* no. 15.

67. John Adams, *Works* (1850-1856), vol. 4, p. 199, and vol. 7, pp. 53-54, as cited by John Agresto, "The Debate over the Nature of Republican Government in the American Founding Period: The Problem of Republican Virtue," Ph.D. dissertation, Cornell University (January 1974), pp. 59-60.

68. Unless otherwise noted, all the quotations in the three preceding paragraphs are taken from *Federalist* no. 10.

69. Jefferson to Dr. Benjamin Waterhouse, June 26, 1822, in *Works* (Federal ed.), vol. 12, p. 243.

70. Ibid.

71. *Engel* v. *Vitale,* 370 U.S. 421, 437 (1962). Concurring opinion.

72. Jefferson, *Notes on the State of Virginia, Works* (Federal ed.), vol. 4, p. 81.

73. Tocqueville, *Democracy in America,* vol. 2, p. 27.

74. Ibid., vol. 1, p. 316.

Chapter 2

1. Alexis de Tocqueville, *Democracy in America* (New York: Vintage, 1945), vol. 2, p. 30.

2. Ibid., p. 27.

3. Ibid.

4. Ibid., pp. 154-155.

5. Thomas Jefferson, *Notes on the State of Virginia,* in *Works* (Federal ed.; New York: Putnam, 1904-5), vol. 4, p. 78.

6. "A Bill for Establishing Freedom," in Jefferson, *Papers,* ed. Julian P. Boyd (Princeton, N.J.: Princeton University Press, 1950-), vol. 2, pp. 545-546.

7. *Negre* v. *Larson,* 401 U.S. 437 (1971).

8. Ibid., p. 471.

9. *Gillette* v. *United States,* 401 U.S. 437, 469 (1971).

10. "Compulsory school attendance laws and the great expenditures for education both demonstrate our recognition of the importance of education to our democratic society" (*Brown* v. *Board of Education,* 347 U.S. 483, 493 [1954]).

11. *Wisconsin* v. *Yoder,* 406 U.S. 205, 215 (1972). See Berns, "The Importance of Being Amish," *Harper's* (March 1973): 36-42.

12. *Estep* v. *United States,* 327 U.S. 114 (1946).

13. *West Virginia State Board of Education* v. *Barnette,* 319 U.S. 624 (1943). *Yoder* should also be distinguished from *Sherbert* v. *Verner,* 374 U.S. 398 (1963), which was not a criminal case. There the Court refused to allow a state to deny a generally applicable benefit—unemployment compensation—to Adell Sherbert because she, as a Seventh-Day Adventist, refused to work on Saturday and therefore refused to accept a job requiring Saturday work.

14. *United States* v. *Ballard,* 322 U.S. 78 (1944).

15. *Ballard* v. *United States,* 329 U.S. 187 (1946).

16. *United States* v. *Ballard,* at 89.

17. Ibid., at 93.

18. *Prince* v. *Massachusetts,* 321 U.S. 158, 163 (1944).

19. *Wisconsin* v. *Yoder,* at 216.

20. Ibid., at 249, citing *Welsh* v. *United States,* 398 U.S. 333, 343 (1970).

21. *Reynolds* v. *United States,* 98 U.S. 145; 25 L.Ed. 244, 249 (1879).

22. As quoted in ibid.

23. Ibid., at 250.

24. Locke, *A Letter Concerning Toleration,* in *Works* (1812), vol. 6, p. 43.

25. Act of June 24, 1948, 62 *Statutes at Large* 612.

26. *United States* v. *Kauten,* 133 F. 2nd 703, 708 (1943).

27. 62 *Statutes at Large* 612.

28. *United States* v. *Seeger,* 380 U.S. 163 (1965).

29. *Welsh* v. *United States,* 398 U.S. 333, 341 (1970).

30. Ibid., at 339-340.

31. Michael J. Malbin, "The Supreme Court and the Definition of Religion," Ph.D. dissertation, Cornell University (1973), p. 398.

32. *Welsh* v. *United States,* at 345.

33. Philip B. Kurland, *Religion and the Law* (Chicago: Aldine, 1962).

34. *Welsh* v. *United States,* at 358.

35. Locke, *Letter Concerning Toleration,* p. 44.

36. Tocqueville to Corcelle, September 17, 1853, as cited in Marvin Zetterbaum, *Tocqueville and the Problem of Democracy* (Stanford: Stanford University Press, 1967), p. 90.

37. *Dred Scott* v. *Sandford,* 60 U.S. (19 How.) 393 (1857).

38. Abraham Lincoln, speech at Quincy, Ill., October 13, 1858, reprinted in *Collected Works,* ed. Roy P. Basler (New Brunswick, N.J.: Rutgers University Press, 1953), vol. 3, p. 255

39. *The Debates and Proceedings in the Congress of the United States* (cited hereafter as *Annals of Congress*), vol. 1, p. 434 (June 8, 1789).

40. As quoted in Michael J. Malbin, "The Supreme Court and the Definition of Religion," pp. 21-22. I have relied on Malbin's account of this debate.

41. Thomas M. Cooley, *Constitutional Limitations* (Boston: Little, Brown, 1868), p. 471.

42. Joseph Story, *Commentaries on the Constitution* (Boston: Little, Brown, 1873), vol. 2, sec. 1879.

43. *Cantwell* v. *Connecticut,* 310 U.S. 296, 303 (1940).

44. *Bradfield* v. *Roberts,* 175 U.S. 291 (1899).

45. *Everson* v. *Board of Education,* 330 U.S. 1, 15, 16 (1947). Having said this, a bare majority of the Court nevertheless concluded, to the justified dismay of the dissenters, that this busing arrangement did not constitute aid to religion.

46. Ibid., at 11, 13.

47. Ibid., at 31-32, 34.

48. Mark DeWolfe Howe, *The Garden and the Wilderness: Religion and Government in American Constitutional History* (Chicago: The University of Chicago Press, 1967), p. 172.

49. A good account of the long struggle to disestablish the Anglican Church in Virginia (which did not culminate until 1802) may be found in H. J. Eckenrode, *Separation of Church and State in Virginia* (Richmond: Virginia State Library, 1910).

50. Story, *Commentaries on the Constitution,* vol. 2, sec. 1874.

51. *Abington School District* v. *Schempp,* 374 U.S. 203, 222 (1963).

52. Ibid., at 271.

53. *McGowan* v. *State of Maryland,* 366 U.S. 420 (1961).

54. *Abington School District* v. *Schempp,* at 278.

55. Ibid., at 281.

56. See Schempp's testimony quoted by Justice Brennan at 374 U.S. 289, note 68.

57. *Board of Education* v. *Allen,* 392 U.S. 236 (1968).

58. *Walz* v. *Tax Commission,* 397 U.S. 664 (1970).

59. *Lemon* v. *Kurtzman,* 403 U.S. 602 (1971).

60. *Early* v. *DiCenso; Robinson* v. *DiCenso,* 403 U.S. 602 (1971).

61. *Levitt* v. *Committee for Public Education and Religious Liberty,* 93 S. Ct. 2814 (1973).

62. *Committee for Public Education and Religious Liberty* v. *Nyquist,* 93 S. Ct. 2955 (1973).

63. *Sloan* v. *Lemon,* 93 S. Ct. 2982 (1973).

64. *Meek* v. *Pittinger,* 95 S. Ct. 1753 (1975).

65. *Tilton* v. *Richardson,* 403 U.S. 603 (1971).
66. *Hunt* v. *McNair,* 93 S. Ct. 2868 (1973).
67. Leo Pfeffer, *Church, State and Freedom,* rev. ed. (Boston: Beacon Press, 1967), p. 325.
68. As quoted in ibid., p. 332.
69. Ibid., p. 335.
70. Ibid., p. 334.
71. Ray Gibbons, "Protestantism and Public Education," *Social Action,* 15 (February 15, 1949): 18-19, as quoted in Pfeffer, *Church, State and Freedom,* p. 339.
72. Ellwood P. Cubberley, *Public Education in the United States: A Study and an Interpretation of American Educational History* rev. ed. (Boston: Houghton Mifflin, 1934), p. 294.
73. *United States* v. *Macintosh,* 283 U.S. 605, 625 (1931).
74. *McCollum* v. *Board of Education,* 333 U.S. 203, 217 (1948).
75. Pfeffer, *Church, State and Freedom,* p. 337.
76. *Marbury* v. *Madison,* 1 Cranch 137, 163 (1803).
77. Alexander M. Bickel, *The Supreme Court and the Idea of Progress* (New York: Harper and Row, 1970).
78. Anson Phelps Stokes and Leo Pfeffer, *Church and State in the United States* (New York: Harper & Row, 1964), p. 427; *Reynolds* v. *Nussbaum,* 115 N.W. 2nd 761 (1962).
79. Pfeffer, *Church, State and Freedom,* p. 338.
80. Ibid.
81. Tocqueville, *Democracy in America,* vol. 1, p. 318.
82. Story, *Commentaries on Constitution,* vol. 2, sec. 1874.
83. Edward S. Corwin, *A Constitution of Powers in a Secular State* (Charlottesville, Va.: Mitchie Co., 1951), p. 116.
84. *Meek* v. *Pittinger,* 95 S. Ct. 1753 (1975).
85. U.S. Supreme Court Briefs and Records, 330 U.S. 1 (1947), "Appellee's Brief," at 28.
86. Ibid., "Brief of the American Civil Liberties Union as *Amicus Curiae,"* at 7, 9-11.
87. *Pierce* v. *Society of Sisters,* 268 U.S. 510 (1925). The charge against the Court was made by Max Lerner. See Robert F. Drinan, S.J., *Religion, the Courts, and Public Policy* (New York: McGraw-Hill, 1963), p. 118.
88. U.S. Department of Commerce, Bureau of the Census, *Statistical Abstract of the United States, 1974* (Washington, D.C.: Government Printing Office, 1974), p. 124.
89. See Donald A. Giannella, "Lemon and Tilton: the Bitter and the Sweet of Church-State Entanglement," in *The Supreme Court Review, 1971,* ed. Philip B. Kurland (Chicago: University of Chicago Press, 1971), pp. 195-199.
90. As quoted by Justice Reed in his dissenting opinion in *McCollum* v. *Board of Education,* 333 U.S. 203, 245, note 11 (1948).
91. *Goss* v. *Lopez,* 95 S. Ct. 729, 740 (1975).
92. Ibid., at 749, note 22.
93. *Papish* v. *Board of Curators,* 410 U.S. 667 (1973).
94. Cubberley, *Public Education in the United States,* p. 757.
95. *Congressional Record* (daily edition), April 17, 1975, p. S6011. On a nationwide basis, Senator Bayh reported, the public elementary and secondary

schools experienced, in the years of 1970-1973, a 77.4 percent increase in assaults on teachers, an 85.3 percent increase in assaults on students, a 36.7 percent increase in robberies of students and teachers, and a 40.1 percent increase in rapes and attempted rapes; other types of assault showed comparable increases.

96. *Federalist* no. 55.

97. It is clear from the debates that the constitution of the Senate, for example, was calculated to enhance the quality of Senators. See Max Farrand, ed., *Records of the Federal Convention* (New Haven: Yale University Press, 1937), vol. 1, pp. 151-52. (Madison's speech, June 7, 1787.)

98. *Annals of Congress,* vol. 1, p. 731.

99. *Gillette* v. *United States,* 401 U.S. 437, 459 (1971).

100. *Wisconsin* v. *Yoder,* 406 U.S. 205, 215 (1972).

Chapter 3

1. *Cantwell* v. *Connecticut,* 310 U.S. 296 (1940).

2. Thomas Jefferson, *The Papers of Thomas Jefferson,* ed. Julian P. Boyd (Princeton, N.J.: Princeton University Press 1950), vol. 2, p. 546.

3. Zechariah Chafee, Jr., *Free Speech in the United States* (New York: Atheneum, 1969), p. 28.

4. Dumas Malone, *Jefferson and His Time.* Vol. 3: *Jefferson and the Ordeal of Liberty* (Boston: Little, Brown, 1962), p. 393.

5. Jefferson to Abigail Adams, September 11, 1804, in *The Writings of Thomas Jefferson,* ed. Andrew A. Lipscomb and Albert E. Bergh (Washington, D.C.: Thomas Jefferson Memorial Association, 1903-1937), vol. 11, p. 51.

6. Leonard W. Levy, *Jefferson and Civil Liberties: The Darker Side* (Cambridge, Mass.: Belknap Press, 1963), p. 15.

7. Ibid., p. viii.

8. James Madison to Jefferson, February 8, 1825, in Madison, *Writings,* ed. Gaillard Hunt (New York: Putnam, 1900-1910), vol. 9, p. 220.

9. Jefferson, *Works* (Federal ed., New York: Putnam, 1904-05), vol. 4, pp. 79-80; "A Bill for Establishing Religious Freedom," *Papers,* ed. Boyd, vol. 2, pp. 545-546.

10. Leonard W. Levy, *Legacy of Suppression: Freedom of Speech and Press in Early American History* (Cambridge: Belknap Press, 1960).

11. John Bach McMaster and Frederick D. Stone, eds., *Pennsylvania and the Federal Constitution, 1787-1788* (Philadelphia, 1888), p. 308; as quoted in Levy, ibid., pp. 201-202. Italics supplied by Levy.

12. Sir William Blackstone, *Commentaries on the Laws of England,* bk. 4, chap. 11.

13. Levy, *Legacy of Suppression,* p. viii.

14. Ibid., pp. 104-105.

15. For an account of these events see John C. Miller, *Crisis in Freedom: The Alien and Sedition Acts* (Boston: Little, Brown, 1951).

16. Francis Wharton, *State Trials of the United States During the Administrations of Washington and Adams* (Philadelphia: Carey and Hart, 1849), p. 689. Callender's words appear originally in his pamphlet, *The Prospect Before Us.*

17. Ibid., pp. 322-332. Cobbett was later to be sued for libel by Benjamin Rush and fined $5,000 plus costs—by a wide margin the heaviest fine assessed in a libel action during this period.

18. *Gazette of the United States,* August 16, 1799, p. 3. It serves to illustrate the thesis of this chapter to point out that Bache was clearly intended to be one of the principal targets of the Federalist Sedition Act and that Cobbett was later indicted and convicted by the Republicans under the common law of Pennsylvania. Cobbett referred to Bache and Duane as "vagrant scribblers, who blacken the sides of these detestable trumpets of sedition and rebellion" (*Gazette of the United States,* August 17, 1799, p. 3).

19. Approved June 18, 1798; 1 *Statutes at Large* 566-569.

20. Approved June 25, 1789; 1 *Statutes at Large* 570-572.

21. Approved July 6, 1798; 1 *Statutes at Large* 577-578.

22. Approved July 14, 1798; 1 *Statutes at Large* 596-597.

23. The most extensive coverage of the enactment of the Alien and Sedition Acts and the subsequent trials is to be found in James Morton Smith, *Freedom's Fetters: The Alien and Sedition Laws and American Civil Liberties* (Ithaca: Cornell University Press, 1956).

24. Thomas Evans, "An Address to the People of Virginia Respecting the Alien and Sedition Laws, by a Citizen of the State" (Richmond, 1798).

25. *The Debates and Proceedings in the Congress* of the *United States* (cited hereafter as *Annals of Congress*), 5th Cong., 2nd Sess., vol. 2, p. 1955.

26. *Nishimura Ekiu* v. *United States,* 142 U.S. 651, 659 (1892).

27. *Fong Yue Ting* v. *United States,* 149 U.S. 698, 705, 711 (1893).

28. *Annals of Congress,* 5th Cong., 2nd Sess., vol. 2, p. 1989.

29. *Dred Scott* v. *Sanford,* 19 How. 393 (1857).

30. *Annals of Congress,* 5th Cong., 2nd sess., vol. 2, p. 1310.

31. Ibid., p. 2028. Six of the remaining ten came from Pennsylvania, two from New York, one from Massachusetts, and one, Matthew Lyon, who was to be one of the victims of the Sedition Act, from Vermont.

32. Ibid., vol. 1, p. 575. Only five of the sixteen votes in favor were cast by slave-state senators, one each from Maryland, North Carolina, and South Carolina, and two from Delaware. I am counting northern states as nonslave even though the process of emancipation had not yet been completed by 1798.

33. *Annals of Congress,* 4th Cong. 1st sess., p. 1291. The vote was on the resolution for carrying the treaty in effect.

34. The question of the formation of political parties in America lies outside the scope of this study, but it is worth remarking that most studies of this subject, particularly the more recent ones, ignore the extent to which this issue of slavery was one of the issues that lay behind this political event. Cf., e.g. William Nisbet Chambers, *Political Parties in a New Nation: the American Experience, 1776-1809* (New York: Oxford University Press, 1963), with John Quincy Adams, "Parties in the United States" (1829), p. 1, in *Adams Papers,* film 469, reel no. 246. Adams did attribute the birth of parties to the "establishment of Slavery," among other factors.

35. See Smith, *Freedom's Fetters.*

36. *Annals of Congress,* 5th Cong., 2nd sess., vol. 2, p. 1963.

37. Ibid., p. 1968.

38. Ibid.

39. *Debates in the House of Delegates of Virginia, Upon Certain Resolutions Before the House. Upon the Important Subject of the Acts of Congress Passed at Their Last Session, Commonly Called the Alien and Sedition Laws* (Richmond: Thomas Nicholson, 1818), p. 37. The debates are reprinted as Senate Document no. 873, 62nd Cong., 2nd sess. Except when indicated otherwise, the original volume, a copy of which is in the Library of Congress, is cited here, and cited hereinafter as *Virginia Debates*.

40. Smith, *Freedom's Fetter*'s, p. 53.

41. *Virginia Debates*, p. 20.

42. Ibid., p. 21. The law referred to was contained in sections 2 and 3 of "An Act for reducing into one, the several Acts and Parts of Acts respecting the Powers and Duties of the Executive," enacted November 16, 1792. See *A Collection of all such Acts of the General Assembly of Virginia, of a Public and Permanent Nature*, etc. (Richmond: Augustine Davis, 1794), p. 85. It is reprinted in *The Revised Code of the Laws of Virginia*, vol. 1 (Richmond: Thomas Ritchie, 1819), pp. 142-143.

43. Ibid., p. 24.

44. *Annals of Congress*, 5th Cong. 2nd sess., vol. 2, p. 2097.

45. Ibid., p. 2102. Cf. Blackstone, *Commentaries*, vol. 4, chap. 11.

46. Levy, *Legacy of Suppression*, pp. 259-260.

47. *Annals of Congress*, 5th Cong., 2nd sess., vol. 2, pp. 2105-2106.

48. Ibid., p. 2152.

49. Ibid., pp. 2148-2149.

50. Ibid., p. 2153. (For a discussion of Livingston's definitive views on criminal libel laws, as reflected in his draft System of Penal Law for Louisiana, see pp. 144-145.)

51. Ibid.

52. Charles Warren, *Jacobin and Junto* (Cambridge: Harvard University Press, 1931), p. 97.

53. Levy, *Legacy of Suppression*, p. x.

54. *Annals of Congress*, 5th Cong., 2nd sess., vol. 2, pp. 2140-2142.

55. Ibid., p. 2160. In his inability to "conceive" of a law "laying such restraints upon speech," Gallatin was displaying a somewhat limited imagination. See, for example, *Hague* v. *C.I.O.*, 307 U.S. 496 (1939); *Kunz* v. *New York*, 340 U.S. 290 (1951); *Poulos* v. *New Hampshire*, 345 U.S. 395 (1953).

56. Ibid., p. 2163. James Morton Smith overlooks this critical fact of Gallatin's position. See Smith, *Freedom's Fetters*, esp. pp. 141-142.

57. Ibid., p. 2167.

58. Ibid., p. 2171.

59. Harry Kalven, Jr., "The New York Times Case: A Note on 'The Central Meaning of the First Amendment,'" in *The Supreme Court Review, 1964*, ed. Philip B. Kurland (Chicago: University of Chicago Press, 1964), p. 205.

60. Malone, *Jefferson and the Ordeal of Liberty*, pp. 396-397, 394.

61. Adrienne Koch and Harry Ammon, "The Virginia and Kentucky Resolutions: An Episode in Jefferson's and Madison's Defense of Civil Liberties," *William and Mary Quarterly*, ser. 3, vol. 5, no. 2 (April 1948): 174.

62. Jefferson to Madison, August 23, 1799, Rives Papers, Library of Congress, as reprinted in Koch and Ammon, ibid., pp. 165-166. I have not seen the origi-

nal, which, according to Koch and Ammon, had never before been printed in full. Only a fragment of it appears in Jefferson, *Works* (Federal ed., 1905), vol. 9, pp. 77-78.

63. Jefferson to Nicholas, Sept. 5, 1799, in *Works* (Federal ed., 1904-05), vol. 9, pp. 79-81.

64. Koch and Ammon, "Virginia and Kentucky Resolutions," pp. 167, 168.

65. Frank Maloy Anderson, "Contemporary Opinion of the Virginia and Kentucky Resolutions," *American Historical Review,* vol. 5 (Jan., 1900), 238.

66. Ethelbert Dudley Warfield, *The Kentucky Resolutions of 1798: An Historical Study* (New York and London: C.P. Putnam's Sons, 1887), pp. 37-38.

67. Jefferson, *Works* (Federal ed., 1905), vol. 8, pp. 471, 476-477.

68. Speech by James Hamilton at Walterborough, S.C., October 1828, as quoted in William W. Freehling, *Prelude to Civil War: The Nullification Controversy in South Carolina, 1816-1836* (New York: Harper and Row, 1965, 1966), p. 152.

69. Jefferson to John Taylor, June 1, 1798, in *Works* (Federal ed., 1905), vol. 8, pp. 430-433.

70. Jefferson to Taylor, November 26, 1798, in ibid., p. 481. Italics supplied.

71. Koch and Ammon, "Virginia and Kentucky Resolutions," p. 167.

72. "Address of the General Assembly of the People of the Commonwealth of Virginia," *Journal of the [Virginia] House of Delegates,* January 15, 1799, pp. 88-89.

73. *Virginia Debates,* p. 31.

74. Ibid., p. 47.

75. Ibid., pp. 74, 76.

76. Ibid., p. 86.

77. "Mr. Mercer said he would not take up the time of the committee in making any observations upon [the Sedition Law]. He was willing to let the proof of its unconstitutional quality rest upon the argument of the gentleman from Caroline" (ibid., p. 38).

78. Ibid., p. 121.

79. Ibid., p. 134.

80. Ibid., pp. 156-157

81. *Acts of the General Assembly of the Commonwealth of Virginia,* passed at the session begun October 1, 1792. This law, as amended, is also printed in *Laws of Virginia* (Richmond, 1819), chap. 162 (vol. 1, pp. 590ff). Virginia enacted a sedition law in 1776, levying a fine up to £20,000 and providing for imprisonment up to five years for anyone who "by any word, open deed, or act, advisedly and willingly maintain[s] and defend[s] the authority, jurisdiction, or power, of the king or parliament of *Great Britian...* " [Hening's, *Laws of Virginia,* vol. 9, p. 170]. A list (not complete) of the various laws against freedom of speech and action adopted by the states against loyalists during the Revolution is provided by Claude Halstead Van Tyne, *The Loyalists in the American Revolution* (New York: Macmillan, 1902), app. C.

82. John Taylor's answer to this had already been given: "It would be as just to say, that a state could pass laws for raising fleets and armies, because Congress had done so, as that Congress could infringe the liberty of speech, because the states had done so" (*Virginia Debates,* p. 134).

83. Ibid., p. 116.

84. Albert J. Beveridge, *The Life of John Marshall* (Boston and New York:

Houghton Mifflin, 1916), vol. 2, p. 402. Marshall was not in the legislature at the time, but this, of course, does not preclude his being the author—Madison, the acknowledged author of the resolutions, was not in the legislature either. Beveridge cites as authority three letters: Sedgwick to Hamilton, February 7, 1799; Sedgwick to Rufus King, March 20, 1799; and Vans Murray to John Quincy Adams, April 5, 1799. In the first, Sedgwick says the address "is said to have been drawn by Marshall" (Hamilton, *Works* [1850 ed.], vol. 6, p. 392); in the second, he says for this "masterly performance...we are indebted to the pen of General Marshall" (*The Life and Correspondence of Rufus King* [1895], vol. 2, p. 581); in the third, Vans Murray, in Holland at the time, says he "should think that John Marshall wrote the address," and "*I hope* that J. Marshall did write the address" ("Letters of William Vans Murray to John Quincy Adams, 1797-1803," *Annual Report of the American Historical Association, 1912*, p. 536.

85. *The Address of the Minority in the Virginia Legislature to the People of That State: Containing a Vindication of the Constitutionality of the Alien and Sedition Laws,* (Virginia) *Journal of the House of Delegates,* December 1798. The address was reprinted in the Virginia *Gazette,* January 29, 1799, and in a supplement, February 5, 1799. A copy of the original pamphlet is in the library of Harvard University. An abridged version of it is printed in John P. Roche, ed., *John Marshall: Major Opinions and Other Writings* (Indianapolis and New York: Bobbs-Merrill, 1967), pp. 34-48.

86. Levy, *Jefferson and Civil Liberties,* p. 55.

87. Walter Berns, "Freedom of the Press and the Alien and Sedition Laws: A Reappraisal," in *The Supreme Court Review, 1970,* ed. Philip B. Kurland (Chicago: University of Chicago Press, 1970), pp. 135-142.

88. Levy, *Legacy of Suppression,* p. 6.

89. See Sir James Fitzjames Stephen, *A History of the Criminal Law of England* (London: Macmillan, 1883; New York: Burt Franklin, n.d.), vol. 2, chap. 24.

90. Levy, *Legacy of Suppression,* p. 249.

91. Stephen, History of Criminal Law of England, vol. 2, p. 348.

92. Levy, *Legacy of Suppression,* p. 283.

93. Berns, "Freedom of Press," pp. 138-139.

94. Tunis Wortman, *A Treatise Concerning Political Enquiry and the Liberty of the Press* (New York, 1800), pp. 229-230. Italics supplied.

95. Ibid., pp. 209-210.

96. Levy, *Legacy of Suppression,* p. 283.

97. *Blackstone's Commentaries: With Notes of Reference to the Constitution and Laws of the Federal Government of the United States; and of the Commonwealth of Virginia,* ed. St. George Tucker (Philadelphia, 1803), vol. 1, app. pp. 29-30. First italics supplied.

98. Ibid., p. 175.

99. Madison, *Writings,* (Hunt ed.), vol. 6, p. 358.

100. Ibid., pp. 392-393. Italics supplied.

101. Ibid., p. 388.

102. Ibid., p. 387.

103. Ibid., p. 397.

104. Ibid., p. 395.

105. Ibid., pp. 387-388.

106. Ibid., p. 392.
107. Ibid., p. 334.
108. Alexander Hamilton to Oliver Wolcott, June 29, 1798, in Hamilton, *Works,* ed. Lodge (New York: Putnam, 1904), vol. 10, p. 295.
109. Madison to Jefferson, October 17, 1788, in *Writings,* ed. Hunt (1904), vol. 5, p. 272.
110. Quoted in William Goodell, *Slavery and Anti-Slavery* (New York: William Harned, 1852), p. 413.
111. Ibid.
112. Ibid., p. 414.
113. James D. Richardson, *Messages and Papers of the Presidents* (New York: Bureau of National Literature, 1897) vol. 3, p. 1395.
114. "Report of the Select Committee on Incendiary Publications," February 4, 1836, *Register of Debates,* vol. 12, pt. 4, app., p. 73.
115. *New York Times* v. *Sullivan,* 376 U.S. 254, 276 (1964).
116. *Register of Debates,* vol. 12, pt. 1, p. 383. The second section provided for the dismissal and fining of postmasters convicted of violating the act.
117. Ibid., pt. 4, app., p. 73.
118. Ibid., pt. 1, p. 1128.
119. Ibid., p. 1139.
120. Ibid., pt. 2, pp. 1730-1731.
121. Ibid., pt. 1, p. 1148.
122. Approved July 2, 1836, 5 *Statutes at Large* 87.
123. Leon Whipple, *The Story of Civil Liberty in the United States* (New York: Vanguard Press, 1927), pp. 112-113.
124. *New York Times* v. *Sullivan,* 376 U.S. at pp. 276, 277.
125. Freehling, *Prelude to Civil War,* pp. 310, 333, 83.
126. *Register of Debates,* 24th Cong., 1st sess., p. 4053.
127. *People* v. *Croswell,* 3 Johns. 336, 337 (New York, 1804). The best history of the litigation is in Julius Goebel, ed., *The Law Practice of Alexander Hamilton: Documents and Commentary* (New York and London: Columbia University Press, 1964), vol. 1, pp. 775-848.
128. Thomas Reed Powell, "Kent's Contributions to Constitutional Law," *Columbia Alumni News* 14 (1923): 373.
129. Callender too was described in an indictment as "a person of wicked, depraved, evil disposed, disquiet and turbulent mind and disposition," and charged with maliciously designing to defame President Adams with the intent to bring him into contempt and to excite the good people of the United States toward him. See Smith, *Freedom's Fetters,* p. 344.
130. Theodore Plucknett, *A Concise History of the Common Law,* 4th ed. (London: Butterworth, 1948), p. 470; Stephen, *A History of the Criminal Law of England,* vol. 2, pp. 347-348.
131. See Plucknett, *Concise History of the Common Law,* pp. 456-460.
132. Stephen, *History of the Criminal Law of England,* vol. 2, pp. 304-305.
133. *R.* v. *Tutchin,* 14 Howell's S.T. 1095; *R.* v. *Shipley,* 21 S.T. 847; *R.* v. *Thomas Paine,* 22 Howell's S.T. 358.
134. Stephen, *History of the Criminal Law of England,* vol. 2, p. 350.
135. Ibid., p. 351.
136. W. Blake Odgers, *A Digest of the Law of Libel and Slander* (London: Stevens & Sons, 1881), p. 388.

137. Ibid.
138. I have found most useful Stephen's account, vol. 2, pp. 298-395.
139. 32 Geo. III, c. 60.
140. Stephen, *History of the Criminal Law of England,* vol. 2, p. 359.
141. 6 and 7 Victoria, c. 96.
142. 3 Johns. at 352, 393-394.
143. *Beauharnais* v. *Illinois,* 343 U.S. 250, 265 (1952).
144. Hamilton "reprobated the novel, the visionary, the pestilential doctrine of an unchecked press.... [This] would encourage vice, compel the virtuous to retire, destroy confidence, and confound the innocent with the guilty" (3 Johns. at 352).
145. Kent's conclusion on this point was stated as follows: "...that upon every indictment or information for a libel, where the defendant puts himself upon the country, by a plea of not guilty, the jury have a right to judge, not only of the fact of the publication, and the truth of the *innuendoes,* but of the intent and tendency of the paper, and whether it be a libel or not; and, in short, of 'the matter put in issue upon such indictment or information'" (3 Johns. at 376-377, quoting from Fox's Libel Act, 32 Geo. III, c. 60 [1792]).
146. 3 Johns. at 358.
147. Ibid.
148. Ibid., at 377.
149. Ibid., at 377-378.
150. Ibid., at 379.
151. Ibid.
152. Ibid., at 378. Under *New York Times* v. *Sullivan,* 376 U.S. at 280-281, not only is truth a defense, because recovery depends on "actual malice" defined as "knowledge that [the statement] was false" or was made "with reckless disregard of whether it was false or not," but it is also unnecessary for the defendant to prove truth so long as the victim cannot show that the defamatory statement was made with "actual malice."
153. N.Y. Sess. Laws (1805), chap. 90; New York State Constitution of 1821, Art. 7, Sec. 8. The constitutional provision read: "Every citizen may freely speak, write, and publish his sentiments on all subjects, being responsible for the abuse of that right, and no law shall be passed to curtail, or restrain the liberty of speech, or of the press. In all prosecutions or indictments for libels, the truth may be given in evidence to the jury; and if it shall appear to the jury that the matter charged as libelous, is true, and was published with good motives and for justifiable ends, the party shall be acquitted; and the jury shall have the right to determine the law and the fact."
154. 3 Johns. at 411.
155. Levy, *Legacy of Suppression,* p. 15.
156. *Code of Crimes and Punishments,* arts. 362-398. See *The Complete Works of Edward Livingston on Criminal Jurisprudence* (Montclair, N.J.: Patterson Smith, 1966), vol. 2, pp. 100-108.
157. Ibid., vol. 1, p. 290.
158. Thomas M. Cooley, *Constitutional Limitations,* (Boston: Little, Brown, 1868), p. 615.
159. David Riesman says there were only about 30 cases in New York from 1805 to 1942. See Riesman, "Democracy and Defamation: Control of Group Libel," *Columbia Law Review* 42 (May 1942): 747.

160. Levy, *Legacy of Suppression,* p. 6.

161. Harvey C. Mansfield, Jr., "Thomas Jefferson," in *American Political Thought: The Philosophic Dimensions of American Statesmanship,* ed. Morton J. Frisch and Richard G. Stevens (New York: Scribner's, 1971), p. 37.

Chapter 4

1. *United States* v. *Hudson and Goodwin,* 7 Cranch 32 (1812).

2. Letter to Erastus Corning and others, June 12, 1833, in *The Collected Works of Abraham Lincoln,* ed. Roy P. Basler (New Brunswick, N.J.: Rutgers University Press, 1953), vol. 6, pp. 266-267.

3. *Schenck* v. *United States,* 249 U.S. 47, 52 (1919).

4. *Goldman* v. *United States,* 245 U.S. 474 (1918).

5. *Schenck* v. *United States,* at 52.

6. *Fletcher* v. *Peck,* 6 Cranch 87 (1810).

7. See Samuel J. Konefsky, *The Legacy of Holmes and Brandeis: A Study in the Influence of Ideas* (New York: Macmillan 1957), chap. 9 and pp. 227-231.

8. *Abrams* v. *United States,* 250 U.S. 616, 623-4 (1919).

9. Alfred H. Kelly and Winfred A. Harbison, *The American Constitution: Its Origins and Development*, 4th ed. (New York: W. W. Norton, 1970), p. 678.

10. C. Herman Pritchett, *The American Constitution,* 2nd ed. (New York: McGraw-Hill, 1968), p. 412.

11. *Abrams* v. *United States,* at 630. Dissenting opinion.

12. See Theodore Draper, *American Communism and Soviet Russia* (New York: Viking Press, 1963), esp. pp. 253-258.

13. *Gitlow* v. *New York,* 268 U.S. 652, 667, 668 (1925).

14. Ibid., at 670.

15. Ibid.

16. Ibid., at 657-658, note 2. Italics in original.

17. Ibid., at 669-670, quoting *People of Illinois* v. *Lloyd,* 136 N.E. 505 (1922).

18. Ibid., at 673. Dissenting opinion.

19. Ibid.

20. Thomas I. Emerson, *The System of Freedom of Expression* (New York: Vintage, 1970), p. 48.

21. *Communist Party U.S.A.* v. *S.A.C.B.,* 367 U.S. 1, 147-8 (1961). Dissenting opinion.

22. Felix Frankfurter, *Mr. Justice Holmes and the Supreme Court,* 2nd ed. (Cambridge: Harvard University Press, Belknap Press, 1961), p. 112.

23. Benjamin Cardozo, "Mr. Justice Holmes," in *Mr. Justice Holmes,* ed. Frankfurter (New York, Coward, McCann, 1931), p. 5.

24. Harold Laski, "Mr. Justice Holmes," ibid., p. 148.

25. Robert K. Faulkner, *The Jurisprudence of John Marshall* (Princeton: Princeton University Press, 1968), p. 227.

26. *People* v. *Croswell,* 3 Johns. 336, 358 (New York, 1804).

27. Holmes to Laski, July 28, 1916, in *Holmes-Laski Letters,* vol. 1, p. 8.

28. Holmes, "Natural Law," in *Collected Legal Papers* (New York: Harcourt, Brace & Howe, 1921), p. 314.

29. Holmes to Sir Frederick Pollock, August 30, 1929, in *Holmes-Pollock Letters,* ed. Mark DeWolfe Howe (Cambridge: Harvard University Press, 1941), vol. 2, p. 252.

30. Holmes, "Ideals and Doubts," *Illinois Law Review* 10 (May 1915): 3.

31. *Olmstead* v. *United States,* 277 U.S. 438, 470 (1928). Dissenting opinion.

32. *Buck* v. *Bell,* 274 U.S. 200, 207 (1927). See Walter Berns, *"Buck* v. *Bell:* Due Process of Law?" *Western Political Quarterly* 6 (December 1953): 762-775.

33. Frankfurter, "Mr Justice Holmes and the Constitution," in *Mr Justice Holmes,* p. 85.

34. *United States* v. *Schwimmer,* 279 U.S. 644, 654-5 (1929).

35. *Schneiderman* v. *United States,* 320 U.S. 118, 132, 135, 138, 144 (1943).

36. *Lochner* v. *New York,* 198 U.S. 45, 75-6 (1905).

37. Holmes, "Montesquieu," in *Collected Legal Papers,* p. 258.

38. *Federalist* no. 10.

39. *The Debates and Proceedings in the Congress of the United States,* vol. 1, pp. 454-455 (June 8, 1789).

40. Holmes to Laski, March 4, 1920, *Holmes-Laski Letters,* vol. 1, p. 249.

41. Holmes to Pollock, June 18, 1925, *Holmes-Pollock Letters,* vol. 2, p. 163.

42. *Debs* v. *United States,* 249 U.S. 211, 215 (1919).

43. Holmes to Pollock, April 5, 1919, *Holmes-Pollock Letters,* vol. 2, p. 7.

44. Zachariah Chafee, Jr., *Free Speech in the United States* (New York: Atheneum Press, 1969), p. 84.

45. Alexis de Tocqueville, *Democracy in America* (New York: Vintage Books, 1945), vol. 1, chap. 11.

46. Ibid., p. 273.

47. Ibid., p. 190.

48. Ibid., p. 191.

49. Ibid., vol. 2, p. 342.

50. See, for example, Justice Black's dissenting opinion in *Adamson* v. *California,* 332 U.S. 46, 89 (1947).

51. Tocqueville, *Democracy in America,* vol. 1, p. 188. For a fuller discussion of Tocqueville's argument for freedom of the press, see Berns, "Free Speech and Free Government," *Political Science Reviewer* 2 (Fall 1972); 225-233.

52. Tocqueville, *Democracy in America,* vol. 1, p. 200. Italics in original.

53. Ibid., p. 204.

54. See Leonard W. Levy, *Jefferson and Civil Liberties: The Darker Side,* (Cambridge, Mass: Belknap Press, 1963) chap. 3; and Harry V. Jaffa, *Equality and Liberty* (New York: Oxford University Press, 1965), p. 181.

55. *Abrams* v. *United States* at 630.

56. John Locke, *Second Treatise of Civil Government,* sec. 132.

57. *De Jonge* v. *Oregon,* 299 U.S. 353, 362 (1937).

58. Ibid., at 365. Italics supplied.

59. *Whitney* v. *California,* 274 U.S. 357, 374, 375 (1927). Concurring opinion.

60. Ibid., at 374.

61. *Dennis* v. *United States,* 341 U.S. 494 (1951).

62. *Yates* v. *United States,* 354 U.S. 298 (1957).

63. *Brandenburg* v. *Ohio,* 395 U.S. 444, 452 (1969). Concurring opinion.

64. Ibid., at 456.

253

65. *Keyishian* v. *Board of Regents,* 385 U.S. 589 (1967).

66. *Communist Party of Indiana* v. *Whitcomb,* 94 S. Ct. 656, 662 (1974), quoting from *Bradenburg* v. *Ohio,* at 447.

67. Tocqueville, *Democracy in America,* vol. 1, p. 203.

68. Ibid.

69. Ibid., p. 200.

70. *Dennis* v. *United States,* at 589. Dissenting opinion.

71. *Brandenburg* v. *Ohio,* at 454. Concurring opinion.

72. *Communist Party of Indiana* v. *Whitcomb,* at 662.

73. Robert A. Horn, *Groups and the Constitution* (Stanford: Stanford University Press, 1956), p. 150.

74. *Dennis* v. *United States,* at 582, 584.

75. Charles L. Black, Jr., *The People and the Court: Judicial Review in a Democracy* (New York: Macmillan, 1960), p. 52 and passim.

76. *West Virginia State Board of Education* v. *Barnette,* 319 U.S. 624, 670 (1943). Frankfurter, dissenting opinion.

77. See, for example, Ben J. Wattenberg's catalogue of what has been said by "intellectuals" about the country and its present condition, in *The Real America: A Surprising Examination of the State of the Union* (Garden City, N.Y.: Doubleday, 1974), pp. 13-22.

78. Abraham Lincoln, speech of June 26, 1857, in *Works,* ed. Basler, vol. 2, p. 406.

79. *Whitney* v. *California* at p. 375. Concurring opinion.

80. James Madison, *Writings,* ed. Gaillard Hunt (New York: Putnam, 1906), vol. 6, p. 397.

81. Emerson, *Freedom of Expression,* p. 17.

Chapter 5

1. *Cohen* v. *California,* 403 U.S. 15, 21 (1971).

2. *Davis* v. *Massachusetts,* 167 U.S. 43 (1897).

3. The leading case is *Hague* v. *C.I.O.,* 307 U.S. 496 (1939). On the general question, see Harry Kalven, Jr., "The Concept of the Public Forum: *Cox* v. *Louisiana,*" *The Supreme Court Review, 1965,* ed. Philip B. Kurland (Chicago: University of Chicago Press, 1965), pp. 1-32.

4. *Cox* v. *New Hamsphire,* 312 U.S. 569 (1941).

5. *Cox* v. *Louisiana,* 379 U.S. 536 (1965); *Adderley* v. *Florida,* 385 U.S. 39 (1966).

6. *Kovacs* v. *Cooper,* 336 U.S. 77 (1949).

7. Robert H. Bork, "Neutral Principles and Some First Amendment Problems," *Indiana Law Journal,* vol. 47 (Fall, 1971), p. 21.

8. *Cohen* v. *California,* at 22-23.

9. Ibid., at 18.

10. *Chaplinsky* v. *New Hampshire,* 315 U.S. 568, 571-2 (1942).

11. Ibid., at 572.

12. *Cohen* v. *California,* at 24.

13. *Lehman* v. *City of Shaker Heights,* 94 S. Ct. 2714, 2718 (1974).

14. *Cameron* v. *Johnson,* 390 U.S. 611 (1968).

15. *Cohen* v. *California,* at 25.

16. Ibid.

17. Ibid., at 26.

18. *Gooding* v. *Wilson,* 405 U.S. 518, 521 (1972). See also *Hess* v. *Indiana,* 94 S. Ct. 326 (1973) and *Lewis* v. *New Orleans,* 94 S. Ct. 970 (1974).

19. Nathan Glazer, *Remembering the Answers* (New York: Basic Books, 1970).

20. Alexis de Tocqueville, *Democracy in America* (New York: Vintage Books, 1945), vol. 1, p. 275.

21. *Rosenfeld* v. *New Jersey,* 408 U.S. 901 (1972).

22. *Brown* v. *Oklahoma,* 408 U.S. 914 (1972). For dissenting opinions, see also 408 U.S. 909-913.

23. *Papish* v. *Board of Curators,* 410 U.S. 667, 670 (1973).

24. See Francis Canavan, "Freedom of Speech and Press: For What Purpose?" *American Journal of Jurisprudence* 16 (1971): 95-142.

25. *Stanley* v. *Georgia,* 394 U.S. 557 (1969).

26. Sir William Blackstone, *Commentaries on the Laws of England,* bk. 3, chap. 1.

27. See, for example, the separate dissents of Justices Black and Douglas in *Beauharnais* v. *Illinois,* 343 U.S. 250, 271 (note 4) and 286-7 (1952).

28. Max Farrand, ed., *The Records of the Federal Covention of 1787* (New Haven: Yale University Press, 1911, 1937), vol. 1, p. 9.

29. *Cohen* v. *California,* at 19.

30. James Madison to Thomas Jefferson, February 8, 1825, in *Writings,* ed. Gaillard Hunt (New York: Putnam, 1900-1910) vol. 9, pp. 218-219.

31. Jefferson, *Notes on the State of Virginia,* in *Works* (Federal ed. New York: Putnam, 1904-05), vol. 9, p. 62.

32. This is from the so-called Rockfish Gap report. See Saul K. Padover, *The Complete Jefferson* (New York: Duell, Sloan & Pearce, 1943), p. 1098.

33. *Federalist* no. 55.

34. *Abington* v. *Schempp,* 374 U.S. 203, 281 (1963).

35. Clinton Rossiter, *The American Presidency* (New York: Harvest Books, 1960), p. 108.

36. *West Virginia State Board of Education* v. *Barnette,* 319 U.S. 624 (1943).

37. *Tinker* v. *Des Moines School District,* 393 U.S. 503 (1969).

38. *Goss* v. *Lopez,* 95 S. Ct. 729 (1975).

39. *Papish* v. *Board of Curators,* 410 U.S. 667 (1973).

40. *Keyishian* v. *Board of Regents,* 385 U.S. 589, 622 (1967).

41. *Whitehill* v. *Elkins,* 389 U.S. 54 (1967).

42. *Street* v. *New York,* 394 U.S. 576 (1969); *Smith* v. *Goguen,* 94 S. Ct. 1242 (1974); *Spence* v. *Washington,* 94 S. Ct. 2727 (1974).

43. Roth v. United States, 354 U.S. 476, 489 (1957).

44. *Manual Enterprises* v. *Day,* 370 U.S. 478, 482 (1962); *Jacobellis* v. *Ohio,* 378 U.S. 184, 191 (1964); *A Book Named "John Cleland's Memoirs of a Woman of Pleasure"* v. *Attorney General,* 383 U.S. 413, 419 (1966).

45. *Ginzburg* v. *United States,* 383 U.S. 463, 492, 489-90 (1966). Dissenting opinion. This is the case where the Court upheld the conviction on the ground

that Ginzburg had employed "pandering" in his advertising, a rule constructed for this case alone and never to be applied again.

46. John Stuart Mill, *On Liberty,* chap. 1, "Introductory."

47. For a discussion of the use of obscenity in the works of great comic poets, see Walter Berns, "Beyond the (Garbage) Pale or Democracy, Censorship and the Arts," in *Censorship and Freedom of Expression,* ed. Harry M. Clor (Chicago: Rand McNally, 1971), pp. 69ff. This essay is reprinted in *The Public Interest* (Winter 1971) and in Victor B. Cline, ed., *Where Do You Draw the Line?* (Provo, Utah: Brigham Young University Press, 1974), pp. 25-44.

48. Ian Robinson, *The Survival of English* (Cambridge: Cambridge University Press, 1973), p. 164.

49. Jean-Jacques Rousseau, *Politics and the Arts: Letter to M. d'Alembert on the Theatre,* trans. Allan Bloom (Ithaca: Cornell University Press, 1968).

50. Gotthold Ephraim Lessing, *Laocoön* (New York: Noonday Press, 1961), chap. 1, p. 10.

51. *Rosen* v. *United States,* 161 U.S. 29, 36 (1896), quoting *Commonwealth* v. *Sharpless,* 2 Serg. & R. 91, 102 (1815, Penn.) vol. 1,

52. *Swearingen* v. *United States,* 161 U.S. 446 (1896).

53. *United States* v. *Limehouse,* 285 U.S. 424 (1932).

54. *Commonwealth* v. *Holmes,* 17 Mass. 336 (1821).

55. *The Report of the Commission on Obscenity and Pornography* (New York: Bantam, 1970), pp. 62ff.

56. *Jacobellis* v. *Ohio,* at 195.

57. *Ginsberg* v. *New York,* 390 U.S. 629, 641 (1968).

58. *Miller* v. *California,* 413 U.S. 15 (1973); and especially *Paris Adult Theatre I* v. *Slaton,* 413 U.S. 49, 57-64 (1973).

59. Harry M. Clor, *Obscenity and Public Morality: Censorship in a Liberal Society* (Chicago: University of Chicago Press, 1969).

60. Leslie Farber, "I'm Sorry, Dear," *Commentary* 38 (November 1964): 48.

61. Ibid., p. 53.

62. Hugh Kenner, "The Comfort Behind the Joy of Sex," *New York Times Magazine,* October 27, 1974, p. 69.

63. Bernard Bailyn, *Education in the Forming of American Society* (Chapel Hill: University of North Carolina Press, 1960), p. 16.

64. Alexis de Tocqueville, *Democracy in America,* vol. 2, pp. 204-206.

65. Ibid., p. 207.

66. Ibid., p. 217.

67. Thomas Babington Macaulay, *Critical and Historical Essays* (London: Everyman, 1951), vol. 2, p. 419.

68. Rousseau, *Letter to M. d'Alembert,* p. 124.

69. See Berns, "Absurdity at the *New York Times,*" *Harper's* (May 1973): 34ff.

70. *New York Times,* editorial, April 1, 1969.

71. *Miller* v. *California,* 413 U.S. 15, 24 (1973). See also *Paris Adult Theatre I* v. *Slaton,* 413 U.S. 49 (1973).

72. The *New York Times* asked a "number of prominent people" for their opinions on the 1973 decisions. For their replies (all but one opposing the decisions), see the *Sunday Times,* August 5, 1973, sec. 2, pp. 1, 11, 16.

73. Rousseau, *Letter to M. d'Alembert,* p. 125.

74. Tocqueville, *Democracy in America,* vol. 2, pp. 154-155.

Chapter 6

1. *Adamson* v. *California,* 332 U.S. 46, 89 (1947).
2. *Hague* v. *C.I.O.,* 307 U.S. 496 (1939).
3. *Federalist* no. 10.
4. *Federalist* no. 51.
5. Alexander M. Bickel, *The Least Dangerous Branch* (New York: Bobbs-Merrill, 1962), p. 16.
6. *Furman* v. *Georgia,* 408 U.S. 238 (1972).
7. *Roe* v. *Wade,* 410 U.S. 113 (1973). A 1972 Gallup poll showed 46% to favor legalized abortion and 45% to oppose it, with 9% undecided; but in the same year, which was one year before the Court's decision, the question of whether to legalize abortion was put to the voters in referenda in two states, and in North Dakota 77% opposed it and in Michigan 61%. See Ben J. Wattenberg, *The Real America: A Surprising Examination of the State of the Union* (Garden City, N.Y.: Doubleday, 1974), p. 219.
8. *Lucas* v. *Forty-Fourth General Assembly of Colorado,* 377 U.S. 713 (1964).
9. Robert A. Dahl, *A Preface to Democratic Theory* (Chicago: University of Chicago Press, 1956), pp. 78-83.
10. Ibid., p. 22.
11. *A Book...* v. *Attorney General of Massachusetts,* 383 U.S. 413, 433-441 (1966).
12. *Newsweek,* August 18, 1975, p. 67; Wattenberg, *Real America,* p. 265. Recently, the Court, on procedural grounds, held that Chattanooga, Tenn. could not refuse the use of a municipal auditorium to a company planning to show the rock musical *Hair.* Justice Douglas, in a separate opinion, praised *Hair* for its "pungent social and political commentary [on] the puritanical conventions of the Establishment" (*Southeastern Promotions, Ltd.* v. *Conrad,* 95 S. Ct. 1239, 1249 [1975]).
13. *New York Times* (Paris edition), March 21, 1966.
14. *Wall Street Journal,* October 7, 1974, p. 20.
15. Wattenberg, *Real America,* chap. 19 and passim.
16. Ralph Lerner, "The Supreme Court as Republican Schoolmaster," in *The Supreme Court Review, 1967,* ed. Philip B. Kurland (Chicago: University of Chicago Press, 1967), pp. 127-180.
17. Paul Eidelberg, *The Philosophy of the American Constitution* (New York: The Free Press, 1968), p. 224.
18. "Good Enough to be Free?" *New York Times,* September 7, 1975, sec. 4, p. 17.

Index